T0149226

# Things Everyone Should Know

Thomas R. Gildersleeve

# THINGS EVERYONE SHOULD KNOW

*iUniverse books may be ordered through booksellers or by contacting:*

*iUniverse*
*1663 Liberty Drive*
*Bloomington, IN 47403*
*www.iuniverse.com*
*1-800-Authors (1-800-288-4677)*

*Because of the dynamic nature of the Internet, any web addresses or links contained in this book may have changed since publication and may no longer be valid. The views expressed in this work are solely those of the author and do not necessarily reflect the views of the publisher, and the publisher hereby disclaims any responsibility for them.*

*Any people depicted in stock imagery provided by Thinkstock are models, and such images are being used for illustrative purposes only. Certain stock imagery © Thinkstock.*

*ISBN: 978-1-4917-7052-8 (sc)*
*ISBN: 978-1-4917-7053-5 (e)*

*Print information available on the last page.*

*iUniverse rev. date: 08/21/2015*

# Table of Contents

# Introduction

There are things that everyone should know that our educational system doesn't cover well, if at all. The purpose of this book is to try to rectify this situation.

Everything in this book is something that I've picked up from some other place. My record is unblemished — I've never had an original idea.

However, I started collecting the information that appears in this book before I became sensitive to the idea that I ought to acknowledge my sources. As a result, I've lost track of where I've collected some of this information. Consequently, when I can't remember from where I got an idea, I'm unable to cite the source.

To all of those people whose thoughts I've thus unwittingly stolen, I apologize. I hope that you won't think too little of me ... or sue me.

# CHAPTER ONE

# Knowledge

We have goals that we want to reach. For example, we may be at one place and want to be at another. To get there, we can walk, drive, take a taxi, or hop a train or plane. All of these actions achieve our goal of being transported from one place to another.

However, there are many other actions, such as talking, sleeping or eating, that won't get us where we want to go. To achieve a goal, we must choose one of those few actions, out of the many available, that results in what we want.

How do we choose actions? For example, if we're in the living room and want to be in the kitchen, how do we know that, if we face the kitchen and keep putting one foot in front of the other, we'll end up in the kitchen? What is this *knowledge* that we have that walking transports us, that drinking relieves thirst, that water runs downhill, that dropped objects fall to the ground, and so on?

Knowledge is the memory of experience, both ours and other people's. For example, if every time that we drop an object, it falls to the ground, and if everyone whom we meet tells us that, every time they drop an object, it falls to the ground, we conclude that dropped objects always fall to the ground.

Then we know that, if we have a stone in our hand, we can safely let it go, because it will only drop harmlessly to the ground. It won't fly up and hit us in the face, explode, or float freely in the air.

Knowledge always has this form.

Dropped objects have always fallen to the ground in the past. Therefore, they'll always fall to the ground in the future.

Water has always run downhill in the past. Therefore, it will always run downhill in the future.

Something has always happened in a particular way in the past. Therefore, it will always happen in the same way in the future.

This way of coming to a general conclusion by reasoning from a large number of particular instances is known as *induction*.

But can we be sure that things have always happened in the same way in the past? I have my doubts.

For example, you say that dropped objects have always fallen to the ground in the past. But last night I had this experience.

I went to bed. Sometime later, I dropped a stone, and it grew wings and flew away. Sometime after that, I got up.

Now, here's an experience in which a dropped object didn't fall to the ground. What do you say to that?

You'll say that I was dreaming, and I'll agree with you. To what am I agreeing? I'm agreeing that the experiences that we have when we're dreaming shouldn't be taken into account when we draw up the totality of experience on which we base our knowledge.

Thus, in dreams, dropped objects can do most anything. But in reality, dropped objects always fall to the ground, water always runs downhill, and so on. Since we live and act in reality, not in dreams, it's the real experiences on which we want to base purposeful action.

Here our choice is particularly acute. Cultures have been based on the idea that the really important things happen to people when they're in a dream or trance.

Hallucinogens are taken to achieve the proper state for receiving revelations. When the right person is given what's considered to be a sign, whole groups act on it. And who's to say that such people are wrong?

I can't. You pays your money, and you takes your choice. But for us, we opt to not believe what our dreams tell us.

So it's important for the development of knowledge to distinguish between dreams and reality. How do we do this?

All that we know is our experience. Everything we know we either saw with our eyes, heard with our ears, smelled with our nose, tasted with our tongue, or felt with our body.

This experience is no different when we dream than it is in reality. So when we have an experience, how do we know whether or not we're dreaming?

The answer is that, when we're dreaming, anything can happen. Water can run uphill, and you and I can fly. But in the real world, our experience tends to be consistent with our knowledge as it now stands.

In other words, we distinguish between our dream experiences and the experiences that we have in the real world on the basis of our present accumulated knowledge. If our experiences tend to be consistent with our accumulated knowledge, then they're real. If not, then they're something that we probably experienced when we were dreaming.

You'll notice a certain hesitancy here, embodied in the use of the words "tends to be" and "probably". Our knowledge isn't perfect, so a real experience can be inconsistent with our knowledge. It's these inconsistencies that allow us to refine our knowledge.

When we're dreaming, we don't realize that we're dreaming. It's only after we awake that we can say, of experiences that we had when we were asleep, "Ah, that was just a dream."

This fact has unsettling consequences. For although we're now sure that we're awake and experiencing reality, in a minute we may wake and say, "Ah, but that was just a dream."

In other words, we can't be sure that what we see, hear, smell, taste and feel is reality. We may just be dreaming.

To repeat, knowledge always has the following form.

> Something has always been the case in the past.
> Therefore, it will always be the case in the future.

We just got finished saying that we can't be sure of the first part of this knowledge form — the part that says that something has always been the case in the past. Now let's look at the second part of the knowledge form, the part that says, "Therefore, it will always be the case in the future."

My question is, "What makes you think so? The fact that water has always run downhill in the past doesn't exclude the possibility that, the next time that you look at a stream, it may be running uphill. And the fact that every stone dropped in the past has fallen to the ground doesn't exclude the possibility that, the next time that you drop a stone, it may start rising in the air."

By now you're probably pretty exasperated, and you may exclaim something like, "For Pete's sake! I've always expected something that has always happened in a certain way in the past to happen the same way in the future, and I've always been right."

From a pragmatic point of view, this may be the proper attitude. But as a logical argument, it won't hold.

Look at what you're saying. Once more, the form that knowledge takes is:

> In the past, X has always been the case. Therefore, X will always be the case in the future.

Suppose that we let the X in this form be the statement, "What has happened in a certain way in the past always happens the same way in the future." Then what you're saying is that this specific X has always been the case in the past, and you're trying to persuade me that, therefore, this specific X will always be the case in the future.

But in so doing, you're using the proposition that you're trying to prove. That's not logically permissible.

There's no way out. The fact that something has always been the case in the past can't guarantee that it will always be the case in the future. It may be a useful heuristic, but it can't make claim to unassailable truth.

We've already observed that there are people who believe that what happens to them in dreams is more important than what happens to them in reality and that these people use their dream experiences to guide their actions.

At the time, we said that we have no way to convince such people to do otherwise. They've committed an act of faith, which includes being willing to behave in accordance with this faith.

What we now want to make clear is that deciding to guide our behavior on the basis of inductive knowledge is just as much an act of faith. We're of the belief that using inductive knowledge to guide behavior is the surest way to achieve our goals.

But we can't prove that using inductive knowledge to guide behavior is the surest way to reach our objectives. Our decision remains an act of faith, a commitment to principles on which we're willing to hazard our welfare.

The reason we make this commitment is pragmatic. Use of inductive knowledge to guide our behavior seems to work in that it tends to produce the results that we want.

The body of propositions that we call knowledge isn't constant. What we believed to be the case yesterday isn't necessarily what we believe to be the case today, and what we believe today may not be what we'll believe tomorrow.

We once believed that the world was the center of the universe and that it was flat. As a consequence, we were led into error — that is, actions based on these beliefs didn't get us where we wanted to go. So we refined these beliefs to reconcile them with the new facts that our errors uncovered.

This process continues today. Knowledge isn't an absolute.

Knowledge is a body of beliefs that's the most useful that we can assemble at the moment. Tomorrow we'll be able to refine it further. As we act on our beliefs and make mistakes, we clarify our knowledge to make it progressively more useful in pursuing our goals.

We formulate, store and communicate knowledge with words. A word may have both *connotation* and *denotation*. It's this connotation and denotation that make up the word's *meaning*.

All words have connotation. Connotation is what a word stimulates us to think of.

When you hear the word dog, you may think of a large, longhaired animal. This is your connotation of the word dog.

I may think of a small, shorthaired animal. That's my connotation of the word dog.

Thus, the connotation that the word dog has for you is different from the connotation that the word has for me.

This is true in general. No two people have exactly the same connotation of a word.

However, various people's connotations of a word are similar enough to allow the word to be used in communication. Thus, you may think of a large animal when the word dog is mentioned, I may think of a small animal, Joe may think of a barking one, Pauline of one wagging its tail, and so on. But we all think of a four footed, hairy animal with a tail and can, consequently, talk about dogs.

In fact, if our connotations of a spoken group of sounds or a written group of letters weren't similar enough for us to use them in communicating with one another, they wouldn't be words. Words are sounds associated with groups of letters about which we've a large measure of agreement with respect to connotation.

It's these common connotations that we find in the dictionary. The more scientific the dialogue, the more precisely the connotations of words are defined and the more correspondence there is among people's connotations of the words.

Most words have denotation. Denotation is the relation that a word has to the thing it represents.

If we want to teach a child the denotation of the word dog, we may take him outside, walk around until we find a dog, point to the dog, and say the word, "Dog."

That's our connotation of the word dog. If the child understands what we're about, he develops a conception of a dog from this exercise. This conception is his connotation of the word dog.

From this point on, the word dog has meaning for the child. There's some connotation that comes to his mind when the word dog is mentioned. And he knows that, somewhere out in the world, there are things wandering around that bear some resemblance to his connotation of the word.

Not all denotation is exemplified by pointing. For example, no one has ever seen the Big Bang origination of the universe. But the Big Bang is the explanation that best fits the available observations and mathematical calculations based on the equations that most reliably represent the world as we know it.

We humans are symbolic animals. We're forever inventing, using and modifying words.

We're unique in our use of symbols.

John's dog may be a smart animal. He may be so smart that he recognizes his master's name.

But when the dog hears the name John, his reaction is to start looking for his master. To the dog, the word John is a *signal* to indicate the presence of the word's denotation, just as a clap of thunder is a signal to us to start looking for rain.

In contrast to the dog, when a human hears the word John, his reaction is to respond, "Yes, what about John?" This question is beyond the dog.

A word causes the dog to act with respect to the word's denotation. To the dog, the word is a signal.

A word causes the human to act with respect to the word's connotation. An image is drawn up in his mind, and he prepares himself to receive more information with respect to this image. To the human, the word is a *symbol.*

Our symbolic orientation is what allows us to formulate, store and communicate knowledge. However, it also leads us into talking nonsense by letting us create symbols that have no denotation.

A harmless example of this behavior is the "purple people eater". The concept "purple people eater" draws up an image in each person's mind when it's mentioned. That is, the concept has connotation. Moreover, one person's connotation of a purple people eater is similar enough to another person's that we can talk about purple people eaters.

The above situation is harmless because everybody realizes that the concept "purple people eater" has no denotation. There's nothing that you can point to and say, "There's a purple people eater." Nor is there anything that you can draw to people's attention and use as a basis for reasoning to the presence of purple people eaters.

As long as we create symbols having no denotation and recognize that they have no denotation, we're just amusing ourselves. However, if we create a symbol having no denotation but behave as if it does, we're deluding ourselves.

We then believe in the existence of something that we know nothing about. When we act on the basis of such a belief, we're led into error. That is, our actions result in consequences other than those that we expect.

An example of this kind of behavior is the concept "witch". As Justice Louis Brandeis said, "Men feared witches and burned women." (A xvi)

So it becomes critical to be able to distinguish between symbols that have denotation and those that don't. The general procedure for doing this is to formulate a proposition about what the symbol stands for and then see if the proposition can be empirically verified.

For example, if the symbol is gravity, we can propose to drop a stone and see if it falls to the ground. As we've already pointed out, verifying that the stone did, indeed, fall to the ground doesn't guarantee that it always will in the future. But it lends credibility to the belief that the symbol, gravity, does have denotation.

We have more difficulty in determining whether some symbols have denotation than we do with others. To return to the symbol, witch, we could formulate the proposition that, if a person were a witch, she would be able to make other people sick. Subsequently, certain other people known to an alleged witch might get sick, and the question of whether or not the alleged witch caused the sickness may be difficult to resolve.

Data is often messy, which makes inference difficult (E 157).

To start to round out the subject of knowledge, we have to recognize that what we've been speaking of as knowledge so far is more precisely referred to as *empirical knowledge*, knowledge that can be tested to see if it does, in fact, improve our predictive abilities and, if it doesn't, can be revised to eliminate the errors previously contained in the knowledge. Besides empirical knowledge, there's another body of knowledge, known as *analytic knowledge*, made up of logic and mathematics, that's different from empirical knowledge.

The symbols used in analytic knowledge have no denotation. There's no place that I can take you and show you a one or a seven.

Nor is there any place that I can take you and show you a straight line. I can show you approximations of a straight line, but the straight line, per se, is an ideal concept and has no denotation.

The same thing is true of a point. I can show you approximations of a point, but the mathematical symbol, point, is an ideal concept. For example, it has no dimension, something impossible in the real world.

Yet we rely on logic and mathematics, because unlike empirical knowledge, which is just probable knowledge, analytic knowledge is certain knowledge.

Analytic knowledge is certain knowledge because logic and mathematics are *tautologies*. They consist of nothing but *deductions* made from a set of definitions called *axioms*.

For example, Euclidean geometry has a small number of axioms, and from these axioms are deduced a large number of theorems. We're astounded when we discover some of the theorems that come out of this process.

But the theorems are all implicit in the definitions of the axioms. If we were smart enough, we'd immediately see all of the tautological theorems residing in the axioms, and Euclidean geometry would be dull stuff.

It's their tautological character that makes logic and mathematics unquestionably true. You can't deny the statement that A is A.

There's just one flaw in the claim of mathematics and logic to certainty. Deduction has to start somewhere, so back at the beginning, you have to accept, as premises, a small number of axioms.

Such a necessity gives one pause, because suppose that, against all odds, one of your axioms turns out to be false. In such a case, all is lost. Mathematicians try to protect against such a possibility by keeping their axioms to a minimum and confining them to assumptions that don't lead to contradictions.

Mathematics comes into use in an empirical investigation when its axioms approximate a situation in the real world closely enough to be able to use the deductions from the axioms in furthering the empirical investigation. For example, for small plots of land on the Earth's surface, the Euclidean axioms closely approximate the real situation, and Euclidean theorems can be used to determine certain facts in the situation.

Thus, by determining the angle at which the sun is striking a tree and measuring the length of its shadow, you can figure out how tall the tree is. But for large surfaces of the Earth, Euclidean geometry won't do, for the Earth isn't flat, it's spherical, and to deal with this situation, a different kind of geometry, one with different axioms than those of Euclidean geometry, is necessary.

When used in empirical situations, mathematical equations represent relationships. Symbols are assigned to physical concepts such as motion and electrical current. These symbols are combined in equations to represent the physical relationships involving these concepts.

One of the interesting aspects of this use of mathematics to describe physical situations is that subsequent manipulations of the equations set up to represent recognized physical relationships can predict other phenomena that have previously escaped recognition but that, on investigation, prove to be the case. (S)

Before we leave the subject of knowledge, there's one more topic that we have to cover — quantum physics.

In classical physics, variables are continuous (C 20,24,29). For example, the velocity of an object, subject to a constant acceleration, can be graphically represented by a smooth curve where, at any point in time on the curve, you can pinpoint the object's instantaneous velocity.

However, in the quantum world, the flow of energy isn't continuous. Instead, energy comes in small, discrete packages, called quanta. (C 2) This fact was first detected by Max Planck in 1900 when he was investigating black body radiation.

An object that absorbs light will subsequently re-emit the energy in the form of thermal radiation. The object that most efficiently performs this function is what came to be known as a "black body", since black absorbs all light, and this re-emission was referred to as black body radiation.

By 1900, the needs of the new electric industry had been growing by leaps and bounds. To assist in the development of this industry, the German government asked the German Bureau of Standards (Physikalisch-Technische Reichanstalt) to come up with a formula for how the intensity and frequency of black body radiation varies with temperature. Planck set to work on this problem. (C 36)

The amount of energy radiated by a black body (E) is a function of the frequency (v) of the radiation. By 1901, Planck had determined that the energy radiated wasn't a continuous function — that is, the formula wasn't E = kv.

Instead, the function was discontinuous and came in packets. The amount of energy radiated was some integer multiple of a constant — that is, the formula was E = nhv, where n is an integer and h is the unit in which the packets are measured. (C 37)

This unit came to be known as Planck's constant, which has an extremely small, but nevertheless significant, value. The quantity hv was a packet of energy, which came to be known as a photon (C 52,53).

. Neils Bohr made a signal contribution to our knowledge of atomic structure. He determined that electrons occupy energy levels around the atomic nucleus.

When an electron absorbs energy in the form of photons, it moves to a higher energy level around the nucleus. When an electron emits photons, it loses energy and drops down to a lower energy level. It's this release of photons as the electron drops from a higher to a lower energy level that creates the spectral lines of the atom.

Because photons are quanta of energy, an atom's energy levels can exist only at specific distances from the nucleus. As a consequence, the movement of an electron between energy levels isn't a continuous thing.

When an electron absorbs photons, it doesn't move smoothly from one energy level to the next. Instead, it "leaps" between energy levels in a discontinuous way — it dematerializes at one level and instantaneously materializes at another level. (C 60,61)

All of the above implies that energy comes in the form of particles that we call photons. And yet, there are experiments, most famously the double-slit experiment, that demonstrate that energy is a wave.

So which is it? The answer seems to be that it depends on what experiment we set up to study energy.

If we approach energy from the point of view that it's a wave, then energy behaves as if it's a wave. If we approach it from the point of view that it's a particle, then that's how it behaves. We can know only one side of energy's nature at one time. (C 170,177,180,181)

Electrons move around the atomic nucleus. Consequently, according to classical physics, they have both position and momentum.

It turns out that, in the quantum world, position and momentum are conjugate variables. The more precisely that you determine one by measurement, the less able you are to measure the value of the other.

It's a gradation thing. The more you know about position, the less that you know about momentum, and vice versa.

This indeterminacy is quantified in the uncertainty principle, defined by Werner Heisenberg, and the formula describing this indeterminacy involves Planck's constant. (C 122,153,162,163). The uncertainty principle doesn't say that there are things that we don't presently know. Instead, it says that, in the nature of things, there are things that are unknowable. (C 164)

It's questionable that it makes sense to talk about the position of an electron (C 24,162). In general, what you have is a probability field describing the probabilities that the electron may be located at the various points making up the field (C 133). It isn't until you start looking for the electron that the probability field collapses, one hitherto only probable position becomes real, and all of the other possibilities are eliminated (C 182,183,190,212).

By now, I'm completely at sea. In quantum physics, certainty seems to have gone out of the window. All that we can know about future events is expressed in terms of probabilities (C 212,236). Quantum physics seems throw the concept of the deterministic relation between cause and effect, on which induction is based, into question (C 24,148).

However, physicists disagree with this conclusion. They say that scale matters — that different laws apply to the microworld and the macroworld (C 24). Plank's constant, on which quantum physics is based, is so small that, in the world in which we operate, it ceases to be a factor in the determination of behavior (C 171).

The approach taken by Bohr, Heisenberg and others, generally called the Copenhagen Interpretation, divides the world into two distinct domains, one quantum and the other classical. The quantum domain is governed by the probability field that describes the probabilities of certain real states materializing. (C 190). In the classical domain, behavior is determined by the continuous functions of classical physics.

And yet, no one has found a way to pin down the quantum-classical boundary that separates the two domains. No theory has been developed that tells us where this boundary is, and no experiment has been devised that detects this boundary. (C 219,220)

Which brings us to Schrodinger's cat, a thought experiment developed by the physicist Erwin Schrodinger (C 214).

A cat is enclosed in a steel chamber for an hour. Also in the chamber is a Geiger counter, secured in such a way that the cat can't interfere with it.

The counter contains a small quantity of radioactive substance such that, during the course of the hour, the probability that one of its atoms will decay is equal to the probability that none of the atoms will decay. If an atom decays, the decay is detected by the counter, which then activates a switch causing a hammer to be tripped, which shatters a flask of hydrocyanic acid, the release of which kills the cat. (C 216,217)

Relative to atomic elements, a cat is a big object, clearly a member of the classical domain. The question of whether, during the hour, an atom of the radioactive substance will decay is, on the other hand, in the quantum domain. All that we can know about it is a probability field describing the probabilities that an atom of the radioactive substance will decay at some point during the hour.

But whether the cat lives or dies is a function of whether an atom of the radioactive substance decays. So during the hour, the situation of the cat is equivalent to the situation of the atoms in the radioactive substance.

There's a probability field that describes the probabilities that an atom of the radioactive substance will decay at some point during the hour, and consequently, that probability field also describes the probabilities of the cat living or dying the during the hour. Until the hour is up, that's all that we can know about the condition of the cat.

So, has there been an invasion of the quantum domain into the classical domain? (C 218)

Robert P. Crease and Alfred Scharff Goldhaber, the authors of the book *The Quantum Moment*, say, "No."

The only way in which there can be coexisting possibilities of the living-dying cat is from the point of view of someone outside of the chamber. Inside of the chamber, at every instant during the hour, the cat is clearly either alive or dead.

And in the universe, we're in the cat's position. We deal in certainties, not probability fields. (C 240)

So be it. But quantum theory has proven to be remarkably powerful in predicting, with a high degree of reliability, how matter behaves at the sub-atomic level, and the theory has found practical application in the development of solid-state physics, expanding our ability to fashion things such as transistors, semiconductors, and other such materials essential to the operation of smart phones, tablets, and the other devices of modern information technology (C 275,276) When we're trying to develop confidence that induction will provide us with useful knowledge, the spookiness of the quantum world is disquieting.

The branch of philosophy with which we've been concerned here is *epistemology*, and today, most epistemologists would agree with our conclusions: That the way to knowledge is by induction, and to use words without denotation is to talk nonsense.

Now, you don't have to buy into this idea. As we've pointed out, it's impossible to unequivocally maintain that what we're experiencing is "reality" and isn't a dream, it's often difficult to determine whether the words that we use have denotation, and the uncertainty of quantum physics is disquieting.

We can't prove that induction is the royal road to knowledge. Neither can we demonstrate that there isn't a reality that transcends what we can apprehend with our senses. But if you choose to use words without denotation to develop propositions on which you're going to base your behavior, you're liable to run into trouble, because such propositions can't be tested empirically and you have no way to determine whether or not they're valid.

If you're willing to agree that we should base our behavior on inductive knowledge obtained empirically from what our senses tell us, then certain conclusions follow.

One conclusion is that metaphysics is out. In its concern with the "reality" behind our sense perceptions, metaphysics deals in concepts without denotation and is, thus, something about which we have no way to talk objectively. As Wittgenstein has said, with respect to those things about which it's impossible to speak, one should remain silent. (Actually, his words were, in translation, of course, "Whereof one cannot speak, thereof one must be silent." (Wovon man nicht sprechen kann, daruber muss man schweigen, which is the final statement in Wittgenstein's seminal book, *Tractatus Logico-Philosophicus*. (K 220)))

Just to be clear about it, metaphysics includes religion. In further explication, let me point out that, when the atheist denies the existence of God, he's dealing in the same nonobjective terms as is the believer.

A second conclusion is that ethics is out. It deals with right and wrong, words without denotation.

However, I'm of the opinion that ethics can be restored to respectability through the back door of pragmatism. Such a procedure would seem to be justified, since we accept inductive knowledge on a pragmatic basis.

Some would also reintroduce religion through this same pragmatic back door, although I think that such treatment fatally compromises sincere belief. You should believe because it's useful to do so? Would a benevolent god accept such a cynical profession of faith?

Finally, aesthetics is out. It deals with beauty, another of those words without denotation.

It's also possible to approach aesthetics pragmatically, but the results are superficial — if you like it, it's beautiful. And this conclusion gives you zero guidance on how to create beauty. You just have to trust to your feel and hope that other people feel the same way.

## Sources

The epistemological theory presented here is known as *logical positivism*. Logical positivism was developed by the Vienna Circle, which stood in admiration of Ludwig Wittgenstein and his book *Tractatus Logico-Philosophicus*, and although a contemporary of the Circle, Wittgenstein was never a part of it.

A. J. Ayer, an English philosopher, traveled to Vienna to study with the Circle, and on his return to England, he wrote his book, *Language, Truth and Logic*, which is considered to be the most explicit statement of logical positivism in English. Nevertheless, I got my education in logical positivism from *The Rise of Scientific Philosophy* by Hans Reichenbach.

I got my education in signs, symbols, connotation and denotation from *Philosophy in a New Key* by Susanne K. Langer (Mentor 1951).

(A) Abrams *Speaking*
(C) Crease, Robert P. and Goldhaber, Alfred Scharff *The Quantum Moment* (W. W. Norton 2014).
(E) Ellenberg, Jordan *How Not To Be Wrong* (Penguin 2014)
(K) Kurzweil, Ray *How To Create a Mind* (Penguin 2012)

# CHAPTER TWO

# Ethics

Ethics has to do with right and wrong, words that have no objective referent.

We can point to instances of what we believe are right and wrong behavior. But there's no entity to which we can point and say, "Look, there's right." The same is equally true of right's opposite, wrong. So there's no way to objectively define either term.

While the knowledge that can be accumulated through induction is of immeasurable help in attaining our material objectives in this world, it provides no guidance when it comes to behavior. Since we'd like to be able to live our lives free of the threat of such things as murder, assault, rape and robbery, as well as lesser slights and indignities, it would seem that some guide with respect to right and wrong would be of help. This is a frankly pragmatic appeal.

As such, it has some justification. After all, we don't accept inductive knowledge because we can prove that it's a sure guide for getting us to where we want to go, because we can't make such a demonstration. We accept inductive knowledge because it seems to work — it does, in fact, seem to get us where we want to go. If we can justify inductive knowledge on this pragmatic basis, why not ethics also?

Historically, religion has formed a foundation for ethics. Despite this fact, religion seems to be a weak reed on which to construct an ethic.

Never mind the apparently endless list of atrocities committed in the name of religion. Religion's claim to be the font of ethical knowledge is subject to even more serious question.

Religion deals with terms having no objective referent and must appeal to an alternate source for its justification. There may be revelations and even books of revelations, such as the Torah, Bible and Quran, but a religion is a hierarchy, and the final arbiters of religious thought are the priests whose job it is to interpret the revelations.

So religious conclusions ultimately rest on authority, always a dangerous situation. As Lord Acton said, "Power corrupts." (And he said it in reaction to when the first Vatican Council proclaimed the doctrine of papal infallibility. (M 170))

Then, in the 1800s, a school of ethical thought called *utilitarianism* developed. Its most well known architect was Jeremy Bentham.

Utilitarianism rested on the idea that what was ethical was that which promoted the greatest happiness of the greatest number of people. To happiness, Bentham gave the rather strange name, utility (J), which is why his ethical philosophy has come to be known as utilitarianism.

Unfortunately, the calculus of figuring out what actions promoted the greatest happiness of the greatest number of people was formidable. And utilitarianism suffered from an even more grievous fault.

Who is it who's going to decide of what people's happiness consists? Once more, we're back to the chilling idea of an appeal to authority.

However, utilitarianism did make one contribution. It moved the discussion down from the cosmic struggle between God and the devil to a concern with human beings and their condition, namely, their happiness.

Happiness is a difficult term to define. Pleasure falls into the same category.

But there's no question that we suffer pain, and inability to satisfy our more basic drives, such as thirst and hunger, leads to discomfort and, ultimately, death. At a minimum, we could define pleasure as the avoidance of such pain, agony and disaster.

We can probably do even better than that. Satisfying drives seems to bring some kind of satisfaction that we could call pleasure.

The trouble is that, as we move away from the basic physiological drives to the more peripheral ones, and particularly, when we get into self actuated drives, such as enjoying music or sports, it becomes more and more difficult to make general statements about pleasure. There's just too much variation from person to person.

But perhaps there's a way out. Since there seems to be such variation in the identification of pleasure, why not let each person decide for himself what gives him pleasure and then give him the right to act on the basis of his conclusions? In this way, we arrive at the idea that *freedom*, the right to act in whatever way a person sees fit, can form the foundation for an ethic.

The word, freedom, didn't originate with the Classical Greeks. It's from the Old English. However, the concept of freedom finds its origin in the practices of the Classical Greeks.

Like so many other societies then and throughout history, the Classical Greeks had slaves. And on occasion, they'd grant a slave manumission.

The Greeks then needed a word to describe the new situation in which the manumitted slave found himself. The word they chose was their version of our word, freedom. This provides us with a rough and ready definition of freedom — the absence of slavery.

George Washington recognized that the slave had no motivation to work outside of fear of punishment, and he had whippings administered when he felt that they were appropriate. Washington's observation and practice underline the fact that the slave does what he's told because he's forced to. This gives us a more precise definition of freedom — the absence of *force*.

Thus, freedom is one of those interesting concepts that seem to be most easily defined negatively. Freedom is the absence of force. The more force to which you're subject, the less freedom you have.

How might you go about minimizing the force to which you have to respond?

One way to achieve this state of maximum freedom would be to accumulate enough force so no one else could withstand you. Then everyone, except those whom you chose to exempt, would be your slaves, forced to devote themselves to the satisfaction of your desires and continually at your beck and call. From your point of view, that, indeed, would be a fine state of affairs.

The problem is that everyone would have the same attitude as you. Such a situation would produce a world of strife, rebellion, and continual struggle for power. It would be Thomas Hobbes' state of nature, which he described as "No arts, no letters, no society, and, which is worst of all, continual fear and danger of violent death, and the life of man solitary, poor, nasty, brutish and short."

In such a society, no one would be able to maintain for long a position of dominance. Today's king would be tomorrow's corpse.

An approach to life that wipes out the premise on which it rests can't be sound. So what's the resolution?

The behavior that leads to Hobbes' state of nature is the attempt by people to *exploit* other people, to use them for their own purposes. So, perhaps we could adopt the behavioral principle that we should avoid exploiting people, which means that we should respect the freedom of all other people to act as they wish. If freedom gives us the right to act in whatever way that we see fit, then it should also give everyone else the same right.

This conclusion gives us an ethical principle that applies equally to all people, a rule that places your wishes on the same level as everyone else's: *As long as you avoid the exercise of force against any other person, you're free to do anything that you wish.* If we want to enjoy freedom, we have to constrain our actions to the extent that we avoid subjecting anyone to force.

This is an ethical responsibility. It's not right to subject people to force, and we shouldn't do it.

At a general level, we can say that, if an increase in freedom is good, and a decrease, bad, then ethically, we should be opposed to the introduction of force. Ethically, our approach to behavior should be to reduce force to the minimum possible. Any action on the part of anyone to restrict the freedom of another increases the exploitation in the situation. And with every increase in exploitation, the lowering of the general welfare toward Hobbes' state of nature increases.

You have freedom when you can choose your actions to satisfy your wishes whether they conform to anyone else's wishes or not. The thing that destroys freedom is force.

When faced with force, your choice is narrowed to two alternatives. You can resist or submit.

If you resist, the outcome is in doubt. If you submit, you give up choice.

If you submit, you become a slave. You act according to the wishes of your master, the person who uses force or threat of force to make you submit. The sufficient condition for freedom is absence of force.

A person is a *libertarian* if he subscribes to an ethic based on freedom — the principle that, as long as a person avoids the exercise of force against you or any other person, he's allowed to do anything that he wants.

As another insight into the concept of freedom, consider the following series of situations, which are collectively known as the tale of the slave (N).

1.  You're a slave. What meager possessions you have, a few rags for clothes and a place under a roof to sleep, you hold at your master's sufferance. The products of your efforts go to your master, who uses them as he sees fit. The activities in which your efforts are invested are selected by your master. Your master treats you brutally. You're whipped and otherwise abused at his whim, are often underfed, and receive inadequate medical attention.

2.  Your master acquires other slaves. Ultimately, he owns 10,000 slaves besides you. He treats his other slaves in the same way that he treats you.

3.  Your master publishes a set of regulations concerning slave performance. He whips or otherwise punishes a slave only if the slave violates a regulation.

4.  Your master improves the living conditions of his slaves — supplies more ample clothing, improves the quality of the food, provides more adequate shelter, and arranges for medical services when required.

5.  Your master decrees that his slaves will work for him only three days a week. The slaves can do whatever they want the other four days, but in return, the slaves must provide for their own needs — food, clothing, shelter, medical attention, etc.

6.  Your master allows his slaves to leave the plantation and go wherever they want. He requires only that each slave leaving the plantation send back to the plantation, each week, three sevenths

of the slave's income. The rest the slave may keep to do with as he wishes. Your master retains the power to raise, lower or change the form of the levy on slave income. He also retains the power to recall the slaves to the plantation in case of what he sees as an emergency.

7. Your master turns ownership of the plantation over to the 10,000 other slaves as a group. Of all the slaves, only you aren't included in this ownership transfer. The 10,000 slaves now vote on how the plantation is to be run and what the duties of the slaves to the plantation are. Majority rules on all decisions.

8. If the other slaves are deadlocked on a question, 5000 for and 5000 against, they let you determine the issue.

9. The other slaves decide to treat you just like one of them. Your vote on plantation issues is now mingled with the other 10,000 votes.

The question is: When in the transition from situation one through situation nine did you experience an increase in freedom?

Freedom is the right to choose. So your only increase in freedom came in situation five, when you were allowed to have four days a week to yourself. However, even then, you were still, to a considerable extent, a slave.

In step seven, you turned in a one headed master for a 10,000 headed one. But your slave status didn't change. Even in step nine, where we have adherence to the principle of one-person/one-vote, your control over your actions is small, as is made clear in situation eight.

So what's wrong here? What's wrong is that there's nothing off limits as far as management of the plantation is concerned. It's simple majority rule, and that's it.

We'll return to this problem later in the chapter. Right now, let's look at some of the problems that a libertarian ethic runs up against.

As we've said, the requirement to not use force against other people is an ethical responsibility. The power of an ethical responsibility should never be underestimated.

However, as Paul said, the spirit may be willing, but the flesh is sometimes weak. Given the natural proclivities of humans for gratification and the accumulation of wealth and power, it's not surprising that some exploit others despite the ethical prohibition against doing so.

It's disheartening to realize that, if someone is determined to use force against you, the only thing that will prevent him from doing so is either force or, at the least, the threat of force. This is one of life's hard facts.

If a person undertakes to advance his purposes by exploiting you, the only alternative to submission is to resist, which at the least, involves the threat of retaliation. The promised retaliation doesn't have to be direct.

In many cases, the promise of retaliation isn't direct. The classic case is, "You do that, and my big brother will get you."

Consequently, freedom is a state that we may approach but can't completely reach. A policy of freedom must be to minimize, rather than eliminate, force.

The way that a society minimizes force is to become a political body with a government, which is given the exclusive right to use force. Only the government has police power.

The government has police power to prevent the use of force by one private entity on another. Thus, the government becomes "big brother", to whom recourse is made when you're threatened with violence.

The government's exclusive right to use force presents the danger that those persons representing the government may seize the government's police power to force their will on us. One protection against such power seizure is limitation of the government's ability to use force to those instances where general rules, previously set up, allow for this use. These rules, that describe the limits of the government's police power, are *laws*.

Laws are general. They're worded with respect to everybody and refer to general acts.

Laws don't say that only redheads must replace the property that they've destroyed. Either everybody must make restitution or nobody has to.

Laws don't say that taking a person's life by strangling is murder. They say that taking a person's life is murder regardless of method.

A society in which the extent of the government's police power is limited by laws is living under *the rule of law*. In such a society, the only acts that the government may proscribe are ones that break the law. Under the rule of law, you know that you'll never become subject to the government's police power unless you break the law, knowledge of which is available to you before you act.

The opposite of the rule of law is the rule of people. Under the rule of people, your every action is dependent on the government's arbitrary approval. Under the rule of law, the government's only purpose is to decide whether your action breaks the law.

Under the rule of people, government is represented by the king, dictator or administrator. Under the rule of law, government is represented by the judge. It's the judge's job to interpret the law.

Since law is by nature general, it can never cover particulars. Therefore, law always has to be interpreted.

The interpretation must be made by a judge. And the interpretation made of law varies with the judge making the interpretation. Consequently, it has been maintained that there's no such thing as a rule of law. There's only the rule of people.

Nevertheless, the difference between the force imposed on you by the interpretations of a judge, who must take heed of both the wording of the law and the precedents established by previous rulings on the law, and the power over your action wielded by an administrator, who need appeal only to the power vested in him, marks the distinction between the rule of law and the rule of people.

We introduced the rule of law into the tale of the slave in situation three, when your master set down the regulations, breach of which alone results in punishment. If your actions stayed within the regulations, you didn't have to fear punishment. But you were still a slave and had to do what your master says.

Living under the rule of law is a necessary but not sufficient condition for freedom. The rule of law eliminates capricious punishment. But it doesn't create freedom.

As exemplified in situation three of the tale of the slave, a person can live under the rule of law and still be a complete slave. Your every action is still at the beck and call of your master. The rule of law and slavery aren't incompatible.

Given that a society becomes a political body with a government invested with the responsibility for preventing the use of force by one person on another, the question arises as to which persons in the society are to carry out this responsibility. One answer to this question is democracy, in which the members of the society choose their government by voting.

Democracy has a lot to recommend it. It provides for an orderly transition and resultant continuity of government.

Democracy gives each citizen the feeling that he can participate in the choice of his government, which contributes to political stability. As has been truly said, democracy may not look attractive ... until you consider the alternatives.

But of all the things that democracy is, the thing that it's most touted for is the thing that it's not. Democracy is persistently presented as equivalent to freedom. This is wrong.

There's no connection between freedom and democracy. A society may be democratic and vote itself into slavery.

To choose one's government isn't to have freedom. This fact is demonstrated in situation nine of the tale of the slave, where a one-person/one-vote democracy has been established, but where freedom hasn't increased since your single master gave you the choice of what you wanted to do four days out of seven back in situation five.

Limited government is necessary to freedom. Under a limited government, citizens have rights that can't be taken away by any government, no matter how democratically constituted. In the US, these rights are spelled out in the Constitution.

Here's another situation where a libertarian ethic runs into a problem. A libertarian would prohibit person A from selling person B into slavery because A would be forcing B into a situation where he would no longer be in control of what he wanted to do. Instead, he would be forced to do whatever his master desired.

But what if B wants to sell himself into slavery? If he can find a buyer, B isn't exercising force against anyone else. There's no libertarian reason for preventing B from carrying out the sale.

And if B wants A to act as B's agent and even make a profit from the sale, and if A is willing, once more, no force is being exercised, and a libertarian would have no way of objecting to the sale. And yet, we find the idea of slavery abhorrent. (S1 ch 3) That's why we arbitrarily define our property rights in ourselves (our thoughts, will and action) as inalienable rights, rights not subject to sale.

Nevertheless, voluntary entry into a slavery contract isn't that uncommon. Today, our armed forces are made up of volunteers.

Service in the armed forces could be considered a job. But it differs from other jobs in a vital respect.

With most jobs, if you show up for work on the first day or any other day and you decide that you don't like the job, you can quit. That's not true when you go to work in the military. There you sign up for a fixed term, and once you decide to take the job, you have to stay on it until your term is up.

What's more, while you're serving, you're going to do as you're told. You don't have a choice in the matter.

You get an order, you follow it. In essence, for your term of service, you're a slave.

And a career military person, who reups at the end of each of his terms, spends his adult life as a slave. It's all done voluntarily, with no force exercised. (S1 ch 4) And it's done despite our prohibition about selling oneself into slavery.

But the nation has to be defended. And the alternative to voluntary armed forces is conscription, which once you enter the service, becomes indistinguishable from an enlistment and isn't even voluntary.

The absolute prohibition of slavery is an example of how our values permeate our idea of what's right and override libertarian considerations. Here's another.

There's no connection between freedom and comfort. To be free is to have the ability to choose among actions. With freedom comes the responsibility to live with the results of our actions.

All action is speculation. The future is uncertain.

Freedom to act is the freedom to take chances and make mistakes. Regardless of the discomfort that such mistakes cause, if we want freedom, we must accept the responsibility for our mistakes and deal with their consequences by ourselves.

This brings up the thorny question of *free will*. The concept of free will has been battered by the advances of science, which is based on the concept of *determinism* — that for every effect there's a cause and the result is both predictable and unavoidable. When it comes to human behavior, the thinking is that a person's biological inheritance, the environment in which he was reared, his experiences up to the present moment, and his present circumstances determine what his actions will be and that these actions can't be considered an act of free will.

The most radical statement of this position may have been that of William Goodwin, the father of Mary Shelley, who was the author of *Frankenstein* and the wife of the poet, Percy Bysshe Shelley. Goodwin said that it made no more sense to hold a murderer responsible for a murder than it did to hold responsible the knife with which the murder was committed. Whatever you may think of Goodwin's position, he did put his finger on the core of the problem related to free will, which is that, if a person has no free will, it's pointless to hold him responsible for his actions.

But if a person has foreknowledge that he'll be held responsible for his actions and be expected to live with the consequences of his actions, isn't that one of the circumstances that would bear on his actions in the given situation? So perhaps the solution to the problem of free will is to just dispense with the concept and confine ourselves to maintaining the position that people are responsible for their actions, that they do have to live with the consequences of their actions, and that they should take these facts into consideration when it comes to taking a particular action. (H G 4,115,181,215) It will, then, continue to make sense for those who make good decisions to get rewarded and those who make poor ones to get left behind.

What a person does with his freedom has no bearing on his right to his freedom. Not only is he free to live in a way repugnant to you, work when you traditionally rest, and find his interests in activities that you consider vulgar, he's also free to place his life in jeopardy, be prodigal when he's virile and suffer in his old age, abuse himself, act so as to make himself destitute, and starve. Warn him you can, exhort him you may, help him you can try, but force him you may not.

Freedom allows those with a "social conscience" to give no end of materials, time and effort to any "good purpose" that they wish. It only denies them the right to militate against those who refuse these gifts or decline to participate in the giving.

Suppose that John has made no provisions for his old age. When he becomes so old that he's no longer able to support himself, should we be willing to let him die in the street?

Theoretically, the answer is clear. Yes, we should.

No one is responsible for John but John. If he doesn't provide for himself, he should suffer the consequences.

But are we willing to abide by our convictions in this area? Many of us aren't. Many give to charity to help out those in need.

And that's OK. Charity is a voluntary activity. No one is forcing anyone else to do anything.

But charity typically lacks the resources to completely do the job. What then? Apparently, the majority of us feel that the government should step in.

The high-minded argument goes something like: Everyone has the right to live out his life with at least a minimum of dignity. And it's up to the government to see that this right is respected. The more basic reason may be that we're just not able to stomach the idea of stepping over dead and dying bodies in the street.

In any case, our government has set up a program to see that everyone has some minimum amount of retirement income. That costs money. From where is this money to come?

It shouldn't come from the government's general revenue. That would force people, who don't want to, to contribute to John's welfare.

It's John's welfare about which we're talking here. So he's the one who should pay for it. The government's program forces John to provide for his own retirement even if he doesn't want to.

To suave our conscience about forcing John to do what he may not want to do, the government's program is set up so everyone has to contribute to providing for his retirement in the same way as John has to. The program is designed to be nondiscriminatory and, thus, is considered to be acceptable.

All in all, it's not such a bad program. We're just forcing people to do what they should be doing anyhow.

It seems that this permeation of our behavior with these values is inevitable. People shouldn't be allowed to sell themselves into slavery. People shouldn't have to suffer the extreme consequences of not providing for their retirement. Etc.

We can't live without value-laden attitudes as to what commitments we have to family, community and nation. It's those attitudes that define what we are and that bind us together. (S1 261)

But we have to be careful about this kind of thinking. Every atrocity that Soviet Russia committed against its people was justified on the basis of the argument that it was in their interests. All societies are value laden and some of them, such as Nazism and Communism, go too far in violating individual rights and, consequently, aren't morally acceptable.

Our government guarantees our freedom. If our government is attacked by a foreign nation, our freedom is under attack, and it behooves us to defend our government. Here the call on our responsibilities is the most acute.

At a time of national peril, we may be required to undergo privation in support of our armed forces. We may be compelled to devote ourselves to tasks that don't fit in with our career plans. We may need to give up privileges and undergo inconveniences for the sake of security. We may have to put our lives in harm's way.

All these compulsions are serious restrictions on our freedom that are required to preserve the nation that guarantees that freedom. Here there's room for discussion. What kind of threat justifies what kind of restriction of freedom?

For example, the Fourth Amendment prohibits unreasonable search. But as Richard Posner has pointed out, the more threatening the situation, the more reasonable the search.

If personal freedom is the foundation of ethics, then the ethical principle that we're to follow is that, as long as a person avoids the exercise of force against you or any other person, he's allowed to do anything that he wishes. This principle gives us the definition of a crime.

Obvious examples are the big five — murder (the ultimate denial of freedom), assault (damage to the person), theft (the taking of property by force), arson (destruction of property) and rape (forced sexual relations). Our law code goes on from there, the fine points of which are argued in our courts.

The law is the enumeration of those actions that are anathema to freedom. Laws define the no-no's that are beyond the pale. We have a responsibility to obey the law.

And with respect to law and the police power, we also have other responsibilities. If we feel that a law is unjust, we must work to see that it's repealed. And we must see that the government's power doesn't degenerate into corruption and brutality.

So we need a strong watchdog. Perhaps the best watchdog is the public, so all government operations should take place in broad daylight. Even so, there are some operations, such as the clandestine collection of intelligence, that require secrecy if there's to be any kind of effective operation.

As John Philpot Curran has been misquoted, the price of liberty is eternal vigilance. (What he said was, "The condition upon which God hath given liberty to man is eternal vigilance.")

If we treasure our freedom, we have the obligation to see that our government remains responsible, doing what it should do and not doing what it shouldn't. In a democracy, eternal vigilance is carried out by being active politically and, when government neglects its responsibilities and becomes the tool of individuals and groups, voting the rascals out.

If an increase in freedom is good, and a decrease, bad, then ethically, our approach to behavior should be to reduce force to the minimum possible. Any action on the part of anyone to restrict the freedom of another increases the exploitation in the situation.

With every increase in exploitation, the lowering of the general welfare toward Hobbes' state of nature increases. Even if, in a particular situation, we can't foresee the ill effects of a restriction of freedom, the ill effects will, nevertheless, occur. Our failure to anticipate the undesirable consequences is no argument for instituting the restriction.

With respect to many issues, you can identify the ethically correct position by asking one specific question: In the given situation, is anyone being subjected to violence? That is, is force being using to restrict anyone's freedom of action? If the answer is no, then there's nothing ethically wrong with the action. At the same time, if we find that the application of the libertarian principle of freedom leads to conditions that violate our values, we temper our approach to the issue accordingly.

For example, the government currently spends a lot of time, effort and money prosecuting the production and distribution of drugs. But clearly, the sale of drugs isn't a crime.

No one forces the drug user to use drugs. And selling drugs is no different from selling any other kind of product.

Not only does prosecuting the drug business waste tax dollars, contribute to a burgeoning prison population, undermine the governments of countries where drugs are grown, and finance terrorists, criminalizing this activity results in the creation of extralegal organizations that service the demand for drugs. The objection to extralegal organizations isn't that they provide goods to meet a demand.

What's offensive about these extralegal organizations is the inevitable violence with which they conduct their business. They're, by definition, extralegal and, thus, have no access to courts for the redress of grievances.

Extralegal organizations aren't only suppliers. They're also enforcers. They become so because, unlike legal organizations, they're unable to turn to the police and court system for enforcement of their rights. Decriminalization of the products of these extralegal organizations would eliminate the need for their private enforcement activities.

It's with respect to the question of what our attitude should be toward the use of such things as drugs, tobacco, alcohol and pornography that the distinction between adults and children comes into play. While we've come to the conclusion that a person who has reached his maturity should be responsible for his actions, we have some reason to worry about the judgment of children when it comes to use of what could be damaging products.

It would be nice if we could just leave it up to parents to see that their children didn't misuse these goods, but the fact seem to be that children are more influenced by their peers than they are by their parents. As a consequence, it makes some sense to have society place restraints on the availability of these products for the use of children.

How about prostitution? If there's no extortion involved, prostitution doesn't force anybody to do anything, but it's prohibition forces it onto the mean streets where violence does take place.

Pornography takes on the aspect of a perversion. But again, absent extortion, no one is being forced to do anything. Instead of suppressing pornography, an educational program related to its ill effects would be more productive.

Then there's the issue of punishing crime. One way to respond to an act of violence is to require restitution. That is, the perpetrator of the violence is required to restore the victim to the state that he was in before the violence occurred.

The goal of much civil action is effect restitution. If a person steals, he should restore what has been stolen, at no cost to the victim. Some damages are translatable into money, and in these instances, a person causing damage should compensate the victim for the damage.

Another response to violence is punishment, which is often justified as a deterrent. According to this argument, we don't punish for punishment's sake. What we want when we punish is to discourage violent acts.

As the Marquis of Halifax put it in the 17th century, "Men are not hanged for stealing horses, but that horses may not be stolen." There's merit to the Marquis' argument — that is, people may refrain from violence because they don't want to pay the price of the consequences.

One form of punishment is incarceration. But incarceration isn't only a punishment. It also reduces violence by removing violators from society and the opportunity to commit crime.

Violence can also be reduced by convincing people that it's wrong and something to which resort shouldn't be made. It's to our benefit to rehabilitate, and a period of incarceration should be considered an opportunity to rehabilitate. At a minimum, prisoners should be treated with consideration, not only because such treatment may show them that there's an alternative to violence, but even more importantly, because misusing them is violence and is as much a crime as the violence that put them within our power in the first place.

But beyond restitution, punishment as a deterrent, incarceration as a way to get violent people off of the streets, and rehabilitation, we have the strong feeling that criminals should pay for their crimes. We want to see them punished because it fits in with our sense of fairness. Do the crime, do the time.

The recent residential housing bubble and its aftermath is a prime example of a violation of our sense of fairness. As Thomas Frank put it in his book, *Pity the Billionaire*, the bubble was bred by insatiable, irresponsible greed and epitomized by vulgar, ostentatious consumption and display. When the bubble burst, did those responsible for its buildup get their comeuppance?

Not a chance. They got a bailout.

Those responsible were laden down with billions and our blessings. Today they're rich in a way that you and I will never be able to comprehend. At the same time, through no fault of their own, millions were thrown out of work and countless small businesses failed. (F 27-32,166)

The bailout was a violation of the libertarian principle that people should have to live with the consequences of their actions. But our reaction to the bailout went well beyond objection to the violation of this libertarian principle.

We were outraged that, not only did these people not have to live with the consequences of their actions, they were positively rewarded for their poor judgment. This was an affront to our sense of fairness.

A better scenario for destroying public faith in US institutions couldn't have been contrived. What's the point of hard work, of scrapping for a few dollars more at some lousy hourly wage, when dishonest financial legerdemain is so profitable?

Why play by the rules when they obviously don't apply to everyone? When louts, bullies and corruptionists take home society's greatest rewards?

What should have happened is that all of those people and organizations, whose poor judgment fed by unconscionable greed led to the bubble, should have had to live with the consequences of their actions — the banks that received the bailouts, those greedy ones that took out mortgages that they couldn't afford, and everyone in between. Let them all fail. Let all of the losers go down. (F 54)

Of course, we're not quite that vindictive. Once more, our values come into play. We have bankruptcy procedures so that people aren't reduced to absolute destitution. But they should come out of the experience in radically reduced circumstances.

At the political level, libertarianism translates into rights, actions with which the government can't interfere, such as freedom of expression and privacy. At an economic level, libertarianism translates into the free market, and since education is an aid in navigating the free market, free education for those who can't afford it takes on features of a right.

A libertarian foreign policy would adhere to the principle of the sovereignty of nations. Unless it threatens our vital interests, a foreign nation is free to do whatever it wants.

Employers shouldn't be forced to provide health care coverage for their employees.

No affirmative action. Individuals and organizations should be free to adopt whatever admission policy they want.

If service providers, such as bakers and photographers, don't want to make their services available to certain parties, that's their privilege.

If owners of places of public accommodation want to restrict those whom they're willing to accommodate, that's their right.

Of course, systematic adherence to these rights by one group with respect to another group could result in freezing the second group out of much of public life, which grates against our values, so we proscribe certain discrimination in the interests of diversity.

No minimum wage. Individuals and organizations are free to adopt any payment policy that they want.

Whether you're free doesn't depend on the choices open to you in the circumstances in which you find yourself. You may not have the natural ability to be a basketball star no matter how much you desire and work hard and diligently to attain such a career. You may not have the smarts and education to earn the income that you'd like to enjoy.

There are all kinds of circumstances that limit choice. But that doesn't make you a slave. You're a slave when someone can force you to do what he wants you to do whether or not you want to do it.

Slavery is a function of force, not a function of circumstances. It depends on whether you can act according to your wishes or are subject to another's interests. That a person is caught in circumstances where he has to work at an unsatisfying job that hardly pays enough to provide for life's necessities is regrettable, but it isn't slavery.

Freedom has nothing to do with wealth. Whether you're free and whether you're rich are different questions.

Lack of money may be a condition that limits your choice, but it doesn't reduce your freedom. The only time that your freedom is reduced is when someone uses force on you to compel you to do other than what you'd have done had the force not been applied.

Of course, the options open to a person in extreme economic privation are severely limited, and we question the extent to which we should allow such conditions to exist. We also wonder about the extent to which the person is responsible for his condition. We wrestle with these challenges to our warring principles and values and wonder what the right thing to do is.

Then, there's the question of campaign contributions. From a libertarian perspective, a person or organization ought to be able to contribute as much as they want to a politician's campaign.

On the other hand, we prohibit the bribing of politicians, because it debases government. And to what extent is a campaign contribution different from a bribe?

Sometimes it's not libertarian principles or values that determine things. Instead, hard facts take precedence.

Abortion is an example. Killing a person is murder, and in my book, that's what abortion is. If that was all that there was to it, deciding what position to take with respect to abortion would be a straightforward matter. However:

An abortion is the result of an unwanted pregnancy. And whether an unwanted pregnancy brought to term is worse than an abortion is an open question.

The hard fact is that women who want an abortion are going to get one whether it's legal or not. In fact, the number of abortions performed in countries where it's illegal is greater than the number performed in countries where it's legal (P 343). And legal abortions are safer than illegal ones.

So maybe it's better to legalize abortion. But doing so shouldn't cause us to look on the act as anything other than repugnant and something to be avoided if at all possible, which ought to be most of the time. After all, this is the age of birth control.

A danger of legalizing abortion is that it may come to be considered a form of birth control. My suggestion in this area is that, the first time a woman comes for an abortion, we kill the fetus. The second time that she appears, we save the child and kill the woman.

OK. I know that such an approach is impractical. But it does emphasize the attitude that we should perpetually maintain with respect to abortion.

There's also the question of who gets to do what in society — who gets to join the society's institutions, such as its universities, professions, and public offices? Each institution has the mission of producing certain goods, and this mission should determine who are selected to enter the institution.

For example, the mission of a symphony orchestra is to produce great music, and that means that the people selected for membership in the orchestra should have the best musical talent. Commercial plane flights should be under the command of the best pilots. Surgery should be performed by the best surgeons. To select otherwise would be to pervert the mission of the institution. (S1 178,179,186,Ha 53)

The problem is that there can be debate over what the mission of an institution is. If the mission of a university is to promote the advancement and dissemination of knowledge, then those with the highest academic credentials should be selected to attend.

But if the university also has the mission of promoting diversity in society, then to some extent, considerations of diversity should trump academic credentials. (S1 171,182,191) However, one can't go too far in promoting diversity without compromising the goal of advancing and disseminating knowledge. Judgment and a conservative bent are needed to maintain balance.

## Sources

(F) Frank, Thomas *Pity the Billionaire* (Henry Holt 2012)

(G) Gazzaniga, Michael S. *Who's in Charge?* (HarperCollins 2011)

(H) Hayek

(Ha) Hayes, Christopher *Twilight of the Elites* (Random House 2012)

(J) Johnson, Oliver A. *The Individual and the Universe* (Holt, Rinehart and Winston 1981)

(M) Murphy, Cullen *God's Jury* (Houghton Mifflin 2012)

(N) Nozick, Robert *Anarchy, State, and Utopia*

(P) Pasternak, Charles *Quest* (Wiley 2003)

(S1) Sandel, Michael J. *Justice* (Farrar, Straus and Giroux 2009)

(S2) Sandel, Michael J. *What Money Can't Buy* (Farrar, Straus and Giroux 2012)

# CHAPTER THREE

# How We Decide

I'm going to ask you a question. Please don't think about the question. Just give me your instant, reflexive reaction as to what you think that the answer to the question is.

A ball and bat cost $1.10. The bat costs $1 more than the ball. How much does the ball cost?

If you're like most people, your immediate answer was, "Ten cents." And you'd be wrong.

Check it out. The bat costs $1 more than the ball. So if the ball costs ten cents, then the bat costs $1.10, and the total cost would be $1.20. That's too much.

We could try something lower. How about seven cents?

Then the bat would cost $1.07, and the total would be $1.14. Closer, but still too high.

How about five cents? Then the bat would cost $1.05, and the total would be $1.10. So five cents is the right answer to the question of how much the ball costs.

But we don't even have to resort to the trial and error procedure that we just followed to arrive at the right answer. We could have noodled it out.

The total cost is $1.10. The price differential is $1. That leaves ten cents to be divided between the ball and the bat.

To maintain the price differential, this remainder has to be split evenly between the ball and the bat. So the ball costs five cents, and the other five cents is added to the differential to give the bat price of $1.05.

But we don't even have to noodle it out. We've developed techniques for solving problems such as this ball and bat problem, and by applying these techniques, we can automatically grind out the correct answer to the question. In the case of the ball and bat problem, the appropriate technique is algebra.

Here the unknown is the price of the ball, which we traditionally represent as "x". The price of the bat is then $1 more than the price of the ball, or "x + 1".

If we add these two prices together, "x" + "x + 1", we get a total of $1.10. So:

$$x + x + 1 = 1.1$$

This equation can be solved automatically by applying the appropriate rules. It's so automatic that a computer can be programmed to apply them. But since we don't have a computer, let's apply the rules ourselves.

What we have here is a first-degree equation with one unknown. The first step is to "collect the unknown terms", that is, add them together. "x" plus "x" is "2x", so we have:

$$2x + 1 = 1.1$$

The next step is to get rid of the constant term, the one. We get rid of a number (reduce it to zero) by adding the opposite of the number to the number.

The opposite of a number is the number with the sign changed. So, the opposite of a plus one is minus one, and what we want to do here is add minus one to the left-hand side of the equation.

But if we want to retain the equality of the equation, which if we want to arrive at the right answer, is what we want to do, then whatever we do to one side of the equation, we have to also do to the other side of the equation. So we not only want to add minus one to the left-hand side of the equation, we also want to add it to the right-hand side. Thus, we have:

$$2x + 1 + (-1) = 1.1 + (-1)$$

Reducing this equation gives:

$$2x = 0.1$$

The third step is to convert the coefficient of the unknown term to one. We do this by multiplying the coefficient by its reciprocal.

To find the reciprocal of a number, we flip its numerator and denominator. The numerator of 2 is 2, and the denominator is 1. So the reciprocal of 2/1 is 1/2, and what we want to do is multiply both sides of the equation by 1/2.

$$1/2(2x) = 1/2(0.1)$$

Reducing this equation gives:

$$x = 0.05$$

We've now arrived at the right answer without even thinking about it. All that we had to do was apply an algorithm, a well-known set of steps guaranteed to arrive at the correct answer.

The instinctive, immediate, automatic response of "ten cents" to the question of how much the ball costs is the product of our emotional mind. Trial and error, noodling out a solution, and developing standard procedures for solving classes of problems are products of our rational mind.

Our rational mind is what has given us the considerable control that we have over our environment. Now, if we could only control our own behavior, we might be able to get somewhere. Which might be possible if we were able to learn more about ourselves.

First of all, we shouldn't sell our emotional mind short. The rational mind began evolving about 200,000 years ago with the appearance of modern man. The emotional mind, on the other hand, has been around for around 500 million years and is what has allowed us and our vertebrae cousins to survive and evolve.

Besides, our rational mind can get us into just as much trouble as our emotional one. For example, let's try an experiment.

Suppose that you have a blinking light. Sometimes it blinks red, sometimes green.

Suppose further that there are two buttons, one red, the other green. If you press the red button and, the next time the light blinks, it blinks red, you get rewarded. If it blinks green, there's no reward.

Similarly with the green button. If you press it and the light blinks green, you get a reward. If it blinks red, no reward.

Finally, suppose that, 60 percent of the time, the light blinks red. The other 40 percent of the time, it blinks green.

A white rat will soon figure out that the light blinks red more often than it blinks green, and from that point on, it will just sit on the red button and settle for a 60 percent return.

In contrast, when a person looks at the light, he thinks, "I don't have to settle for 60 percent. If I can figure out the pattern that the light is following, I can get 100 percent."

This is the person's rational mind talking. The rational mind is a pattern seeker.

Fortunately, a lot of the world follows a pattern, so our search for patterns has allowed us to gain considerable control over our world. And if the light in our experiment is following a pattern and the person can figure out the pattern, he can, indeed, win all of the time. However, if the blinking of the light is random, and some significant things in the this world do occur randomly, the person isn't going to be able to realize a 100 percent return, and there's a distinct possibility that he may not do as well as the white rat, which is something that you might keep in mind the next time that you're considering investing in the stock market.

## When You Can Trust Your Emotional Mind

Over time, your emotional mind has evolved into an exquisite decision making machine. (L 17,24,25,100) It operates automatically and is extremely rapid, giving you answers almost instantaneously, which is just what you want if you live in a world where the possibility of being treated as prey is ever present, a situation that has pertained for a large part of our history. Many of us no longer live in such a world, but our emotional mind continues to serve us well.

For example, a typical major league baseball pitch takes about 0.4 seconds to reach the plate. Given that the batter decides to swing at the ball, it takes about 0.25 seconds for his muscles to initiate the swing. That leaves less than 0.15 of a second for the brain to decide whether to swing.

The rational mind, as a newcomer on the evolutionary scene, is, despite its signal contribution in permitting us to achieve our recent ascendancy, unable to process information that quickly. The decision as to whether or not to swing is taken by the emotional mind. (L 25,E 9)

Moreover, when batting a ball, it's essential to rely on the emotional mind. Any attempt to try and involve your rational mind in deciding when and how to hit the ball is going to prevent your emotional mind from doing its job and your effectiveness is going to deteriorate. It's what's known as choking.

Choking doesn't occur just in athletic activities. It can happen whenever performance depends on an automatic delivery developed over a long period of practice. When it comes to choking, opera stars, concert soloists, actors, and speech givers, to name a few, are in the same category as high performing professional athletes. (L)

Becoming a skilled performer requires natural ability. But natural ability alone won't cut it.

In addition to ability, what's needed is practice. The rule of thumb seems to be that, to excel, you have to put in about 10,000 hours of practice to emerge as preeminent in your field. (Gl 40) That's about six years of daily practice five hours a day (K 238).

And this can't be just any kind of practice. It has to be what Daniel Coyle, the author of *The Talent Code*, calls deep practice. This is practice at the edge of your performance ability.

Here you make small mistakes, and for each small mistake, you slow down and figure out how to correct the mistake. This exercise increases your performance level, and you then resume practice at your new edge of performance ability. (C 5,6,18,32,40).

Finally, the practice must take place under the guidance of what Coyle calls a master coach. A master coach is one who recognizes where you are now and who has the experience to guide your practice through the graduated steps that lead to outstanding performance through deep practice. (C 178,184) Feedback that's both immediate and of high quality is essential to the development of exceptional skill (K 241,416).

When people who have gone through such a training regimen are faced with a particular situation, they almost immediately know what the right thing to do is. There's no rational thinking involved. The emotional mind instinctively supplies the answer.

For example, when faced with any particular game configuration on a chessboard, a championship chess player will almost instantly recognize the optimum move to make. This ability doesn't stem from any superiority in analyzing possible moves. There's no analysis involved. Instead, the correct move is the first thing that comes to the champion's mind.

This immediate recognition of the right move occurs because the champion has at his command a vast repertoire of chess positions and their appropriate moves that he has built up over his years of practice. This repertoire doesn't consist of just situations that the champion has himself experienced. It also includes the many positions that have occurred outside of his experience but that he has studied in order to extend the range of his skill. (K 236,238)

Of course, the chess player doesn't rely on just his instincts. They recommend the move. He then checks it out rationally to see if it's correct. (K 237) But usually, it is.

Highly trained and experienced physicians also fit into this category of experts with reliable instincts (K 240). When such a physician is faced with a patient whose complaint lies within the physician's area of competence, he can almost immediately diagnose the patient's difficulty.

Of course, the physician doesn't just act on his instincts. Like the chess player, he first checks out what his instincts tell him. But usually, they're right.

Champion chess players and physicians are experts and their instinctive decisions tend to be on the mark. Is this true of all so-called experts?

Well, it depends. If the expert is operating in an environment that is sufficiently regular to be predictable and the expert has become intimately familiar with this environment and its regularities through experience, both real and virtual, combined with rapid, unequivocal and informative feedback, then he's generally worth of trust (K 240,243,416).

Stock pickers and political scientists trying to make long-term forecasts don't fit into this category. They operate in environments that are irregular and are subject to influences that may have never before been manifested.

High confidence by forecasters, such as a stock pickers and political scientists, in their forecasts is no assurance of reliability. Their forecasts are based on only what they know. There's just too much that can happen and about which these so-called experts don't know to justify trust. (K 239,240,242) Instinct can't be trusted in unstable environments (K 241).

Sometimes expertise is required but the opportunity to gain experience is limited. Virtual practice is then necessary.

For example, virtual practice is characteristic of commercial pilot training. Aircraft difficulties are rare, but when one occurs, it's desirable to have, at the plane's controls, a pilot who instantly knows what to do and how to do it. As a consequence, pilots are trained on flight simulators on how to react under unusual conditions.

Panic narrows perception, so that every part of your being is focused on the immediate problem. The drawback of panic is that it short-circuits the rational mind that, in crisis situations (which tend to be new situations for which the emotional mind hasn't built up a backlog of knowledge), may be helpful in figuring out a more appropriate response. (L 98)

## Heuristics

When you're not in a stable situation that permits the development of reliable instincts, or if, in such a situation, you haven't had sufficient experience, actual or virtual, to develop the skill required for reliable instincts, your emotional mind tends to rely on heuristics, general rules of thumb that it has developed throughout our evolution, to decide what to do (K 11). Often these heuristics lead to good decisions, but they can also lead to error.

For example, to some extent, you determine the distance that an object is from you by how clearly you can see the object. This heuristic has some validity, since the further an object is from you, the less clear it appears.

But this heuristic can get you into trouble. For example, when visibility is poor, use of this heuristic leads you to overestimate the distance separating you from the object.

The emotional mind has a built-in set of fears, such as of spiders, snakes, enclosed spaces, and male strangers, developed by our forbearers to warn them to approach dangerous situations with caution. (Ka).

The reason why what we consider to be "bad" foods (fat, salt and sugar) are so tasty is because they're high in energy and, in our ancestors' time, in short supply, so our forefathers developed a taste for them. Today, the epitome of a tasty food is the french fry, flavored with salt, caramelized sugars, and the beef tallow in which it's fried. (Ka 207,208)

An important thing about the emotional mind is that it operates automatically and is always turned on. Unless you consciously engage your rational mind, your emotional mind will automatically make your decisions for you. (K 28)

Here are some heuristics employed by your emotional mind.

## Risk Aversion

People are risk averse. They shy away from situations in which they might get hurt.

We come by our risk aversion for good evolutionary reasons. Our ancestors were programmed to look for opportunities to eat and have sex, because these activities contributed to the survival of the species.

But trumping both of these proclivities was the urge to avoid harm, which could be fatal and wouldn't be good for the preservation of the species. As a result, evolution encouraged us to shy away from even the threat of harm.

We treat threats as more urgent than opportunities. Opportunities may recur, but one misstep in a deadly situation, and it's all over. (K 282,301,302)

We're risk averse by nature. It's part of our emotional mind. The emotional mind feels a loss more than it enjoys an equivalent gain (L 76,K 297).

This fact is borne out by the fact that, when the price of a good goes down, such as an item in the grocery store, people will buy more of it, just as economic theory predicts. Similarly, when the price goes up, people buy less.

But people respond more to a price drop than they do to a price rise. The price drop is seen as a gain, which people like, but a price rise is seen as a loss, and consequently, people try to avoid it by reducing their purchases proportionately more than they increase their buying when an equivalent price drop occurs. In fact, buying drops about twice as much for a given price increase as buying increases for an equivalent price drop. (K 296,349)

People's inordinate response to what looks like a bargain may explain the endurance of what are known as charm prices — 99 cents, $1.98, $2.95, etc. (P1 186,189,191)

Marketers can take advantage of the disproportionate response that people make to a price drop. Rebates are an example.

A rebate is unquestionably a reduction in the sales price of a product. As such, it encourages people to buy.

But why would a marketer go to the bother of dealing with a rebate? Why not just reduce the price and be done with it?

The reason is that rebates get the marketer the sales, but to a significant extent, he doesn't have to make good on the rebate. People buy because the rebate signals a price reduction, but then, about 40 percent of the people, buying a product with a rebate, never bother to submit the rebate for collection.

In addition, rebate checks are sent in unmarked envelopes that look and feel like junk mail and that, consequently, are not uncommonly treated in the same way — they get thrown away unopened. As a result, the marketer offering a rebate is able to offer a sales price to its customers without having to actually reduce its revenue as much as the rebate would indicate. (P1 177,178)

Here's another example of risk aversion. Suppose that you're given the choice between two options. You can choose between receiving $850,000 for certain or taking a gamble where there's a 90 percent chance of winning a million dollars and a ten percent chance of not getting anything at all.

The second option is uncertain, and statistics gives us a rational method for valuing it. The method is called expected value, and it goes like this.

The expected value of a proposition is the sum of the payoffs multiplied by the probabilities of the payoffs. So in the case of the second option above, the expected value is a million dollars multiplied by 90 percent plus nothing multiplied by ten percent — $0.9(\$1000,000) + 0.1(\$0)$, or $900,000.

That's $50,000 more than $850,000. So by all rational means, you should choose to take the second option. After all, odds of 9 to 1 are very good, and you're almost certain to win the million dollars.

On the other hand, if you take the second option, there's always the chance that you could end up winning nothing, which means that, not only did you not win anything, you also passed up the opportunity to be given $850,000 certain.

As a consequence, most people opt to take the $850,000 and forgo the opportunity to win a million dollars. The possibility that, if you choose the second option, you could end up with nothing makes you risk averse, and you opt to play it safe by getting the $850,000 certain, even though the second option has an expected value of $900,000. Your aversion to the possible loss determines your choice.

The fundamental characteristic of this class of risk aversion is that you have a choice between the certainty of a very large benefit and the chance to realize an even greater benefit at the, admittedly small, risk of ending up without realizing anything. In this case, your risk aversion leads you to choose certainty over the chance of gaining an even greater amount, no matter how good the chances are. (K 280,285)

An interesting characteristic of this class of risk aversion is that, if it's a one-time situation, your risk aversion leads you to choose the certainty over the risky chance. But if the situation can repeat many times, it then becomes more reasonable to take the gamble, because over time, it will pay off more than will the certainty.

At a more practical and everyday level, risk aversion is what makes residential house insurance a viable business. If you own the house in which you live, the chances are that it represents the vast majority of your assets.

Under such conditions, if your house were destroyed, the loss would be devastating, a loss that you wouldn't want to experience. As a consequence, each year, you pay an insurance company a premium so that, if your house is destroyed, the insurance company will reimburse you for the value of your loss.

But the chance that your house will be destroyed is extremely low. If you multiply your house's value by this low probability, you'll arrive at an amount that's less than the sum of the premiums that you're going to pay the insurance company over the course of your life.

The difference is what gives the insurance company its profit. Your aversion, to the possibility of a total loss on the destruction of your house, leads you to insure against this loss, despite the fact that, from a purely economic point of view, it's a poor choice.

The fundamental characteristic of this class of risk aversion is that you have a choice between the remote possibility of experiencing a devastating loss and the certainty of avoiding the loss by assuming a cost that's more than the expected value of the loss but much less than the loss itself. In this case, your risk aversion leads you to choose the certainty of avoiding a very large loss at the expense of paying more than the expected value of the loss in exchange for the certainty.

This class of risk aversion also has the characteristic that it appears differently when the event is singular than when it repeats. If it's a one-time situation, such as house insurance, it may not cost much to insure against the possibility of a large loss and remove the worry that the possibility of such a loss would otherwise cause. But if the situation can repeat many times, it may then becomes preferable to take the chance of an infrequent, large, but not devastating, loss than be subject to a continuing drain of small but steady losses. (K 320,321)

For example, if a company is sued for a large sum for a defective product and it's expected that only this one dissatisfied customer is going to sue, then it's not overly costly to settle with this one complainant and avoid the remote, but possible, chance that a jury may go wild and ratify the plaintiff's outsized claim. However, if this suit is just the first of what's expected to be a large number of similar suits, then it pays to fight the suit so as to abort repeat suits.

The same kind of reasoning pertains to negotiating with kidnappers. If the kidnapping is an isolated thing and the possibility of recovering the victim is good, it may pay to meet the ransom demand. But if the kidnapping is the act of terrorists bent on financing their activities through ransoms for kidnapping victims, paying the ransom will just encourage repeat kidnappings.

There are situations where the aversion to taking a large loss can lead to the eventual realization of an even larger loss. These situations arise when just a slim chance of avoiding the loss exists. In these situations, people shy away from taking the loss and, instead, pursue the remote possibility of avoiding the loss with the almost certain result that they're going to end up even worse than they were when they could have taken the hit and cut their losses.

The classic example of this kind of risk aversion is the poker hand where you started out with a reasonably good set of cards, but as the hand progressed, another player has improved his cards to the point where it has become evident that the cards that you're holding is an almost sure loser. However, you've already put so much money into the pot that you're reluctant to fold and take the loss.

So instead, you stay in the hand and continue to put money into the pot on the slim chance that you may improve your cards to the point where you can win the pot. This behavior makes no sense, but the money already committed to the pot is a reference point, and throwing good money after bad is common.

Another example of this kind of situation is when a residential real estate bubble bursts. The price that a homeowner's house would have brought at the top of the market is a reference point, and accepting anything less looks like a loss. So the homeowner holds out for a better price than the market offers and finds that he can't sell his house at all. A person who won't accept loss takes actions that worsen his position. (Pl 101,133)

A third example is the nation that continues a war long past the point when defeat is almost certain, because it's too difficult to accept defeat (K 319). It seems to me that this is what happened to the South in the Civil War.

At any point, the South could have cashed in and cut its losses. But it continued to battle until its ability to fight was exhausted, and it ended up being devastated.

A less catastrophic but similar case is when you continue to pour time and effort into a project that has gone disastrously wrong and shows little possibility of ever succeeding. Daniel Kahneman, winner of the Nobel Prize in economics for his work with Amos Tversky on how people aren't always rational when it comes to making economic decisions, describes his experience in just such a project, where the team, on which he was working, carried on long after any reasonable chance for success had disappeared. The irony was that the project was to develop a book on how to plan rationally. (K 253)

The fundamental characteristic of this class of risk aversion is that you have a choice between an almost certain, large loss and a remote possibility of avoiding the loss, even though pursuing the remote possibility will almost inevitably lead to an even larger loss. In this case, your risk aversion leads you to choose the remote possibility of avoiding a large loss at the expense of a course of action that will, almost inevitably, lead to an even larger loss. (K 280,285)

We've now covered three classes of risk aversion.

1. Large certain gain versus the possibility of an even larger gain combined with the remote possibility of no gain at all
2. Remote possibility of a large loss versus guarantee against the loss at a price that's more than the expected value of the loss
3. The nearly certain loss of a large amount versus the remote possibility of avoiding the loss with an even worse outcome if the attempt fails

These situations differ. But they have a common characteristic — they each involve the possibility of a large loss, to which we're averse. So we try to avoid it.

However, there are situations in which we're attracted to risk. This is when the amount at risk is small relative to the potential gain.

A good example is the lottery (K 327). Here there's a very large payoff, and the price of a ticket is really small.

But the odds of winning are even smaller. If you were to multiply the payoff, large as it is, by the probability of winning by buying one lottery ticket, the expected value would be less than the price of the ticket, inexpensive as it may be. Nevertheless, the size of the prize is such that people buy in.

The damage of taking a one-time fling on the lottery is minimal. You could write it off as a form of entertainment.

But repeated buying of lottery tickets is irrational. You're just building up a larger and larger loss in the face of essentially no chance to win. When it comes to the lottery, Fran Lebowitz had it right: "I figure you have the same chance of winning the lottery whether you play or not." (P2 77)

Loss aversion is an impediment to conflict resolution. If you conceive of your concessions as losses, whenever you make a concession, you're going to consider yourself as getting the worse of the deal. And your opponent is going to reach the same conclusion with respect to himself. The result is that both sides are reluctant to make concessions, the opposite of compromise. (H 75)

Present versus Future Gains and Losses

The emotional mind values current gains over future ones, even if the future ones are better payoffs. There's a sociobiological reason for this phenomenon. When you're a hunter-gatherer, what you can get now is worth more than almost anything that you could gain in the future.

The predilection to favor current gains over future ones seems to explain why people charge more on their credit cards than they're able to pay off at the end of the month. Being able to take advantage of that bargain, even if it's for something that you don't really need, is more compelling than the future requirement to pay interest that's going to eat up any gains that you might have made on taking advantage of the sale.

The average household is currently carrying over $9000 in credit card debt. The average number of credit cards per person is 8.5. More than 115 million American carry month-to-month balances on their credit cards. (2009)

Favoring present pleasure over future pain might also have been involved in the creation of the subprime mortgage. Hey, why worry about ballooning interest payments in the future? I can move into a house NOW. (L 86,87)

The development of the prefrontal cortex, where rational thought takes place, occurs rather late in life. It's doesn't reach full maturity until the early 20s.

This creates a problem when it comes to dealing with teenagers. Their emotions are at full throttle while their rationality is still stunted.

For example, how do you get high school students to apply themselves to their studies? Emphasizing the importance of getting a high school diploma doesn't cut much ice. Graduation date is a long ways away but getting together with your buddies is something that you can do right now.

Some states, such as West Virginia, have approached this problem by revoking the driver's license of students who aren't performing academically. Not getting a diploma is far in the future, but not having wheels is happening right now. (L 114)

When rewards are immediate and costs long-term or when costs are immediate and rewards long-term, temptation comes into play. In the case of 401(k)s, both factors are in operation. Not signing up involves no reduction in take home pay, and a financially cramped retirement is a long ways away. Signing up involves an immediate decrease in take home pay, while a comfortable retirement is a long ways away.

Temptation operates in other critical areas. Eating all of that yummy food is immediately rewarding. Getting fat, with all of its attendant medical problems, is longer term.

Exercise is costly. It requires a current expenditure in time and effort. The benefits of a longer, healthier life are longer term. (T 73)

Framing

In 1973, the psychologist David I. Rosenhan reported, in *Science* magazine, an experiment carried out by him and seven confederates. They got themselves committed to psychiatric hospitals in five different states by complaining of hearing a voice repeating the words "empty", "hollow" and "thud". Once in, they stopped complaining of their symptoms and maintained that they felt fine and were fit to be released.

The length of their stay before release was an average of 19 days with a range of from seven to 52 and during which they were bombarded with an astounding variety of powerful drugs, which they discretely deposited in the toilet. None of the seven were pronounced healthy. Each was ultimately discharged with a diagnosis of schizophrenia in remission, except for one, who received a diagnosis of bipolar disorder.

One hospital, not involved in the experiment, upon hearing of the study, expressed skepticism. Rosenham told it that he would send them some pseudopatients and challenged it to spot them.

In fact, he sent no one, but over a period of a few months, the hospital rejected ten percent of people applying for admission as shams. It was a clear demonstration that, while expectation may not be everything, it comes close. (H 141,142)

The above is an example of framing. The decision is based on the way in which the situation is presented.

Here's another example. Look at this situation. Would you choose program A or program B?

The US is preparing for an outbreak of an unusual Asian flu expected to kill 600 people. Two alternative programs, A and B, have been proposed to combat the flu. If program A is adopted, 200 people will be saved. If B is adopted, there's a 1/3 probability that all 600 people will be saved and a 2/3s probability that no one will be saved.

Most people choose program A.

Now look at this situation. Again, would you choose program A or program B?

The US is preparing for an outbreak of an unusual Asian flu expected to kill 600 people. Two alternative programs, A and B, have been proposed to combat the flu. If program A is adopted, 400 people will die. If B is adopted, there's a 1/3 probability that no one will die and a 2/3s probability that all 600 people will die.

Most people opt for program B.

But the two situations are identical. The only difference between the two is that the first is expressed in terms of saving lives, while the second is expressed in terms of loss. Loss aversion causes people to shy away from program A in the second situation while favoring it in the first. (K 436,437)

Suppose that you're on the verge of buying a $25 pen when someone tells you that, if you walk 15 minutes down the street, you can get the pen for $18. Most people will take the time to buy the lower priced pen.

Now suppose that you're on the verge of buying a $255 suit when someone tells you that, by walking down the street for 15 minutes, you can get the same suit for $248. Most people won't bother.

These people are comparing the savings with the price of the purchase, which is irrelevant but frames the decision situation. The relevant question is: Is walking down the street for 15 minutes worth $7 to you? (A 19,20)

Given the choice of buying something that comes in three prices, people tend to buy the version with the middle price. Wine stores take advantage of this tendency by arranging their wines by price.

For example, you'll find the chardonnays lined up from lowest to highest price. The wine store does this because it knows that most people aren't going to buy the highest priced wine but also don't want to appear cheap, so they go for the middle, where the biggest markup is. (A 4)

Once more, framing influences the buying decision. Personally, I love this kind of product display.

I always buy the item at the bottom of the price hierarchy and work my way up until I settle on something that I like. Most of the time it's the item at the bottom of the price list.

On the other hand, I've bought some terrible wines this way. Fortunately, I don't drink wine, so someone else has always had to drink the wine and tell me how bad it was.

Here's another example of how framing influences buying habits. A restaurant can improve its profit by adding a high priced item to its menu.

Few people will order the highest price meal on the menu. But they do tend to order the second highest priced item, the price of which can be manipulated so that it has the highest profit margin. (A 4)

Also, Coach offers a $7000 alligator handbag. Each Coach flagship store carries one or two such bags.

Coach doesn't expect to sell these bags. But their prominent display in the store makes its $2000 ostrich handbag seem to be more reasonable priced. (P1 158)

Markdowns are an example of how marketers can take advantage of framing to encourage people to buy. For example, suppose that a price tag reads "Regular Price $48, On Sale for $40".

This is a price reduction come-on encouraging people to buy. But many customers have no idea of what the regular price should be, and the advertised "regular price" may, in fact, be a markup. (Pl 191)
Try this exercise.

You paid $10 for a ticket to a show. When you get to the theater, you discover that you've lost the ticket. Would you buy another ticket?

Now try this exercise.

You go to a theater to see a play for which the ticket price is $10. When you step up to the ticket booth, you discover that you've lost a $10 bill. Would you still buy a ticket?

More people say that they'd buy a ticket at the ticket booth in the second situation than say that they would in the first case. The explanation again seems to be framing.

People keep mental accounts. In the first case, the initial ticket purchase price of $10 was entered into the "ticket purchase" account. When it came time to replace the lost ticket, a second $10 purchase would have to be entered into the "ticket purchase" account, which would bring the cost of the show up to $20 for a $10 ticket, something many people choose not to do. In the second case, the lost $10 would be debited to the general cash account and buying the ticket would still cost only $10.

All obfuscation, because the two situations are identical. In both cases, you've lost $10 and the only pertinent question is whether you want to spend $10 to see the show. (K 443)

Then there's the endowment effect. A wine collector will sell his wine, but only a higher price than he's willing to pay for it. When he's selling, it's his wine, which falls into a different category than the wine he buys, which is other people's wine. (K 293,294)

The above examples of framing lead to conclusions that don't make much sense. But framing can be used for the benefit of both society and the people involved. For example, if when you're hired, you're enrolled in the company's 401(k) plan unless you opt out, more people will participate than will if, when you're hired, you won't participate in the 401(k) plan unless you opt in. (T 8,83)

Organ donation happens more often if, when you sign up for a drivers license, you're automatically enrolled in the organ donation program unless you opt out than if, when you get your license, you're not enrolled unless you opt in. In Austria, when the default case is participation, almost everyone is part of the program. In Germany, where the opposite is the case, participation is 12 percent. In Sweden, where you're in unless you opt out, participation is 86 percent. In Denmark, where you have to opt in, it's four percent. Similar cultural backgrounds, but participation is a function of the way in which the choice is framed. (K 373)

Words and other stimuli activate, or prime, mental processes that influence subsequent thoughts or actions. (Pl 94) For example, people who are asked if they're going to vote (that's it — no pressure, no exhortation, nothing but a question) are more inclined to vote, by about 25 percent, than those who aren't asked. (T 69,70)

When numerical values are involved, priming is known as anchoring. (Pl 94). Here's an example.

Suppose that you have to guess the population of Milwaukee. If you're from Chicago, with a population of three million, you say, "Well, Milwaukee is a city, but it's smaller than Chicago. Maybe its population is a million."

However, if you're from Green Bay, with a population of about 100 thousand, you say, "Well, Milwaukee is larger than Green Bay. Maybe its population is 300 thousand."

Actually, Milwaukee's population is about 600 thousand. (T 23) The population of where you're from is the anchor, and from this anchor, you adjust to arrive at a number that sounds reasonable to you.

If the plaintiff in a liability lawsuit prevails, he's compensated for the expenses that he has incurred as a result of his mistreatment by the defendant plus an additional award to compensate him for his pain and suffering. It's up to the jury to decide what the appropriate compensatory award should be.

Theoretically, the amount of the award should vary with the extent of the pain and suffering. But there's no objective way to scale a monetary award to an intensity of suffering.

As a result, the amount that a jury decides to award is typically determined by the amount for which the plaintiff asks. So the recommended approach is to ask for a lot.

The jury won't give the plaintiff everything he asks for, but if he asks for a lot, he'll get more than he would if he had asked for less. The amount asked for is an anchor from which the jury adjusts. The more you ask for, the more you get.

The rule applies in any bargaining situation. And it pays to get your bid in first. The person who names the first number establishes the stronger anchor. (P1 1,17,18,19,110,204,211)

<u>Representativeness</u>

Try this exercise.

Linda is 31 years old, single, outspoken, and very bright. At college, she majored in philosophy. As a student, she was deeply concerned with issues of discrimination and social justice, and also participated in anti-nuclear demonstrations.

Below are listed eight activities in which Linda may be engaged after graduating from college. Rank the activities in descending order according to how likely you think that it is that Linda will end up in the activities, where 1 is most likely, and 8 least likely. If you think that two or more of the activities are equally likely, you may assign them the same rank number, in which case the number of different numbers that you use will be proportionately less than eight.

Rank    Activity

_____.    Linda is a teacher in elementary school.
_____.    Linda works in a bookstore and takes Yoga Classes.
_____.    Linda is active in the feminist movement.
_____.    Linda is a psychiatric social worker.

_____. Linda is a member of the League of Women Voters.

_____. Linda is a bank teller.

_____. Linda is an insurance salesperson.

_____. Linda is a bank teller and is active in the feminist movement.

The two critical activities in this exercise are "bank teller" and "bank teller and active in the feminist movement". If Linda is a bank teller and active in the feminist movement, then she is, by definition, a bank teller.

Consequently, no matter how high or low you rank these two activities, to be logically sound, at best, you must indicate that "bank teller" and "bank teller and active in the feminist movement" are equally likely futures for Linda. And since there's probably some possibility that Linda will end up being a bank teller without being active in the feminist movement, you probably ought to indicate that it's more likely that Linda is just a bank teller than it is that she's both a bank teller and active in the feminist movement. This is just a particular instance of the rule that, the more detail you add to the description of something, the less likely you are to find it (K 160).

Nevertheless, people doing this exercise show a distinct tendency to indicate that it's more likely that Linda is a bank teller and active in the feminist movement than it is that Linda is just a bank teller. You may be one of them.

This is an example of the heuristic known as representativeness. Given the description of Linda's activities in college, being a bank teller may be an unlikely future for her in any case, but if that's where she ends up, it's just more representative of the Linda whom we knew and loved in college for her to also be active in the feminist movement, and we choose our ranking on the basis of this representativeness rather than on the basis of logic. (T 26,27 P 88,89)

Representativeness is a good heuristic for predicting people's behavior. But you can probably appreciate the extent to which it can lead into error by realizing that another name for representativeness is stereotype.

Availability

Here's an example of the availability heuristic. The question is: Which is greater: The number of six letter words having "n" as their fifth letter or the number of six letter words ending in "ing"?

Most people go for the "ing". That's because of the availability bias.

We can easily conceive of a lot of words ending in "ing". It's harder to think of words with an "n" in the fifth letter.

However, here our emotional mind has, once more, led us astray. If we think about it, we may realize that all of the six letter words ending in "ing" have an "n" in their fifth letter and the probability is high that there's at least one six letter word not ending in "ing" that, nevertheless, has an "n" as its fifth letter. So the better bet is that there are more six-letter words with "n" in the fifth letter. (M 28)

Availability also comes into effect when, for example, a doctor is exposed to a large number of similar cases, such as during an epidemic or when the doctor is in a line of work (emergency room) where people frequently appear with, for example, the DTs. The next case comes along and it has similarities to the previous cases, so it gets lumped in with the others without adequate investigation of the particulars.

Related is "the last bad experience". After having made a mistake, the investigator tends to look for the evidence that he had previously overlooked to the exclusion of other evidence. (G 65,188)

Another example of availability is the extent to which things are covered in the media. For example, because of the media attention given to breast cancer, women in their forties are more likely to believe that their chances of developing breast cancer is one out of ten, while in fact, it's more like one out of 250 (S 271).

Because every plane crash is spread all over the front pages, you probably get on a plane with some trepidation. But you get into your car without a second thought.

Nevertheless, when you board your next domestic flight, your chances of dying are one in 60 million. The figure for the next time that you get into your car is one in nine million. (Sh 58)

The exposure effect is related to availability. Given that your initial reaction to somebody or something is, if not positive, at least neutral, the more that you're exposed to the person or thing, the more you grow to like the person or thing. (I 149)

If an example of a circumstance is available to us, we're likely to believe in the general existence of the circumstance. For example, we read about female celebrities who have children when they're in their 40s. Consequently, we believe that it's not unusual for a woman to have a baby when she's in her 40s, despite the fact that, in general, women in their 40s have difficulty having children and, most commonly, fail to do so. (J 179,180)

## Confirmation Bias

When an investigator gives disproportionate weight to data that supports a proposition that he desires to establish, he's operating under the influence of confirmation bias. It causes the investigator to value information confirming his proposition more highly than information that runs contrary to it.

Or he may reach a conclusion on the basis of preliminary data and then subsequently favor further information that supports his conclusion to the exclusion of information that may refute it. One way in which confirmation bias can be brought into operation is when a problem is presented to an investigator with an accompanying suggested solution. (G 47,65,146,150,154)

Here's an example of how confirmation bias works. You're told that you'll be given a string of three numbers that follows a rule and that you're job is to determine what the rule is.

You're to conduct your investigation into the nature of the rule by proposing other three number strings, and for each proposed string, you'll be told whether or not the string conforms to the rule. You can continue this investigation for as long as you wish, but when you become convinced that you've determined the rule, you can state the rule. You'll then be told whether or not you have correctly identified the rule, and if you're incorrect, you'll be told what the rule really is.

Here's the string of numbers that you're given.

2 4 6

Try it. What string of numbers would you propose to test the rule that you think that the given string follows?

If you're like most people, the rule that most readily pops into your mind is that the string is a series of even numbers increasing by two. To confirm this hypothesis, you might propose a string such as:

8 10 12

In response, you're told that the proposed string does, indeed, conform to the rule. You're encouraged. So, you might propose something really wild, like:

116 118 120

Again, you'd be told that your proposed string conforms. If you're somewhat creative and suspect that things might not be quite what they seem, you might decide to try out the idea that maybe the rule is just that the numbers have to increase by two and can be even or odd. So you might propose:

1 3 5

Again, confirmation. By now your confidence is overwhelming. So you state your rule: Numbers increasing by two.

But it turns out that you're wrong. The rule is: Any string of increasing numbers. So 1 2 3 follows the rule, as does 16 128 405. −6 -4 -2 even follows the rule.

All of the way through this exercise, you did nothing but seek evidence that would confirm the hypothesis that you had in mind. What you need to do, to progress in determining the nature of the rule, is to seek out evidence that would disprove your hypothesis.

You took a first step in this direction when you proposed odd numbers rather than even ones. That disproved the hypothesis that the rule involved even numbers.

But you didn't follow through. You then should have tried a string such as 1 2 3. Confirmation of this proposed string would disprove the idea that the numbers had to be separated by two.

If you had then tried -6 -4 -2, confirmation would have disproved the idea that the numbers had to be positive. But it wouldn't be until you proposed something like 3 2 1 and received the information that this string <u>doesn't</u> confirm to the rule, that you would have started to get a fix on what the rule might be. It's the negation of hypotheses that leads to the development of better hypotheses.

The way to buttress a proposition isn't to seek out confirming information. Instead, you should look for evidence that tends to throw doubt on the proposition. It's from the continuing failure of such a search to turn up any such evidence that the support for the proposition grows. (To 139) Here's another example.

You have a deck of cards. Each card has a letter on one side and a number on the other. The hypothesis is that, if a card has a vowel on one side, then it has an odd number on the other side.

You're given four cards: A, K, 4 and 7. The question is: Which cards do you have to turn over to either disprove or reinforce the hypothesis?

The K card is pretty easy. There's no point in turning it over, since whatever's on the other side, it's irrelevant as far as the hypothesis is concerned.

But you want to turn over the A card, because if it has an even number on the other side, the hypothesis is disproved. Most people get this.

They then want to turn over the 7 card, to see if it has a vowel on the other side. I was one of them.

But turning over the 7 card proves nothing. The hypothesis is that, if a card has a vowel on one side, then it has an odd number on the other. It's not that, if a card has an odd number, then it has a vowel on the other. It could have a consonant and not disprove the hypothesis. The other card that you have to turn over is the 4 card, because if it has a vowel on the other side, then the hypothesis is disproved.

Premature Closure

An explanation is discovered, after which investigation is suspended, even though there may be alternative explanations (G 185).

It's dangerous to judge ability by short-term results. Think about money managers.

Here's a relevant case. Leonard Koppett developed a system that, by the end of January, would predict the direction of the market for the coming year. It worked from 1979 through 1989, missed in 1990, and was then correct every year through 1997.

His system? Whenever the team from the National Football League won the Super Bowl, the market would go up. Otherwise, it would go down. (M 71,177)

Conventional Wisdom

Here's an example of conventional wisdom: If something costs more, it's better.

Yet one blind taste test concluded that Smirnoff, a relatively cheap vodka, was the best tasting, favored over, among other vodkas, Gray Goose and Ketel One. (M 214,215). People taking a blind taste test run by *The Wall Street Journal* concluded that, among five wines, the best tasting was a Gallo product, by far the lowest priced wine in the test. Conversely, when novice wine drinkers sampled five wines priced from $5 to $90 a bottle, they expressed a preference for the more expensive ones, even though the wine in the five bottles was all the same (I 152).

The Lancome and Maybelline brands of cosmetics both belong to L'Oreal. Their matte foundations are made in the same factories and are nearly identical in composition. Yet even though L'Oreal sells Maybelline New York's Dream Matte Mousse Foundation for $8.99, it still has no trouble getting rid of Lancome Magique Matte Soft-Matte Perfecting Mousse Makeup at $37. (I 156)

Another example of conventional wisdom is bottled water. It's believed, in one way or another, to be superior to tap water, although tap water is perfectly safe.

In fact, federal standards for tap water are more stringent and more strictly enforced than they are for bottled water. Yet, although on a per-gallon basis, Americans pay 1000 times more for bottled water than they do for tap water, in 2007, they drank, on average, 27.6 gallons of bottled water a year, higher than the consumption of milk or beer (I 153,154)

## Status

How often have refrained from contradicting someone who's wrong just because of his status? (Ka 57,58) Or even worse, accepting what someone says simply because he's in authority (S 274).

There's also the halo effect. If a person knows a lot about one subject, there's a tendency to believe that he knows a lot about everything. (S 275)

Steven King, afraid that the speed with which he turned out books would reduce his popularity, began producing works under the name of Richard Bachman. His books continued to sell well, but Bachman's experience was poor. (M 215)

## Remembering Pleasant and Painful Experiences

Your memory of pleasant and painful experiences is a function of your emotional mind, and given a particular experience, your emotional mind will categorize it as pleasant or painful and will record the intensity of the sensation on the basis of the combination of the high point and final point of the experience. The emotional mind will take no notice of the duration of the experience. (K 380,383)

For example, if you take a two-week vacation, you have a particularly pleasant experience during the vacation, and the vacation ends on a high note, you'll remember the overall vacation as a pleasant one, even though, during the bulk of the vacation, nothing notable happened. Similarly, if you had a really bad experience during the vacation and it ended on a sour note, you'll remember it as an unpleasant vacation, even though, during the bulk of the vacation, things went well enough.

Kahneman and his colleagues demonstrated this fact with a telling experiment. Participants went through two trials during which they immersed a hand, up to the wrist, in water that was cold enough to cause moderate but tolerable pain. After each trial, the participants were given a warm towel. (K 382)

During the first trial, the water was kept at a temperature of 14 degrees Celsius and the participants held their hand in the water for 60 seconds. During the second trial, the participants held their hand in the water for 90 seconds. During the first 60 seconds, the water was kept at 14 degrees Celsius. At that point, the person conducting the experiment, without saying anything, open a valve that allowed the water to warm up by one degree. (K 382)

Before beginning the experiment, the participants were told that the experiment would consist of three trials. At the end of the second trial, the participants were given a choice for the third trial. They could repeat the first trial or they could repeat the second one.

Eighty percent of the participants chose to repeat the second trial. They thus chose to experience 30 seconds of needless pain simply because, in the second trial, the ending experience was less painful than the ending experience of the first trial. (The third trial was never conducted.) (K 382,383,408)

This bias of our emotional mind causes us to favor a short period of intense joy over a long period of moderate happiness and to be inclined to give up the opportunity for a long happy period if it's anticipated that it will end badly (K 409). Not a good way to conduct your life (K 385).

Planning

When planning a project, the tendency is to look at the particular project and figure out what's going to happen and how long it will take. A better approach would be to look at similar projects that have been undertaken in the past and see what happened to them and how long it took for them to be completed.

The second approach would provide a baseline for your planning, which can then be modified to take into consideration the particulars of your project. Concentration on the particular project, to the exclusion of other similar projects, tends to result in confining consideration to the best-case scenario, which means that the contingencies that characterize already undertaken projects are given short shrift. (K 247,248,251,252)

Confining planning to the best-case scenario generally results in unjustified optimism (K 253). No one getting married believes that they're going to get divorced. Yet the sad, hard fact is that 50 percent of marriages end in divorce. (T 32)

Undue optimism may also explain why nations go to war and why people litigate and start small businesses (K 253). The chances that a small business in the US will survive for five years are about 35 percent (K 256). Sixty percent of restaurants are out of business within three years. In general, people make more money selling their skills to employers than they do by going into business for themselves. (K 257).

## Distraction

Being distracted by something may cause you to not notice something that's fairly obvious. The classic example is a one-minute video of two teams of three players each, one in white shirts, the other in black. They move around and each team passes a basketball between them.

People watching the video are asked to count how many times the white team passes the ball. After 35 seconds, a person dressed in a gorilla suit walks to center stage, thumps his chest, and after nine seconds, leaves. When the observers are later interviewed, 50 percent of them report not seeing the gorilla, even when they were asked if they had noticed anything unusual. (S 272)

## Small Samples

A study of the incidence of kidney cancer in the 3141 counties of the US revealed that the incidence of kidney cancer is lowest in those counties that are mostly rural, sparsely populated, and located in traditionally Republican states in the Midwest, South and West. The reaction to this finding is unsurprising.

The fact that the counties with the lowest incidence of kidney cancer were found in Republican states was probably not significant. But the fact that the counties were rural had meaning. The low incidence was undoubtedly the result of clean rural living — no air or water pollution and access to fresh food with no additives.

The study also showed that the incidence of kidney cancer is highest in those counties that are mostly rural, sparsely populated, and located in traditionally Republican states in the Midwest, South and West. Once more, the result can be easily explained. The high incidence must be the result of the poverty of the rural life style — no access to good medical care, high fat diet, and too much alcohol and tobacco.

In fact, the key factor here is that rural counties have small populations. With small populations the rural counties have a better statistical chance of exhibiting extreme outcomes, chances that are reduced when sample size is increased. (K 109,110,111)

The admonition is as simple as it's ignored — don't trust what small samples tell you. Not doing so can lead to pernicious consequences, as the following case demonstrates.

In a survey of 1662 schools in Pennsylvania it was found that six of the top 50 schools were small, an overrepresentation by a factor of four. As a result, the Gates Foundation made an investment of $1.7 billion in the creation of small schools, sometimes by splitting large schools into smaller units.

The Foundation was joined in this effort by a dozen other prominent institutions, such as the Annenberg Foundation and the Pew Charitable Trust. Also participating was the US Department of Education's Smaller Learning Communities Program. (K 117)

A deeper investigation would have revealed that, not only do the best schools tend to be small, so do the bad schools. Small schools aren't better or poorer on average, they're simply more variable. If anything, large schools tend to produce better results, especially in the higher grades, where curriculum options are greater. (K 118)

Randomness plays a role in determining how big a sample you need to make an informed decision. The more the randomness, the bigger the sample that you need. For example, if you're wondering about sprinter ranking, you have to observe only a few trials to determine who the fastest sprinters are, because they'll beat the slower ones every time. Randomness (or luck or chance, as randomness is generally referred to when speaking of sports) plays little part in a sprint.

But in a sport where luck plays a bigger part, you need a larger number of trials to determine which individual or team is the best. (Ma 26). For example, the World Series is a farce. The teams tend to be more or less equal. Even if one team has an unusually large 55-45 advantage, assuming that luck is normally distributed (which seems to be reasonable), it would take 269 games to determine the better team with a five percent level of confidence. (M)

Regression to the Mean

One of the things that Kahneman did in his career was to teach flight instructors in the Israeli Air Force about the psychology of effective training, during which he told them about the training principle that rewards for improved performance work better than punishments for mistakes. The instructors disagreed. They pointed out that, when they praised a cadet for an exceptional performance, they generally found that, the next time, the cadet didn't perform as well, while when they castigated a cadet for poor execution, the next time, the cadet typically improved. (K 175)

As Kahneman pointed out in his book, *Thinking, Fast and Slow*, the instructors were both right and wrong. They were right about the cadets' performance, but they were wrong about the reason for it.

After an exceptionally good performance, regardless of whether or not the cadet was praised, on his next venture, he typically returned to a more average level of performance. The same was true for the cadet with the poor performance. He had a bad day, and whether or not he was chewed out, his subsequence performance was usually more average. (K 175,176)

This is an example of the regression to the mean, which merely means that behavior tends to fluctuate but averages out toward a mean. It's a statistical fact with which our emotional mind, which is biased toward finding causes for behavior, has a lot of trouble contending. Regression to the mean has an explanation but doesn't have a cause. (K 182)

It's important to appreciate that, when talking about regression to the mean, the mean being referred to isn't the mean of an individual's performance over time. It's the mean of the performance within the population to which the individual belongs.

Once more, the combination of skill and luck involved in the activity being performed is a determining factor in the regression to the mean. If performance is overwhelmingly the result of skill, then the skillful participant will be able to consistently keep his performance well above the mean. In this case, you can predict the participant's future behavior on the basis of his past performance.

But if luck is the dominant factor, then any deviation from the mean is, almost invariably, the result of a lucky, or unlucky, fluke, and it's unlikely to continue. Here your better predictor of future performance is average performance. (Ma 28,206,207)

Statistics

The emotional mind doesn't deal well with statistics. Ellen Peters, a psychologist at Ohio State gave research volunteers a chance to win money by randomly selecting a jellybean from one of two jars. If a volunteer selected a red jellybean, he won.

One jar contained 100 jellybeans, nine of which were red. The jar was labeled "nine percent red beans". The other jar contained ten jellybeans, one of which was red. It was labeled "ten percent red beans".

Even though, clearly, a ten percent chance is better than a nine percent one, many of the volunteers were conflicted, because one bottle had nine red beans in it while the other had only one. (U 140,141)

Collecting Information from a Group

The more effective way of collecting information from a group is to confidentially solicit each person's judgment rather than by conducting an open public discussion among all of the group members, where more forceful personalities tend to dominate and may inhibit the expression of good information by less assertive people. (K 245)

The Ultimatum Game

The game goes like this. A "proposer" is given an amount of money, typically, $10. He has to split this money with a "responder".

The character of the split is up to the proposer. He can split the money 50-50, 60-40, whatever he wants, ranging from giving it all away to keeping it all for himself.

The kicker is that the responder gets to decide whether to accept the proposer's offer. If he does, then both keep whatever the proposer's split provides for. However, if he rejects the proposal, then neither gets anything. (P1 110,111)

When the game is played, the most common proposal is 50-50. But rationally, even a 90-10 split should be acceptable to the responder. After all, $1 is better than nothing.

But in fact, that isn't the way responders react. They tend to accept as little as $3, but a $2 offer is just too little. They'd rather not get anything rather than let the proposer get away with such an unfair deal.

It's a common situation. There are pushy people intent on having their own way. To some extent, you put up with it. But too much is too much, and ultimately, you rebel.

The most likely to rebel are high testosterone males (they react aggressively but they don't initiate conflicts.). So if you're going to push, it pays to know whom you're pushing. Pick on women, men with wedding rings (married men have lower testosterone levels than single ones), or men whose ring fingers are shorter than their index fingers (men with longer ring fingers are more competitive — during gestation, they had greater exposure to the androgens that determine sex, which extends ring finger length). (P1 111,112,249,250,251)

The ultimatum game has been played all over the world. One of the interesting correlations is that, the more widespread a trading economy is in the society in which the game is being conducted, the more likely it is that the proposer will offer a deal that the responder is inclined to accept. Where there was little trade, the attitude of the proposer seemed to be, "It's mine, and I'll keep it," and the responder's attitude was, "I don't expect anything from you, and anything you give me, no matter how picayune, I'll accept." Another interesting correlation is that, in societies where gifts come with strings attached (you're now indebted to the gift giver), even generous proposals were turned down. (P1 122,123)

Rejecting an unacceptably low proposal involves a cost. But it's considered to be worthwhile, because it results in punishment of the proposer for engaging in unfair, disgusting behavior.

And disgusting seems to be the right word. MRI scans of responders indicate that, when they receive an unacceptable proposal, their insula cortex is activated. This area of the brain is also triggered by foul odors. We have the same reaction to what we consider moral failing as we do to rotting meat or feces. (P1 114,168 Ka 230)

There's an interesting theory that maintains that the willingness to punish at cost is what creates social solidarity. Here's the argument.

There's a segment of society, maybe 25 percent, who are "saints". They contribute to the common good out of sense of responsibility, regardless of what everyone else is doing.

Another segment of society, maybe another 25 percent, are "free loaders". They take advantage of the benefits provided by collective actions but make no contribution themselves.

The rest of society is made up of "moralists". The moralists resent the actions of the free loaders, and as long as the free loaders continue to get away with their exploitation, the moralists refuse to contribute to the common good.

Given the situation described thus far, it's clear that, no matter how sincere the saints, their actions, by themselves, are never going to result in a society with social solidarity. Instead, the society is on its way to disintegration.

However, if the moralists are given the opportunity to punish the free loaders for their actions, the moralists become willing to sacrifice some of their own self-interest to see that punishment is carried out.

The motivation of the moralists isn't to get the free loaders to conform. What they want is retribution for the misbehavior of the free loaders. That's why they're moralists.

So, in effect, the moralists are willing to support a police force and a retributive judicial system. They're willing to support a welfare system if the free loaders are frozen out. By getting the satisfaction of seeing the exploiters and free loaders punished, the moralists become willing to make their own contribution to the common good.

As a consequence, the balance tips in favor of contributing to the common good. It's the moralists that make social solidarity possible. (T 119-122,136)

The next question is: Do proposers who make acceptable offers do so because they're responding to a sense of fairness, or are they just trying to frame the game so that they assure themselves that responders don't turn down their proposals? The dictator game provides answers (more than one) to this question.

## The Dictator Game

In the original dictator game, the proposer proposed the split and the responder took whatever split the proposer proposed. The responder couldn't reject the proposal.

Under these conditions, proposers continued to make acceptable offers. Chalk up one for a sense of fairness.

But wait. A refinement was then introduced.

Each proposer received an envelope that generally held ten singles and ten bill sized sheets of blank paper. In privacy, he then removed ten slips from the envelope. He could remove all ten of the singles, all ten of the blank sheets, or some combination of singles and blanks.

The envelope was then returned to an attendant, who delivered it to a responder.

Some of the original envelopes contained just 20 blanks, in which case, the proposer just removed ten blanks and returned the envelope to the attendant. So a responder never knew which proposer prepared the envelope that the responder received, and if the envelope contained ten blanks, the responder didn't know whether this was a choice of the proposer or if the proposer simply had no choice.

Under these new circumstances, 60 percent of the proposers kept all ten of the singles. So the proposers in the original game weren't responding to a sense of fairness. Instead, they were trying to avoid being identified as greedy. Peer pressure has a lot to do with behavior. (Pl 117,118,119)

Peer Pressure

Perhaps the most impressive demonstration of peer pressure is the following experiment. A group of people are repeatedly shown two lines, one of which is longer than the other and are asked which is longer.

Actually, only one member of the group is the subject of the study. All of the other members are confederates of the investigator, and sometimes, they identify the shorter line as the longer one.

Ultimately, most subjects go along with the group decision. One of these studies determined that, if the subject had just one other person who agreed with him, the extent to which he went along with the group decreased to one fourth. (Z 264)

Peer pressure can be a good thing. It inclines people toward behaving the way society thinks that they should. (Pl 119) But that isn't necessarily the case. Think of mobs.

Authority

Perhaps the most discouraging example of the pernicious use of authority is the experiment carried out by Stanley Milgram. The subject was seated at a console controlling the electricity to which a person on the other side of a wall from the console was apparently being subjected.

The control on the console was clearly calibrated and indicated such levels as "painful", "dangerous" and "fatal". The administrator in charge of the experiment was dressed like a doctor in a lab coat, and he explained to the subject that the purpose of the experiment was to determine how well a person learned when subjected to punishment.

The subject was given a set of questions to ask the person on the other side of a wall. Communication was through a speaker in the wall.

If the test taker on the other side of the wall answered a question incorrectly, he was to be given a jolt of electricity. With each incorrectly answered question, the electricity level was to be increased.

At some point in this escalation, when a jolt was applied, a cry of pain could be heard from the other side of the wall. As the level of the electricity applied continued to be increased, all sounds from the other side of the wall eventually ceased.

Nevertheless, the administrator instructed the subject to continue the experiment. At some point, a few of the subjects refused to go on. But most carried on until the control was set at its highest possible level.

In her book, *The Sociopath Next Door*, Martha Stout argues passionately against giving in to this tendency to defer to authority and encourages people to question any authority that directs them to do anything that violates their conscience (St 156,157).

But as bad as the human tendency to defer to authority is, the perverse aspects of human nature get even worse.

Evil

In his book, *The Lucifer Effect*, Philip Zimbardo documents the fact that evil is banal. Given a situation in which evil can be practiced with impunity, in general, it will.

If we want to avoid evil, we shouldn't allow situations, in which it can occur, to develop. When evil occurs, Zimbardo places responsibility for its occurrence on the system (typically, the society) for allowing the situation, in which the evil takes place, to develop. (Z x,xi,9,10,211,226,445,446).

In 1971, Zimbardo conducted a chilling experiment, the Stamford Prison Experiment. He was a professor at Stamford, and he outfitted the basement of the psychological department as a prison.

Both the guards and the prisoners at Zimbardo's "prison" were college students who had volunteered to participate in the experiment, and they were screened in advance for "normalcy" (no criminal record, no emotional or physical disability, no intellectual or social disadvantage or advantage, passage of various personality tests), and they were randomly assigned to their roles.

Zimbardo's initial interest was in how the prisoners would react to their situation. He tried to set up the situation so that it resembled a real prison as much as possible.

Consequently, his briefing of his guards was as follows. There couldn't be any physical abuse. But the prisoners were to have no privacy, there would be constant surveillance, the prisoners would be permitted to do only what the guards told them to do, they would wear uniforms with numbers on them, and they would be addressed by number only, no names.

The idea was to create a feeling of powerlessness in the prisoners. Zimbardo wanted to see what they'd do under such circumstances. However, it was the guard behavior that surprised him. (Z 20,55,196)

Almost immediately, the guards began harassing the prisoners, requiring them to engage in all kinds of pointless drills, berating them for purported failure to perform, punishing them by taking away their blankets, pillows, and cots, forcing them to engage in demeaning activity such as cleaning the toilet bowl with their bare hands, and ultimately, getting them to simulate sodomy. By the second day, a prisoner had to be released because he was in emotional disarray.

By the fourth day, another prisoner had broken down and had to be released. On the fifth day, two more prisoners had to be released. Although the experiment had originally been scheduled to run for two weeks, by the sixth day it was spiraling out of control and was shut down (Z 78,107,159,160,178).

Zimbardo also served as an expert witness for Staff Sergeant Ivan Frederick II, the MP who was in charge of the night shift on Tiers 1A and 1B at Abu Ghraib. The situation at Abu Ghraib was that the MPs were given no direction as to how to conduct themselves and received no supervision.

In addition, the prisoner interrogation room at Abu Ghraib was in Tier 1A, and even though it was against policy, the interrogators allowed the MPs to observe interrogations. After seeing what took place during interrogations, what the MPs did on the prison floor seemed like child's play.

Moreover, the interrogators explicitly asked the MPs to soften up the prisoners to assist the interrogators in doing their job. And the only general direction that the MPs got from their higher ups was that they wanted the prisoners to be broken so that interrogation would be more successful (Z 331,349,352,358,383).

Besides a situation making evil possible, other factors promoting evil are (Z :219,221,222,258,295,301):

1.  What the psychologists call deindividualisation. The easiest way to think of this is probably as anonymity. The less a person is identified, the more prone he is to engage in evil. His personal accountability is reduced. A mob is a good example. This factor is enhanced if the system endorses the evil action, thus giving permission for it to be engaged in.
2.  The need to be accepted, to belong to the group. If everyone is doing it, the harder it is to resist engaging in evil.
3.  Dehumanization. The less human and the more inferior the victim appears to be, the easier it is to subject him to evil.

Visual System Heuristics

Optical illusions reveal the heuristics that our visual system uses to make sense of our world. For example, in the following figure, which line is longer, line A or line B? (Li 67)

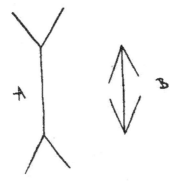

If you measure the two lines, you'll determine that they're the same length. The interesting thing about this example is that, even after your rational mind has determined that the two lines have the same length, your emotional mind continues to tell you that line A is longer than line B. This is the Muller-Lyer illusion.

There's an explanation for this. Our visual system makes various assumptions about what different visual clues imply, and it uses these assumptions to make sense of the world around us. In the Muller-Lyer illusion, the arrows at the ends of line B suggest that you're looking at the edge of two walls joining together close to you. In contrast, the arrows at the ends of line A suggest that you're looking at two walls that are meeting far away in the distance.

While lines A and B have the same length, the arrows at the ends of the lines suggest that line A is far away and that line B is close to you. Evolution has taught our visual system that, the further away something is, the smaller it will look. Consequently, our visual system concludes that line A is larger than it really is and that line B is smaller than it really is.

## Miscellaneous

I suspect that there's a name for the phenomenon that I'm about to describe, but I don't know what it is. Consequently, the label "Miscellaneous".

The more the number of people who witness an emergency, the less likely it is that anyone will intervene to help. The explanation seems to be that, the larger the number of witnesses, the more each witness excuses himself from doing anything because he thinks that someone else will step in. (Z 315)

## Appendix

Here's another example of how our emotional mind leads us astray.

John, who's married, is looking at Jane, who's looking at Bill, who's unmarried. The question is: Is anyone who's married looking at anyone who's unmarried? There are three possible answers.

1. Yes
2. No
3. There's insufficient information to make a determination

Most people choose answer 3. But the right answer is answer 1. Here's the reasoning.

Jane is either married or unmarried. If she's married, she's looking at Bill, who's unmarried. If she's unmarried, then John, who's married, is looking at her.

So no matter what Jane's marital status is, someone who's married is looking at someone who's unmarried. We just don't know who the someone is.

## Sources

(A) Ariely, Dan, *Predictably Irrational* (HarperCollins 2008)
(C) Coyle, Daniel, *The Talent Code* (Random House 2009)
(E) Eagleman, David, *Incognito* (Random House 2011)
(Gl) Gladwell, Malcolm, *Outliers* (Little Brown 2008)
(G) Groopman, Jerome, *How Doctors Think* (Houghton Mifflin 2007)
(H) Harris, Sam, *The Moral Landscape* (Simon & Schuster 2010)
(I) Iyengar, Sheena, *The Art of Choosing* (Hachette 2010)

(J) Jay, Meg, *The Defining Decade* (Hachette 2012)

(K) Kahneman, Daniel, *Thinking, Fast and Slow* (Farrar, Straus and Giroux 2011)

(Ka) Kaplan, Michael and Ellen, *Bozo Sapiens* (Bloomsbury 2009)

(L) Lehrer, Jonah, *How We Decide* (Houghton Mifflin 2009)

(Li) Lieberman, Matthew D., *Social* (Random House 2013)

(Ma) Mauboussin, Michael J., *The Success Equation* (Harvard Business School Publishing (2012)

(M) Mlodinow, Leonard, *The Drunkard's Walk* (Random House 2008)

(P1) Poundstone, William, *Priceless* (Farrar, Straus and Giroux 2010)

(P2) Poundstone, William *Rock Breaks Scissors* (Little, Brown 2014)

(S) Shermer, Michael, *The Believing Brain* (Henry Holt 2011)

(Sh) Sherwood, Ben, *The Survivors Club* (Hachette 2009)

(St) Stout, Martha *The Sociopath Next Door* (Random House 2005)

(T) Thaler, Richard H. and Sunstein, Cass R., *Nudge* (Yale U 2008)

(To) Tough, Paul, *How Children Succeed* (Houghton Mifflin Harcourt 2012)

(Tu) Turchin, Peter, *War & Peace & War* (Pi 2006)

(U) Ubel, Peter A., *Critical Decisions* (HarperCollins 2012)

(Z) Zimbardo, Philip, *The Lucifer Effect* (Random House 2007)

# CHAPTER FOUR

# Money

Consider two people. Suppose that they both want both venison and corn.

Each of these two can spend part of their time hunting deer and the rest of their time raising corn. Each consumes the fruits of his hunting and farming.

We refer to the circumstances in which such people live as a *subsistence economy*, which is one in which each person consumes his own production. In a subsistence economy, there's no market and the general welfare is low.

As an alternative to a subsistence economy, one person can devote himself to hunting and the other to farming. The hunter can exchange venison for corn with the farmer. The hunter and farmer then make up an *exchange economy*, an economic system in which producers exchange *goods*, such as venison and corn, with one another.

In such an economy, people are offered the opportunity to produce for a *market* in which goods are exchanged. It's on the basis of an exchange economy that a *division of labor* is constructed. And the division of labor is the foundation on which increased *production* is built.

In an exchange economy in which goods are swapped directly, the method of exchange is known as *barter*. Barter has drawbacks.

Suppose you have venison and want corn. You must find a person who has corn and wants venison.

You may find several people with corn who don't want venison. You may also find people who want venison but have no corn.

With none of these people can you trade. As has been aptly observed, barter is frequently characterized by a want of coincidence, rather than by a coincidence of wants.

But unlike venison or corn, which few people want all of the time, there are some goods that most people want at least most of the time. Gold is such a good.

So, if you can't find a person with corn who wants venison, you may be able to find a person with gold who wants venison. You trade your venison for gold. Then, since almost everybody wants gold, it's easy to find a person willing to trade corn for gold.

You trade your venison for gold, not because you want to make jewelry, but because you know that it's easy to trade gold for whatever you want. As this feature of gold becomes more known, more sellers of goods become willing to exchange their goods for gold.

Each seller builds up a store of gold, which is the form in which he holds his *wealth*. He holds his wealth in gold because he knows that, when he wants something, it's easy for him to get the thing as long as he has gold to offer.

As soon as everyone begins to hold his wealth in gold, it's easier for you to sell your venison. All that you have to do is find a person who wants to buy. Presumably, he'll have some gold with which to carry out the transaction.

In the above situation, gold has acquired a new characteristic. In addition to being a *commodity* (a good that's desired for consumption), it's now also a *medium of exchange.*

Venison is no longer exchanged for corn or potatoes. It's exchanged for gold.

Corn is no longer exchanged for venison or potatoes. It's also exchanged for gold.

And so on. Gold becomes the medium through which the exchange of goods is carried on.

Here gold is called *commodity money*, since although it's used as a medium of exchange, it's also wanted for consumption in its own right. You want gold because you can buy venison and corn with it. But you also want it because it's decorative.

Many goods have been used as a medium of exchange: cattle, hides, gold, silver, leafs of tobacco, cigarettes, and candy bars, to name a few. Each has a disadvantage.

Cattle aren't divisible for small change. Leafs of tobacco deteriorate with handling. Gold is so rare that coins of low value are so small that they're hard to keep from being lost.

You hold your wealth in gold. To protect your gold, you should store it in a vault. But vaults are hard to get.

Sam is a goldsmith. He has lots of gold and a large vault in which to keep it.

You make an arrangement with Sam. You put your bag of gold in Sam's vault for safekeeping.

Sam tags your bag, to show that it's yours, and gives you a receipt for it. When you need to buy something, you give your receipt to Sam, he gives you your gold, and off you go to the market.

You've deposited your gold in Sam's vault. The deposit that you've made is a *demand deposit*, because anytime that you want, you can give your receipt to Sam and demand that he give you your gold.

Other people become aware of your arrangement with Sam. Soon Sam has many bags of gold in his vault, and most people are walking around with one or more of Sam's receipts in their pockets.

One day, you're in a hurry to buy something from Dave. Perhaps he's just made a knife.

Dave is willing to sell his knife to you. But if you don't buy it right away, he's going to sell it to Carol.

You haven't got time to go to Sam's to get your gold. So you offer Dave your vault receipt for the knife. Dave accepts.

In this way, *paper money* is introduced. People buy and sell with vault receipts. The receipts are backed by the gold in Sam's vault.

Vault receipts now serve as the medium of exchange. When you buy corn, you pay for it in vault receipts. When you work, or sell your services, you get paid in vault receipts.

Vault receipts have none of the disadvantages of commodity money. They can be issued in all kinds of denominations. There are vault receipts for small amounts of gold to be used in minor transactions and vault receipts for large amounts to be used in major transactions. Deterioration isn't a problem since, when a receipt becomes worn, Sam exchanges a new one for it.

Vault receipts can be issued in a standard size convenient for handling. The amount of the receipt is represented by the number on it, one ounce of gold, two ounces of gold, etc.

Unlike gold, vault receipts are of insignificant value in themselves. You can't only buy venison and corn with gold, you can also make jewelry and teeth with it. Vault receipts, on the other hand, can't be eaten or worn for clothes. They have value only as a medium of exchange.

The value of a vault receipt derives from the fact that all buyers and sellers agree that the vault receipt stands for a certain amount of gold. Buyers and sellers agree in this way because they know that, when they want to, they can go to Sam, present their vault receipts, and get the amounts of gold that they've agreed that the vault receipts stand for.

At this point, Sam's vault is just a checkroom. You bring gold to Sam. He tags it and gives you a receipt. When the receipt is presented to Sam, he turns over the gold that was given to him when he issued the receipt.

But over time, Sam discovers that gold is gold. One ounce is indistinguishable from another. So Sam stops tagging gold.

When you bring gold to be deposited in Sam's vault, he just tosses it into a common pile. When you present a receipt, he weighs out the ounces called for by the receipt from his common pile and gives them to you. Once the gold in Sam's vault is mingled, his vault becomes a gold warehouse, or *central bank.*

In the United States, the government had the central banking job of running the gold warehouse. The gold warehouse receipts that the government issued, while the United States was on the gold standard, were dollars. Anytime that you wanted, you could take a dollar to the central bank and get the specified amount of gold for it.

The United States went off of the gold standard in 1933. At that time, as far as the United States citizen was concerned, the correspondence between a dollar and a gold warehouse receipt disappeared.

The central bank still issues dollars. But they're no longer gold warehouse receipts. You can't exchange them for gold.

Instead, dollars are just *fiat money*. They constitute a medium of exchange because the government says that they do.

The government says that all of the dollars that it issues are "legal tender for all debts, public and private". In fact, it prints this dictum right on its dollar bills. *Legal tender* is whatever the government says must be accepted in payment of debts.

Legal tender is something that the government requires a creditor to accept as payment of a debt, although this requirement doesn't hold for day-to-day transactions. A seller can decline to accept legal tender as payment. (J 43)

We now come to the point where I'm going to deviate from the customary use of a term. I'm going to use the unmodified term, *money*, to refer to the medium of exchange provided by the government. To some extent, this is a conforming definition, in that, from time to time, people refer to what people use as money but that isn't issued by the government as a *money substitute*.

But in general, people use the word money to refer to anything that's used as money, whether it's issued by the government or is a money substitute. In particular, when people speak of the money supply, they're referring to this undifferentiated collection of government issued money and money substitutes.

That's not how I'm going to use the term, money. When I use the term, I'm referring to just the money issued by the government. And when I talk about the *money supply*, I'm referring strictly to the money in the economy that's supplied by the government.

In the past, money has consisted of coins made of precious metal, such as gold or silver, commonly referred to as *specie*, or a combination of specie and paper money that can be exchanged with each other. However, today, money is universally paper money that constitutes legal tender only.

The government also issues coins made of a base metal (an inexpensive alternative to a precious metal) that are used for small change. These coins are, to some extent, also legal tender, but only in small amounts.

Basically, coins are just tokens, created for convenience only. The amount of these tokens that the government says must be accepted for payment of debts is small, amounting to a few dollars. Consequently, these coins are insignificant in any discussion of money, and therefore, we're going to ignore them.

The disadvantages of money are that it's easy to lose and it's too negotiable. If you have a $100 bill and lose it, you've lost the ability to buy $100 worth of goods.

If Mary finds the $100 bill that you lost, she can use it as money. No one, including you and Mary, has any way of knowing if the $100 that she's using is the one that you lost. All $100 bills look the same, and one is as good as the next.

At this point, Jack comes up with an idea. He opens a money warehouse.

You bring money to Jack and deposit it in his money warehouse. Jack notes in a book how much you've deposited and gives you some blank warehouse receipts.

Then if you want to buy a knife from Dave for five dollars, you fill out a warehouse receipt to say that Jack is to pay Dave five dollars whenever he wants it, and sign the receipt. In this way, nobody can get money for the receipt, or *cash* it, but Dave.

When Dave cashes the receipt, Jack reduces by five dollars the balance of money that you've deposited in his money warehouse. Periodically, Jack sends you a *statement* showing how many dollars of money you have left in his money warehouse.

Such blank receipts that can be filled in for any amount payable to a specified person are *checks*. A money warehouse is a *bank*. And what you have at the bank is a *checking account*.

Checks have none of the disadvantages of money. Until they're filled out, they're worthless. That is, the bank won't cash, or honor, them. So if you lose them, you've lost nothing.

Even after you fill one out to Dave, the only person to whom it's worth anything is Dave. He's the only one who can cash, or negotiate, it. So Dave can lose the check without harm.

Moreover, if your checks are numbered and the check that Dave lost was your check number 20, you can tell the bank not to honor that check, and you can then write Dave another one. In this way, Dave gets his money, and you're protected against the possibility of

Dave finding the original check and cashing two checks in payment for just one transaction.

We use the checks with which Jack supplies us as a medium of exchange. We continue to use money for small transactions. But once price becomes more than a minor matter, we resort to writing checks.

So far, nothing has really changed. True, we're using checks as a medium of exchange, rather than money alone.

But every check we write is backed up by money in the bank. Consequently, even though our buying power is more a function of our ability to write checks than it's a function of the money that we have in our pockets, over all, the *buying power* in the economy is still represented by the money supply.

However, let's continue. Sometimes we take a check that we've received to the bank and cash it.

But mostly, we just deposit the checks, which we've received, in the bank. In this way, we replenish our checking accounts so that we can write more checks. As a consequence, few checks are ever presented to Jack with a request for money.

Perhaps Jack has $10,000 is his bank. It's unlikely that, on any one day, Jack pays out more than $200 in money. And it's possible that, on the same day, $200 or more are deposited.

Jack's depositors have the right to write checks for $10,000. These checks are used as a medium of exchange. For each dollar for which a check is written, there's a dollar of money in Jack's bank.

But on any one day, the public sees only about $200 of this money. The other $9800 of money in Jack's bank could disappear without dampening our willingness to accept checks for payment of debts. And Jack takes advantage of this fact. He does so as follows.

Suppose that Jack has just started his bank. You deposit $100 of money in it. Then Jack's deposits total $100.

Jack gives you checks, which you can fill out for a total of $100. You use these checks as a medium of exchange.

So there are liabilities on Jack's bank for $100 of money. That is, there's the possibility that Jack may have to pay out as much as $100 to cash checks that you've written.

Jack knows that just about everybody does most of their buying with checks, that these checks are deposited in checking accounts to replenish the accounts, and that few checks are ever cashed. However, some might be. Jack doesn't want to get caught short.

So Jack decides to keep $10 of your money in his bank, just in case. This is Jack's *reserve*. It's a 10 percent reserve, since it amounts to 10 percent of his deposits. This leaves Jack $90 with which to work.

Suppose that Alice needs $90. Jack tells Alice that he'll give her $90 now if she'll return it to him a year from now with an interest payment of $6.

Alice agrees. The exchange is made. What's the effect of this loan?

The effect is to increase buying power. When you had $100 in money, it represented a certain amount of buying power. When you deposited your money in Jack's bank and received checks, $100 of money went out of circulation in the economy, checks for $100 went in, and buying power remained unchanged.

But when Jack loaned Alice $90, buying power increased. You've still got the ability to write checks for $100, which you're using as a medium of exchange, and Alice has $90, which she's also using as a medium of exchange. Buying power has increased by $90.

But this increase in buying power doesn't stop here. Suppose that George has also just started a bank and that Alice deposits the $90 that she got from Jack in George's bank.

There are now, in the economy, checks on Jack's bank for $100 and checks on George's bank for $90, and there's still no change in buying power since it went up by $90 when Jack loaned Alice $90. But if George also keeps just 10 percent of his deposits, or $9, on reserve and loans the other $81, say to Barbara, buying power increases by another $81.

And so it goes. If every bank follows a policy of keeping a 10 percent reserve and loaning out the rest of its deposits, it can be shown that, for every dollar of money deposited in the *banking system*, which is what we call the collection of banks in the economy, $10 of buying power can show up in the economy.

In other words, a 10 percent reserve policy can increase buying power by as much as 900 percent over the money deposited in the banking system. This increase consists of the money substitute, made up of bank loans, created by the 10 percent reserve banking policy.

In general, any reserve policy other than for 100 percent — that is, any *fractional reserve banking* policy — increases buying power through the creation of the money substitute of *bank credit*. It isn't necessarily true that a bank will issue bank credit to the extent allowed by its reserve policy, but it can and makes every effort to do so, since it's the interest that it earns on its loans that constitutes much of its revenue (the rest of its revenue comes from the fees that it charges for its services).

While a significant factor in buying power, bank credit is, nevertheless, only one form of credit. In general, credit is a money substitute that's used as a medium of exchange and comes into existence whenever an exchange is made on the basis of "Don't pay me now. You can owe it to me." A familiar example of credit, other than bank credit, is when you put something on your aptly named credit card. In general, *any kind of credit adds to buying power.*

The next concept with which we have to deal here is *dollar velocity.* To get a start on what we mean by dollar velocity, let's begin with a single dollar that belongs to you.

Let's suppose that you buy something from Dolores for one dollar. The dollar, which used to belong to you, now belongs to Dolores. If Dolores just holds onto the dollar, the dollar represents the exercise of some amount of buying power.

But if, in turn, Dolores buys something from Ed for one dollar, the dollar passes through two pairs of hands, and what we now have is the exercise of twice as much buying power as we had before. There's still just one dollar, but its velocity (the speed at which it moves from one pair of hands to another) has doubled.

So buying power isn't just a function of the number of dollars in the economy. It's also a function of the velocity at which these dollars move through the economy. The faster that the dollars move, the greater the buying power.

In general, *buying power is the sum of the money and money substitutes in the economy, this sum being multiplied by the velocity at which the dollars, making up this sum, move through the economy.* I'm now going to invent a term and refer to this buying power as the *dollar supply.*

My term, dollar supply, is roughly equivalent to the conventional term, money supply. However, even here I've deviated. The conventional term, money supply, refers to the sum of money and money substitutes in the economy. Velocity isn't included.

It's the amount of the dollar supply that's one of the factors in determining the price of goods. The other two factors are the demand and supply of these goods.

We want the price of goods to vary with supply and demand, because that provides for the efficient allocation of goods. But we don't want prices to vary because of changes in the dollar supply, because that threatens the ability of the market to accurately reflect the demand and supply of goods.

So we want to be able to control the dollar supply, so that it doesn't, by itself, influence prices. To do so, we have to be able to measure the dollar supply.

However, it's not clear how one would go about measuring the dollar supply. The reason is that no one is clear about what should and shouldn't be included when you're counting up the dollars in the dollar supply.

The inability to come up with a precise definition of the dollar supply is why the Fed (the Federal Reserve Bank, our central bank), in particular, and economists, in general, have so many definitions of what makes up the dollar supply. Let's take a look at some of these definitions.

First, there's the legal tender issued by the government. This is what I've called money. Milton Friedman calls this legal tender "high powered money", since when it enters the banking system, the fractional reserve banking policy of the banking system allows the banking system to introduce several dollars of bank credit into the economy for every dollar issued by the government.

The next most narrow definition of the dollar supply is what the Fed calls Ml. Ml is the sum of *currency* and the dollars deposited in checking accounts. Currency is the dollars held by the public — that is, not in bank vaults but, instead, carried around in pockets and stuffed in mattresses. You can see that this definition of the dollar supply is broader than that of the money supply, since it involves bank credit as well as money.

Next comes M2. M2 is Ml plus the dollars deposited in savings accounts plus the dollars deposited in money market deposit accounts plus the dollars invested in money market mutual funds plus the dollars invested small denomination (less than $100,000) time deposits, such as certificates of deposit.

Ml and M2 are the most commonly used measures of the dollar supply. They're characteristically referred to as measures of the "money supply", which as I've pointed out, uses the term, money supply, differently than I'm doing here.

However, there's also M3. It's M2 plus all time deposits other than those already included in M2, such as large denomination certificates of deposit.

Charles P. Kindleberger, who spent a good bit of his life studying credit and had come to believe that it's almost infinitely expandable, reported that he was aware of as many as seven (Ml through M7) levels of the dollar supply that have been defined. His contention was that you can take this kind of definition on indefinitely.

Notice that none of these definitions of the dollar supply include the concept of dollar velocity. Some economists maintain that dollar velocity is stable — that is, that while it changes over time, the change is gradual and predictable, with the consequence that dollar velocity can be ignored when determining the dollar supply (M 323,324).

Others contend that dollar velocity is variable and unpredictable and is, therefore, a vital factor in the determination of the dollar supply (M 332). For example, if two economies have the same sum of money and money substitutes, the one in which a dollar moves through four hands in a year has a dollar supply double that of the one in which a dollar moves through just two hands a year.

Since we aren't able to identify all the sources of credit (one reason being that, when credit is needed and no existing form is available to satisfy the need, new forms of credit tend to arise) and we have no reliable way to measure dollar velocity, how can we be sure of what we're talking about when we so glibly refer to the dollar supply?

In any case, the dollar supply, no matter how you define it, varies on a moment-to-moment basis. However, if we're going to try to figure out what's going on when dollars are being used as a medium of exchange, we can't let too many variables keep changing all over the place. We've got to keep most of these variables constant, so that, when one of the remaining variables changes, we can see what effect it has on the other few variables that, at the moment, we're allowing to vary.

Initially, in the following discussion, one of the things that we're going to hold constant is the dollar supply. As we've said, we aren't sure what the dollar supply is, but whatever it is, in the following discussion, we're going to assume that it doesn't change over time, even though we know that this assumption is at variance with the world as we know it.

Despite the artificiality of this assumption, we're anticipating that, by making it, we'll be able to get some insight into what happens when we use dollars as a medium of exchange. So until we say that it's no longer so, all of the following discussion presumes that the dollar supply is a constant amount, whatever that amount is.

The *purchasing power* of a dollar is the array of all of the goods that a dollar can buy. This is the "price" of a dollar.

The price of a dollar is what the consumer price index tries to measure. If you've exposed yourself to any of the controversy over what procedures should be used to come up with the consumer price index for any one point in time, then you can see that, just like the dollar supply, no one has any good idea of how to measure the purchasing power of a dollar.

As a consequence, the concept of the purchasing power of a dollar is in good company with the concept of the dollar supply. We don't know how to measure either one, but we continue to maintain that they're useful concepts.

As we've said, the purchasing power of a dollar is the price of a dollar. When we speak in such terms, we're thinking of a dollar as a good.

The price of a good is fixed at the point where the supply curve for the good intersects the demand curve for the good. So the purchasing power of a dollar (that is, the price of a dollar) can be found at the point where the supply curve for dollars intersects the demand curve for dollars.

It's easy to figure out what the supply curve for dollars looks like. We're assuming that the dollar supply is fixed. Therefore, the supply curve for dollars is a vertical line. That is, no matter what the purchasing power of a dollar is, the number of dollars made available remains constant.

The demand curve for dollars is just like any other demand curve. It slopes downward to the right. That is, the greater the purchasing power of a dollar (the price of a dollar), the fewer the number of dollars that will be demanded.

This makes perfect sense. The more that a dollar will buy, the less the number of dollars that we need.

This information about the supply and demand curves for dollars is summarized in the following figure. Notice that, while this supply-demand chart has many similarities to other supply-demand charts, it has one significant difference.

Each supply-demand chart shows the supply and demand for a particular good. The quantity of the good is charted along the horizontal axis of the chart, and the price of the good is charted along the vertical axis.

In most supply-demand charts, the vertical axis is marked off in dollars, since that's how we measure the price of most goods. However, in the case of money, the price of the good is the purchasing power of the dollar, and the good, dollars, is charted on the horizontal axis.

As we've said, the purchasing power of a dollar — that is, the price of a dollar — is to be found at the intersection of the supply curve for dollars and the demand curve for dollars.

With the information shown in the following figure, we can now abandon our assumption about the size of the dollar supply not changing and investigate what happens when the dollar supply changes. Let's first ask: At any particular point in time, is there any particular significance to the size of the dollar supply?

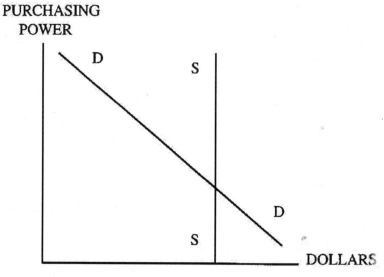

The Demand (D) for and Supply (S) of Dollars

To place a particularly sharp point on this question that we've just asked, let's suppose that, given the situation in the following figure, we all wake up tomorrow to discover that everything related to dollars has doubled: your bank account, your salary, your debts, the prices in the supermarkets and department stores, and so on. Would anything change?

Well, both the supply and demand curves in the above figure would now be twice as far away from the vertical axis as they were yesterday. But as far as purchasing power is concerned, the curves would still intersect at the same price for the dollar.

So there would be no change in the purchasing power of a dollar. In terms of goods bought, it would have the same value as it did yesterday.

Even though, as demonstrated above, at any particular point in time, the size of the dollar supply is immaterial to the operation of the economy, the size of the dollar supply in an economy may change, and the process of this change is material. The general scenario is as follows.

Let's suppose that the dollar supply is in the process of expansion. This is known as inflation. This is just one of several possible examples of inflation.

In general, *inflation* is defined as an increase in prices. But inflation can occur for number of reasons. One is when the dollar supply increases. Another is when the supply of goods decreases. A third is when the demand for goods increases.

Remember our assumption that we're going to hold everything constant but those things on which we want to concentrate, so we can see what the effects are of changing these things that we allow to change. Right now, we're holding the supply of and demand for goods constant, so that we can see what are the results of an increase in the dollar supply.

As can be seen from the above figure, an increase in the dollar supply causes the supply curve to move to the right. If for the moment, we assume that nothing else in the economy changes — that is, if we do a static analysis — we can see that the demand curve for dollars will now intersect the supply curve at a lower dollar price. Thus, one result of inflation is the reduction of the purchasing power of a dollar.

This lowered purchasing power benefits debtors and penalizes creditors. This is because loans are defined in terms of dollars. If between the time that a loan is made and the time that it's repaid, inflation has reduced the purchasing power of a dollar, the debtor pays back to the creditor less purchasing power than he borrowed from the creditor.

You can see what kind of effect this situation would have on the economy. Given that inflation is going to eat away at the purchasing power of a dollar and that, consequently, debtors are going to pay off creditors with less purchasing power than they borrowed, creditors are going to demand an interest rate high enough to compensate them for their loss of purchasing power.

The greater the potential loss of purchasing power due to inflation, the higher the interest rate will be. The higher the interest rate, the less likely people will be to borrow. And finally, the less borrowing there is in the economy, the more stunted is the development of capital plant, the wellspring of our general welfare.

The conclusion is that inflation caused by an increase in the dollar supply is an enemy of our welfare. It will have the impact just described above.

However, everything else in the economy won't remain static. The economy will adjust to a one time inflationary event. The economy will ultimately reach the equilibrium that we described when we conducted our thought experiment on the overnight doubling of everything related to dollars. Nevertheless, the short-term effect will still be a disruptive distortion of the relationship between debtors and creditors.

But more importantly, if the increase in the dollar supply is a continuing (rather than a one time) thing, the increasing spiral of inflation results in serious economic dislocation. Runaway inflation that destroys an economy is almost invariably a result of the government starting down the inflationary path of increasing the money supply and finding that the resulting disruption makes breaking its money printing habit increasingly difficult.

The money supply is under the control of government. Governments don't necessarily mismanage the money supply. But they do it often enough to generate concern.

For example, there's the question of how well the Fed has performed in terms of preserving the integrity of our money supply. The Fed was formed in 1913. In 2012, a dollar bought less than what a nickel would have purchased in 1913.

Over time, production becomes more efficient, and productivity increases — that is, more is produced with the same amount of resource input. If we were to hold the dollar supply constant, then over time, prices would drop, since there would be more goods to buy with the same amount of dollars. This is *deflation.* The result of deflation is to increase the purchasing power of a dollar.

This increased purchasing power benefits creditors and penalizes debtors. If between the time that a loan is made and the time that it's repaid, deflation has increased the purchasing power of a dollar, the debtor pays back to the creditor more purchasing power than he borrowed from the creditor.

Another negative consequence of deflation is that, in response to declining prices, people and organizations are inclined to delay purchases in anticipation of lower prices tomorrow. This depresses current consumption and, in turn, current production, and the economy slows down. This isn't what we want our economy to do.

To avoid such a development, central banks try to counteract this negative effect of increasing productivity by increasing the dollar supply just enough to offset the price decline that would otherwise occur. Unfortunately, central banks characteristically overestimate productivity increases, and the result is persistent, creeping inflation.

In fact, for some reason that escapes me, the Federal Reserve has a policy of not allowing the inflation rate to fall below two percent. This doesn't strike me as a good policy.

Sources

(J) Johnson, Simon and Kwak, James *White House Burning* (Random House 2012)
(M) McConnell *Economics*

# CHAPTER FIVE

# Property

For markets to operate, the buying and selling of goods must take place as a matter of course. For this to happen, each buyer must be assured that, when he has bought something, he then owns it — that is, that the thing becomes his *property*. He must, as a result of his purchase, come into a *clear title* to the thing. For this to happen, the seller of the thing has to have had clear title to the thing when he offered it for sale.

Buying isn't the only way to obtain *ownership* of something. The previous owner of the thing can, instead of selling it to you, give it to you as a gift.

And facilitating the exchange of goods isn't the only function of clear title. Perhaps even more important is that, if you want to borrow money and put up your property as collateral, you must be able to demonstrate clear ownership of the property.

Ownership is sometimes given a mystical cast, as if some bond exists between the owner and the thing owned. We refer to <u>my</u> house, <u>my</u> car, and so on. Even when we go to work in someone else's office, we tend to refer to <u>my</u> desk, <u>my</u> stapler, etc., even if we don't own these things.

But there isn't any such tie between us and property. Ownership isn't a direct relationship between people and things. Instead, ownership inheres in the rights that people have with respect to things. These rights are the owner's *property rights*.

The concept of an easement is an example of the fact that ownership inheres in rights rather than in things. Suppose that you own a plot of land and that you give your neighbor the right to run a gas line under a corner of your property.

While you retain most of the rights to your property, there's now a restraint on these rights. You can subsequently, as we say, "sell your property". But what you're really selling is your rights to the land, not the land itself. And these rights don't extend to the gas line cutting across the corner of your land.

The right to the gas line remains with your neighbor. He may sell it along with his other property rights when he sells his land.

But you no longer own the right to the gas line running across your land. You can't sell the gas line, because you've already given it away.

When a buyer buys your property rights, he agrees that he has no rights to the gas line. He can't remove it or force its removal. This restriction is spelled out as an easement on the deed documenting your property rights.

Thus, while we generally think of property as a thing, it is, in fact, a bunch of rights related to the thing. These rights can be separated and disposed of individually. Thus, you can sell the mineral rights to your land without relinquishing your right to use the land in other ways.

The importance to the operation of a free market of unquestioned ownership rights is emphasized by the lengths to which we go to see that ownership chains aren't broken. If an owner dies without stating his preferences with respect to the inheritance of his property rights — that is, if he dies intestate ("in testate" — without a testament, or will), we have laws that spell out how the property rights are to pass on.

The difficulties that are created when property rights aren't clear are illustrated by the squabbles surrounding fishing rights at sea. Although it has historically not been treated as such, the sea is equivalent to land.

The sea can be surveyed, and thus, bounded, just like land. The fact that, in the sea, water and wildlife move over the plot isn't material.

Water and wildlife move over land, too. This doesn't create insurmountable difficulties in defining bounded property rights on land.

There is the problem that ships move over the sea. And sea-lanes aren't analogous to roads and railroad tracks. But sea-lanes shouldn't present so much of a problem that an accommodation couldn't be worked out if a committed effort to create ownership rights to areas of the sea were made.

For example, the right of a ship to pass over your piece of sea could be considered an easement on your property rights. And these ship lane rights could be restrictively defined so that no ship would be allowed to pollute your sea property with impunity.

Another example of the difficulties that arise when property rights aren't clear is the case of flowing water. Originally, our concept of the rights to flowing water was borrowed from English common law and was known as the doctrine of riparian rights — every landowner on the banks of water has equal rights to the water, but no landowner can use the water in such a way that the rights of the other landowners is reduced.

Thus, suppose that you buy a plot of land across which flows a stream. In purchasing the plot, you buy certain rights to the stream.

But these rights aren't unlimited, since the stream flows off your land onto other land. The owners of this other land also have rights in the stream.

You can do anything you want with the water in your part of the stream as long as your actions don't infringe on the rights of the owners downstream. For example, you can build a mill on the stream and even dam the stream to create a millpond as long as you don't interrupt the flow of the stream. Thus, if you were to dam the stream to divert its water for irrigation of your land and, in so doing, were to reduce the flow downstream, you'd have exceeded your rights in the stream.

Initially, the doctrine of riparian rights worked fine in the US. However, at the time that the more arid western parts of the country were being developed out West, the dominant theme in the nation was to get the land into operation as soon as possible.

The idea was to get what water there was into production, and the faster, the better. As a result, a doctrine different from that of riparian rights, the doctrine of prior appropriation, was adopted.

Basically, this doctrine was first come, first served. If there wasn't enough water left over for latecomers, that was just too bad. This departure from the doctrine of riparian rights may have served the times, but it has now come back to haunt us in terms of the contention going on over who has the rights to the water available in the West.

In their natural state (that is, before any work has been done on them), there are only two things that can be owned: land and animals. Anything that's permanently attached to the land, such as vegetation, is part of the land.

From these two things, land and animals, all other goods flow. The goods are first extracted as raw material and then worked on to transform them into more specific things.

In the US, there is, and never has been, any unowned land. However, there are still wild animals, animals in their natural state, that wander about. If you can capture a wild animal while it's on your land, you can claim ownership of the animal.

This ownership comes about by a process called *appropriation*. By capturing the wild animal, you've, so to speak, "mixed" your labor with the natural state of the animal and established ownership.

There's little question that wild animals can be made property by appropriation. Theoretically, appropriation is how ownership of land is also first established.

And appropriation is the only theory that has ever been put forward for establishing first ownership rights to land. The question of first ownership of land is critical, since essentially all goods ultimately derive from the land.

A thing moves through a chain of sellers and gift givers in its passage from one owner to another. During this passage, the nature of the thing can be changed by work done on it by various owners. This work transforms the thing from a more natural state to a more processed state.

However, this chain of buying and gift receiving can't be traced back indefinitely. At the beginning of the chain, there has to have been a first owner. How did this first owner come by his ownership of his land?

According to the theory of appropriation, the first owner came by his property rights to his land by mixing his labor with it. In some way, he had to improve it. To take a few examples, he could have cultivated the land, he could have engaged in mining on it, or he could have done nothing more than build a home on it.

Once improved, the land becomes the property of the first owner and his heirs forever, provided that none of them choose to either sell it or give it away. Moreover, the ownership that they possess over the land pertains to any use to which the land can be put, regardless of whether any of them had ever before put the land to this use.

In addition, a landowner can't abandon his ownership, no matter how hard he tries. If he chooses, he can let the land lie follow, but it remains his.

In summary, land can be appropriated just once. The theory of appropriation as the basis for first ownership was devised by John Locke.

Well, the theory of appropriation is a great theory. And it's true that, in the frontier days of the US, people did go beyond the edge of civilization and carve homesteads out of the wilderness. (Don't talk to me now about Indians. We'll get to them later.)

But to maintain what these pioneers thought of as their ownership rights, they did a lot more than just improve the land. They stood over it with guns and banded together with neighbors to discourage expropriation.

And when civilization did reach the boundary of what these pioneers thought of as their land, they had to contend with the government, which by clear title, really owned the land. Fortunately, at that time, the government had lots of land, and in the case of most homesteaders, who were technically just squatters, the government was more than willing to reward these intrepid pioneers with title to the land on which they had worked so hard to develop and defend.

Theories are fine. But when it comes to practicalities, people don't necessarily pay much attention to theories. The blunt fact of the matter is that first ownership rights are almost always established by conquest.

For example, when William the Conqueror successfully invaded England in 1066, all of England became his property by right of conquest, and he could do with it as he willed. And did he ever. It's estimated that, by 1071, when William completed the pacification of

England, 99 percent of the land had moved from Saxon into Norman hands, with of course, no compensation.

In this regard, the US has been lucky. Its first lands were ceded to it by England as a result of successful revolution, although a lot of Tories, who owned property in the colonies before the revolution, had their property expropriated. (Once more, don't talk to me now about the Indians. I promise you, we'll get to them later.)

Florida was ceded to the US by Spain as compensation for damages to US commerce during the Napoleonic wars. The Louisiana territory, the Gadsden Purchase, and Alaska were purchased from France, Mexico and Russia, respectively.

The Oregon territory was ceded to the US by England. Only the Southwest and Hawaii came into US possession by conquest, although technically, both were ceded to the US in the treaties that ended the conflicts.

Thus, there has never been any unowned land in the US.

Some colonists had claim to plots of land granted by England. But the bulk of the land making up the US passed directly into the hands of the government. In each segment of the country, as the land came into government ownership, the government has tended to respect the prior private claims to the land and then disposed of the rest by selling it, giving it away, converting it into parkland, or letting it lie fallow.

And now, let's talk about the Indians. We didn't respect their prior claims to the land because the claims weren't private, they were tribal — the Indians' claims didn't conform to the Western concept of property.

The Indians wanted to retain a tribal form of life and roam over vast expanses of land without developing it. The Westerners, on the other hand, wanted to make the land productive, or if you prefer, exploit it. At bottom, the dispute between the Indians and us was a culture clash, and the fundamental clash was over the concept of property.

Just like the Mexicans in the Southwest that we took over as a result of the Mexican War and the Spanish, French and Creoles in the New Orleans that we purchased from the French, the Indians could probably have joined the US polity if they had wanted to.

Many Indians did, in fact, give up tribal life and meld into the Western population. But the bulk of the Indians chose not to join the Westerners and to, instead, continue their tribal ways.

So a clash was almost inevitable. The two groups disliked each other right from the start, and each thought that it had the superior way of life. The result was that the strong imposed its way of doing things on the weak.

The Indians really had just one choice: assimilation or annihilation. Resisting the surge of white settlers into the west was like telling the tide to not come in.

But the Indians thought that their way of life was superior and that white civilization couldn't possibly endure. So they were washed away.

What we did was abhorrent. We killed off the Indians with our germs and our guns, and we expropriated their lands. We engaged in genocide at Sand Creek, and we let the Indian killers, who thought that the only good Indian was a dead one, have their way.

It's regrettable, but it was in the best tradition of historical practice and is now over. We have little choice but to accept the situation and move on.

The overriding rule seems to be: If land comes into a government's hands by conquest and this government can sustain and solidify its conquest, then ownership rights are determined by this government. However, if the conquering government is unable to sustain and solidify its conquest, then the property rights existing before the conquest retain their validity.

Thus, even though, during WW II, property rights in Poland became Germany's and Russia's by right of conquest, neither could sustain and solidify its conquest. As a result, the property rights in existence before the German and Russian invasions are being given respect in the courts of law.

Despite the rather shaky foundations on which property ownership ultimately rests, we would be remiss if we questioned them too closely. In a world in which people can find little on which to come to a meeting of the minds and in which this disagreement threatens a societal breakdown, the concept of property rights is one of the few things on which people tend to agree and which unquestionably contributes to the stability, as well as the prosperity, of society.

As Hernando De Soto has pointed out in his book, *The Mystery of Capital*, the citizens of the poor countries of the world possess savings sufficient to remove them from poverty. For example, if the US were to raise its foreign aid to the level recommended by the United Nations, 0.7 percent of national income, it would take us 150 years to transfer, to the world's poor, resources equal to that which they already possess. The reason that poor countries remain poor is that the property rights to these resources are defective.

Houses are built on land with no record of ownership and businesses are unincorporated. In the communities within which these "properties" exist, there's agreement as to who owns what. But there's no official title, blessed by the government, to these property rights.

As a result, this property can't be used as collateral for loans. Thus, it can't be converted into capital, which is the engine of prosperity.

And let's make no mistake about it. Property rights are rights established and enforced by the government. Without a strict rule of law with respect to property rights, we'd find ourselves in the same unenviable position occupied by the citizens of undeveloped nations.

There are a few shadowy areas on the fringes of the concept of property rights. For example, does the owner of an animal have the right to treat it cruelly? Does the owner of a wetland have the right to fill it in and build a subdevelopment on it?

In general, we resolve such questions by having the government establish regulations that restrict behavior toward property that our values cause us to find repugnant. The remaining disputation has to do with how restrictive these regulations should be, and if the restriction results in a loss of value to the owner, what compensation from the government he's entitled to.

The concept of property rights raises several interesting considerations. One is the question of the alleged conflict between property rights and the creation of pollution.

According to the doctrine of riparian rights, no owner of a section of flowing water has the right to reduce the rights of the other owners of this water. A factory has no right to pour pollutants into a stream, since in so doing, it reduces the rights of the owners downstream.

Property rights to air are more complicated. But the situation isn't materially different from the case of water pollution.

As we've pointed out, things in their natural state aren't personal property. Thus, free flowing air is no one's personal property.

Of course, not all air is free flowing. Some people condition air.

These people have mixed their labor with the air and acquired it by appropriation. Their ownership is manifested by the fact that their conditioned air is packaged. That is, it's marked off by a boundary, such as walls or containers.

The fact that something is free and, therefore, is no one's personal property, means that the thing belongs equally to us all. It's property that we hold and use in common.

When a factory pours fumes into free flowing air, it's not exercising its right. Instead, it's infringing on our rights by damaging our common property.

Air and water pollution aren't examples of defects in property rights. Instead, they're a failure on our part to protect our property rights. As in all other cases of property rights violation, the remedy is legal action to compensate for and end pollution damage.

Of course, this isn't the approach that we've taken to the problem. With our propensity to turn to the government to solve our problems, we've opted for regulation, and we now have the EPA (Environmental Protection Agency) and all of its attendant bureaucracy. It would have been interesting to see what our tort lawyers could have done with a class action suit of property owners against polluters.

Most of our property rights are alienable. That is, if we choose, we can give them up, either as a gift or in exchange for value.

However, because of our values, we've decided that certain property rights should be inalienable. We shouldn't be able to give them away or sell them.

Inalienable property rights have to do with each person's ownership of himself. You exercise dominion over your thoughts, will and action.

Moreover, you're prohibited from transferring these property rights. To do so would involve slavery, which our values cause us to reject.

Such a definition of ownership raises the question of the legitimacy of employment. If a person accepts employment, isn't he entering into a slavery contract? Isn't he agreeing to exchange some of his inalienable property — his thoughts, will and actions — in return for goods, usually money?

The answer is, "No." What the employee agrees to transfer for his wage is the product of his thoughts, will and actions, not his thoughts, will and actions themselves.

This point may be clarified by considering the situation of the author. The author deals in his thoughts, which are his inalienable property.

However, what he does is set down his thoughts on paper and then sell or give away this paper in the form of a manuscript. He doesn't sell or give away his thoughts. He sells or gives away the product of his thoughts.

And the author has the right to sell or give away the manuscript, because it belongs to him. He acquired the paper and then mixed his efforts with the paper to produce the manuscript.

The question of the truth of the author's thoughts are immaterial to the question of his ownership. His thoughts and the manuscript resulting from his thinking belong to him, true or false.

Then there's the question of privacy. The concept of privacy revolves around the use of information about a person.

The question is: What right do I have to use information about you? Do I have any such right? And if I do, is this right limited? Or is it unrestricted, so that I can put the information to any use that I see fit? It should be apparent from these questions that the issue of privacy is the right to use information — that is, the property rights to information.

If you post information about yourself on a social website, can anyone with access to that site use this information in any way that he wants to? When you buy something, a record is made of that purchase. Is this purchase information in the public domain, available for use by anyone, or is it your private information?

In these instances, the question of privacy has to do simply with the right to use information. In other instances, the question of the truth of the information is also raised.

Then we get into the area of "libel" and "slander". The basis for a libel or slander suit is that every person has a "property in his own reputation", for which he can look to the courts to uphold.

If we think about this issue, it should become apparent that a person's reputation is what others think of him. Therefore, the right to use these thoughts lies with the people to whom they belong.

In short, a person has no such thing as a property right in his reputation. This is just one instance of the general rule that there's no basis for the idea that freedom of thought and speech should be restricted.

Now, let's return to the question of privacy in general. If a person's rights aren't infringed — that is, if he isn't forced to testify against himself and isn't subjected to unreasonable search and seizure, then there are no restraints on how information about him is used.

For example, Al has a right to purchase or receive as a gift a copy of Barbara's thoughts about Charlie; record the copy of these thoughts in any form that he wants; and sell, give away, or otherwise use this recording in any way that he wants. The question of whether Barbara's thoughts are true is immaterial to the question of ownership and the rights accorded by that ownership. It may be in Al's interest to show the record on Charlie to him and have him correct it, but Al is under no obligation to do so.

All the above is true when it comes to dealing in noncoercively collected information. However, the government collects some information about people coercively. We have the choice of either yielding up the information or being punished.

An example is your income tax form. You know what would happen to you if you refused to provide the information requested on this form.

The government would use force to coerce you into testifying against yourself. Thus, your rights are being violated.

There's a minimum of information that a government must have about its citizenry to carry out its responsibilities. The government has the right to force people to provide this information.

Consequently, information provided under duress should be handled under the most stringent of privacy safeguards. However, restrictions on the use of noncoercively collected information about people represents an intrusion into the free actions of individuals.

Finally, how about blackmail? Is blackmail a crime? That is, is it an exercise of private force to coerce you into doing something that you wouldn't otherwise choose to do? (That is, incidentally, the definition of *crime*.)

If the information forming the basis of the blackmail is noncoercively acquired, then the blackmailer has the right to use the information as he sees fit. One use of information is to suppress it.

The blackmailer has the right to enter into an agreement with you, the "victim", where in return for value, the blackmailer agrees to suppress the information. If the blackmailer fails to live up to this agreement, then you have the basis for taking legal action against the blackmailer to collect damages.

Of course, to make your case, you'd have had to execute a written contract with the blackmailer (would he have cooperated in executing such a contract?), that contract would have had to spell out the information to be suppressed, and the contract would have to be presented in court, which would negate your purpose in the first place.

Maybe you could have a closed door court session or present the contract to the court under seal. I simply don't know. But blackmailing does present an interesting problem with respect to property rights.

# CHAPTER SIX

# Government

It's a violent world. And in a violent world, you have to protect yourself. Trying to do it by yourself is inefficient, and what's worse, generally ineffective.

The standard solution to the problem of protection against violence has been to band together with others to provide for a common defense against other bands. To be effective in providing for this common defense, it's necessary for your band to adopt a command structure. Those with leadership roles in this command structure have the responsibility for deciding how the band is to deploy itself in its defense and arranging for training the band members in their roles in the band's defense.

But just because your band is committed and prepared to do battle if its existence is threatened by another band, it's nevertheless not the case that all confrontations between bands are decided by battle. Sometimes, the leadership of the contending bands get together and resolve the situation through negotiation. Ideally, they may agree on arrangements that minimize the possibility of conflict in the first place.

The band's governing structure not only provides for the common defense and foreign relations. It also restrains violence within the band. Confrontations within the band are investigated and resolved by the leadership, and sanctions are imposed on those who disrupt domestic tranquility.

All members of the band support their leadership in its defense, foreign relations, domestic policing, and judicial functions. Either that, or you don't belong.

Today, containment of violence is carried out by nations. And national governments still perform the communal functions of defense, foreign relations, policing, and adjudication.

The expense of carrying out these functions is met by means of general taxation, in which all share. However, taxation is a forceful transfer of our money to the government and, as such, is legalized theft.

This makes taxation a contentious issue. When does taxation cease to be an obligation to support a responsible government and become extortion in the pursuit of unjustified ends?

Police power and the defense are unquestionably justified government functions. Without them, we'd be reduced to Hobbes' state of nature, where there are "[n]o arts; no letters; no society; and which is worst of all, continual fear and danger of violent death, and the life of man, solitary, poor, nasty, brutish, and short."

But the government does things other than what's called for by the police power and defense. Support for these other things is provided by taxation.

And because taxation is theft, we want to keep it down. So we should minimize the things in which the government is involved.

Deciding how to keep government involvement down to essentials is difficult. The general principle to be followed here seems to be something like this.

We have a free market economic system in which the drive for profit produces a cornucopia of goods to meet our needs. When this economic system is effective in performing this function, the government should get out of the way and let the system do its job.

But we also have vital needs that a free market system doesn't meet. We've just looked at two — providing for the common defense and insuring domestic tranquility. Private armies and police forces aren't unitary and, consequently, serve special interests rather than the common good.

In these instances, the profit motive of the free market doesn't produce the goods that we want. It's in these areas, where the profit motive doesn't work, that government involvement is required.

But following the principle of letting the profit motive do its job when it's effective and involving the government when it's not isn't an easy one to follow. There are some clear-cut cases, but there are others where making the decision is more difficult. Let's first look at a case where the intervention of the government is clearly called for — childcare.

For our society to operate at peak efficiency, we want it to be peopled by citizens that are equipped to work effectively in our economic system and be responsible in their political activity. And since, if there's any purpose to life, it's to enjoy a rewarding one, we also want our people to be in a position to do just that. For all of these reasons, providing everyone with a quality education is essential.

One requirement here is the existence of a quality school system. What it takes to put together a quality school system is a subject of debate.

But leaving that question to one side, when it comes to providing our children with what it takes to grow into responsible, productive and emotionally mature adults, a quality school system, as difficult and expensive as it is to develop and maintain, is just a beginning. More is necessary.

Classically, the expectation has been that all of this "more" would be provided by parents (or substitute caregiver). However, time has demonstrated that, in a significant number of cases, parents don't have the wherewithal or commitment to make this provision.

A pregnant woman needs to eat a nutritionally healthy diet, refrain from smoking, drinking, and using drugs, and get proper medical care, so that she produces a healthy baby. If she isn't doing so, because she has insufficient resources or doesn't have the requisite knowledge or incentive to carry out this responsibility, then help must be provided.

From the day that a child born, he needs to have a nutritionally healthy diet in order to support his growth. If his parents aren't able or willing to provide this diet, then alternate provisions must be made.

For the first few years of a child's life, he needs to be able count unqualifiedly on the support, care and love of a caregiver 24 hours each day, so that he can develop the ability to manage stress, bounce back from failure, see that his current conditions aren't his destiny and that they can be changed, keep working toward a goal even when there's no immediate external reward involved, deliver on his commitments, act responsibly, be able to tell right from wrong and behave accordingly, and get along and cooperate with other people. If the child's parents don't know how to provide this care, then they have to be trained, so that they can carry out this responsibility.

Before entering the school system, a child needs to have the experience required to be able to exercise self-discipline, pay attention, and follow directions, experience typically garnered in free play with other children, often provided in preschool daycare groups. If a child's parents aren't in a position to provide this kind of milieu, then alternate provisions must be made.

When a child enters kindergarten, in order to be able to learn how to read and write, he has to be able to distinguish words, syllables and phonemes in the spoken language, and he has to be able to hold a pencil and make shapes with it. If parents are unable or unwilling to provide this preK education, once more, alternate provisions must be made.

In none of these necessary areas is there the opportunity to make a profit by providing these services. As a consequence, it's up to the government to pick up the slack.

Now, let's look at a case where the government should get out of the way and let the market do its job — health care.

The market is often thought of as an undifferentiated thing. This is a mistake. There are, at least, three types of markets.

One is the classic market, the one identified by Adam Smith at the dawn of the dismal science, which operates as follows.

A producer develops a more economical way of producing a product. As a result, he can afford to offer a lower price for his product and take market share away from his competitors.

To stay in business, his competitors have to reduce their price. To do so, some will either copy the first producer's innovation or come up with a better alternative. Some may not be able to do either and will leave the market.

The result is that the producers remaining in the market are the more efficient ones, customers get the product at a lower cost, and the economy as a whole is more productive. Both the individual customers and the collective (the economy as a whole) benefit.

In this classic market, a producer can also compete by developing a superior product, in which case, a similar weeding out process takes place — the producer's competitors must counter the producer's superior product by improving their own product, reducing the price on their current product, or some combination of the two. If they fail to do so, consumers won't buy their product and they'll be driven out of the market.

In any case, the nature of the classic market is to encourage the development of both better products and more efficient production techniques.

A second market is the positional market. The characteristic that distinguishes a positional market is that what's being competed for isn't a superior product or a lower cost production process that will attract customers and improve profit. Instead, the competition has to do with the relative position of a person with respect to his competitors in a zero sum situation — if one competitor moves up in the ranking, of necessity, some other competitor must move down.

It's not the absolute size of the payoff that counts in a positional market. It's the size relative to the size of the payoff for the other competitors.

I make more money than you do. My mansion is bigger than yours. My car is faster than yours. My daughter's wedding made your daughter's look second rate. Look at the size of my yacht.

For example, if you set your sights on buying a bigger house, and through dint of significant sacrifice and effort, succeed in doing so, you've improved your individual circumstances with respect to your housing. But other things being equal, the supply of houses hasn't changed.

When you moved up in the housing hierarchy, others, of necessity, moved down. You haven't changed the overall situation. Only one person can live in the best house on the block.

All that you've done by bidding for your house in this positional market is to increase the price of housing, which just makes it more difficult to find the resources to meet other requirements. You've moved money out of other markets and into the housing market.

In these positional situations, where it's relative, rather than absolute, return that's significant, even if the competitors are fully informed and are acting without external restraint, pursuing individual goals doesn't guide resources to their most valuable uses. The competition for relative position is maladaptive for the collective.

When it comes to these positional situations, no single actor can benefit the collective by refusing to compete. No individual person, by declining to compete for a bigger paycheck, larger house, faster car, more lavish wedding ceremony, or more luxurious yacht, can prevent the pursuit from taking place.

The third market is the financial market. A financial market isn't a positional market. And it isn't a classic one either.

Classic markets are stable. If price gets out of line in a classic market, the forces of supply and demand push the market back toward equilibrium.

That doesn't happen in financial markets. They're unstable.

In a financial market, incentives are perverse. Instead of pushing toward the center, they push toward the tails.

Whether the situation is good or bad, it tends to be pursued to excess. In reaction to fear, depressions are intensified. In reaction to greed, prices continue to be bid up until the bubble bursts.

Positional markets are dysfunctional. Here government action is appropriate. One approach would be to get rid of income taxes and replace them with a progressive consumption tax.

Financial markets aren't as dysfunctional as positional ones. Financial markets do provide societal benefits. They enable buyers and sellers to meet efficiently, they provide liquidity by means of their ability to convert illiquid assets, such as land, buildings and machines, into liquid assets, such as loans, bonds and stock, and they create derivatives that allow people and organizations to lay off risk.

But financial markets are unstable. They need to be regulated, and here the government has a role. One of Obama's dismal failures was that he came into power with a war chest of overpowering political capital at the time of the best opportunity to institute financial regulation since the Great Depression and what he produced was the 2300 page Wall Street Reform and Consumer Protection Act that did just about nothing and left the financial institutions that were too big to fail even bigger than they were before the residential housing bubble burst.

However, unlike positional and financial markets, classic markets work best when left alone. Laissez faire, as they say. Government intrusion into classic markets just distorts them and reduces their effectiveness.

There are goods, such as fire fighting and local roads, that the market can't provide. Volunteer activity helps in these areas. But when the need becomes substantial, it becomes necessary for the government to step in and supply the goods.

Health care isn't a good that the market can't supply. And the health care market isn't a financial market. It's not a positional one either. It's a classic market. The conclusion to be drawn is obvious.

If the health care market were left to operate without interference, people would pay for their health care expenses out of their own pocket. As a consequence, they'd become more informed with respect to health care choices and exercise more discretion in making these choices. In response, care providers would be encouraged to compete for the health care dollar.

This would contribute to the alleviation of the fundamental problem of our current health care system, which is the continuously escalating cost of health care. It would be the opposite of what we have now, where people use health care indiscriminately, because they don't pay for it out of pocket.

It's blanket health care coverage, provided to groups where the same premium is paid for each individual covered, that lies at the bottom of our ever-increasing health care costs.

People, typically old and lonely, show up in the ER with complaints for which no physical basis can be found, because they crave attention.

Terminally ill patients are subjected to extensive and painful treatment because the family insists that everything be done to keep the patient alive and the administration of pain modulating drugs would be fatal.

Patients demand a treatment for which there's no justification and shop around until they find a doctor who's willing to accommodate them.

People use a high cost drug when a low cost generic would be just as effective, because medical insurance won't pay for the generic but will pay for the higher priced drug.

People believe that, if it's new, it has to be better. Why trust your doctor to use a stethoscope to listen to breath sounds in your chest when you can get an X-ray? And why settle for a $60 X-ray when you can get a $2000 CT scan? After all, the insurance is paying for it. And your doctor may be happy to accommodate you.

It goes even further. There's pressure to approve and provide treatment even if there's no scientific evidence that the treatment is effective.

After all, the treatment might work. And if you're suffering and the treatment is covered, why not give it a try?

Once more, your doctor may be happy to accommodate you. He might even suggest or recommend the treatment.

All of these things happen because the persons calling for the treatment don't pay for it. Instead, it's covered by group insurance, on which the premium has already been paid, mostly by an employer or the government.

Health insurance is primarily group coverage with a fixed fee for each person covered. This isn't true for any other type of insurance.

Insurance companies are happy to offer life, automotive, property and casualty, and liability insurance coverage on an individual basis with risk-based premium pricing. But they're leery of individual health insurance, because they're afraid of adverse selection.

It wasn't until Blue Cross and Blue Shield, nonprofit organizations, demonstrated that the problem of adverse selection could be avoided by offering services to groups on a fixed fee per individual basis that insurance companies began to get into the business.

Then, in 1942, the government passed the Stabilization Act, which limited the wage increases that firms could offer in pursuit of workers but which also allowed them to offer employee health plans as a recruiting incentive, plans the premiums for which could be considered a company expense and, therefore, a reduction in the profit on which the company had to pay taxes. Soon, an employer who didn't offer health insurance as part of an employee's compensation package was locked out of the labor market.

Beginning in 1965, Medicare provisions began to be added to this mix. And now, we have Obamacare.

Instead of encouraging the growth of a market for individual health care insurance policies and getting the benefit of its advantages, we've pushed the expansion of group health care and suffered the ever-escalating costs that come with it.

Health care is a necessity. But so are food, clothing and shelter.

We recognize that the food, clothing and shelter markets are classic markets. We let them operate without interference and, as a result, harness the incentives that classic markets generate to produce food, clothing and shelter with higher quality and in more abundance at a lower cost than is possible under any other economic system at the same time as we provide welfare for those who have difficulty accessing these markets.

We should do the same thing with respect to health care. Why would we settle for a system that will produce lower quality health care in less abundance at a higher cost, when we know how to do better? And for those people who can't afford health care, there's welfare — Medicaid and other similar federal and state programs.

None of this means that health care insurance will disappear. Health care costs can be catastrophic, and the only reasonable response to this situation is insurance.

The objection to our current health care insurance industry is the poor quality of personal insurance being provided. But the reason for the poor quality product is the lack of competition that would force insurance companies to do better.

The personal health insurance market is anemic. The bulk of people have their health expenses paid by a government or employer provided plan. Imagine the vibrant market that would spring up if every individual bought his own health insurance.

Insurance companies would have to improve their product or lose out in the marketplace. The policy type that would probably dominate such a health care market would be one that covers catastrophic costs only. This is exactly the type of coverage that our current group plans don't offer.

There would be risk-based premiums. After all, why does someone with a preexisting condition want health insurance?

Because he doesn't want to incur the expense of treating his condition. Well, neither does the insurance company.

The insurance company would prefer to keep down its expenses so that it can lower its standard premiums and improve its competitive position in the insurance market. So the size of the premiums that it charges varies with the risk involved. The same is true in the automobile liability insurance business, and for the same reasons.

That leaves the case of the person who can afford catastrophic care insurance but chooses not to insure. What happens when he needs care for which he can't pay?

A true libertarian would say, "Too bad. The choice to not insure was freely taken. No one forced the person to do it. So he's just going to have to live with the consequences of his actions. There'll be no treatment forthcoming."

Even I think that that may be extreme. But I can't help also thinking that it would serve as an excellent object lesson.

In any case, we can't let a person who doesn't pay his bills get away scot-free. That would just encourage people to not provide for catastrophic health care expenses. "Why bother?" the reasoning would go, "I'm going to get the treatment anyhow."

Here's a proposal. Pass legislation that requires everyone not eligible for welfare to carry some specified minimum amount of catastrophic health care insurance. That's like posting a great big warning sign that says, "Don't go naked! It's against the law!"

Then, if a person in crisis is brought into an emergency room, he's treated, no questions asked. If it subsequently develops that he's unable to meet the expense, then he's given a slap on the wrist, the expense is absorbed by the state, and the person is excused.

However, in the more usual case, where there's time for deliberation and the diagnosis is for treatment that the person can't afford, he'd be given a choice: Forego the treatment or accept treatment, let the government pay the fees for his treatment, and go to prison for an appropriate number of years for stealing the fees from the government.

Mandatory health insurance would solve the insurance companies' adverse selection problem. The concomitant to mandatory health insurance would be that insurance companies would be prohibited from refusing to provide insurance to high-risk cases.

Outside of providing welfare in the form of Medicaid and other medical plans for those unable to afford to pay for their own health care, requiring mandatory health insurance, and requiring insurance companies to cover all cases regardless of risk, the government should get out of the health care business. In the absence of Obamacare, Medicare, and employer tax deductions for employee health care plans, a vibrant market for individual health insurance would grow to take their place.

Eliminating employer tax deductions for employee health care plans doesn't mean that companies may not continue to offer such plans. They may.

But it does give companies an opportunity to opt out, if that's what they'd like to do. Before Obamacare, which made employer health care plans mandatory, these plans were being phased out, even in the face of a deduction for providing such plans. If this deduction were removed, my suspicion is that, rather quickly, such plans would disappear.

Phasing out Medicare is more complicated. Commitments made should be honored. All those currently covered, whether working or retired, should continue to be covered. But for all new entrants into the job market, Medicare should no longer be a possibility.

Obamacare would be handled in the same way as Medicare — honor commitments made but terminate the program.

For some people, health care is going to be less than adequate. Health care is a good, and that means that there isn't enough to go around.

Rationing is inevitable. Some people are going to die earlier than they would have otherwise, because the health care that they needed wasn't available.

Now, that's ugly. But when a necessity is in short supply, ugly things happen.

One way to carry out this dirty work of rationing health care is to let the faceless government do it. But it would be more productive to let the equally faceless market do the job, because while handling the distribution, the market will, at the same time, also create incentives to increase the quality and quantity of supply and reduce costs, something that won't happen under a system where the rationing is carried out by the government. As a result, while ugly things will continue to happen in a market system, they'll happen less often than in any other kind of system.

Health care and health are different things, a fact that we often ignore. Sure, we want good health care.

But what's of vital interest to us is good health. When it comes to good health, health care is a minor contributor.

The most important thing that we personally can do to stay healthy is to practice preventative care — have an annual checkup, eat a nutritious diet, exercise, take care of our teeth, be conscientious about taking medicine, not smoke, and not do drugs or drink to excess. These are things that you can't legislate.

To encourage healthy behavior, an education program is necessary. And an essential ingredient of such an education program would be risk based health care insurance premium pricing.

Besides preventive care, the other major contributor to good health is such things as pure water, clean air, sewage disposal, getting inoculated, putting on your seat belt and observing the speed limit when you drive, and dare I mention it — climate control. Here the government has a clear role. And with each improvement in these and other similar areas, the need for health care will decline, which will result in an overall reduced health care cost.

Now that we've looked at a case where involvement of the government is clearly called for (childcare) and a case where, basically, the government should get out of the way and let the market handle product production and distribution (health care), let's look at some cases where it's difficult to decide whether the government should get involved.

At present, the government is deeply involved in infrastructure. Should it be?

Take, for example, the national highway system. It was built and is maintained by the government.

But there's little question that private enterprise could have done the job, perhaps even more effectively than did the government. However, the national highway system constructed by the government provided a significant stimulus to the economy.

So, was it better for the government to step in and do the job, or should we have waited for private enterprise to shoulder the undertaking? And if we had waited, would private enterprise have taken up the challenge? It sometimes shies away from ultimately profitable enterprises because of the sizable initial investment involved. For the life of me, I don't know the answer to these questions.

Fundamental scientific research is another area in which private enterprise seems reluctant to take a major role, even though it's dependant on advance in this area. A lot of this essential work is carried on in research universities and is funded by the government.

Government regulation, even something as simple as on which side of the road you should drive, is essential in order to avoid confusion and catastrophe. Perhaps most fundamentally, the government sees to it that contracts are inviolate and that property rights are respected.

Financial markets are unstable and need regulation. We haven't figured out the solution in this area. Despite our regulatory efforts, financial markets still manage to, every now and then, go off of the rails.

We agree that, to some extent, regulation is necessary. The question is: When does regulation become excessive and counterproductive?

The discussion here is heated and fueled by a considerable degree of self-interest. Think about agricultural subsidies. Or global warming.

Finally, we come to welfare. At least for some of the time, some people are incapable of providing for themselves.

What do we do about that? Leave charity to look after them, certainly.

But what do we do when charity has inadequate resources to handle all cases? Then, the government must step in. Our society is too rich to justify ignoring destitute people.

The question is: How much help should be made available? Do we leave a man to starve when, with a minuscule addition to our taxes, he could be fed? The economic forces unleashed by freedom have resulted in a surge of productivity that allows us to consider food pretty much a right rather than a good.

Next in the hierarchy of needs is clothing. There's no necessity for the government to provide clothing for the needy. US citizens contribute so much in the way of clothing to charities that the charities are unable to use it all.

After clothing comes shelter. We do have homeless people. Most of them seem to be people who can't cope.

Providing shelter for these people doesn't seem to be an insuperable problem. Most of the people on the street are there because they decline to enter the shelters that are available for them.

The extent to which we should be providing shelter by means of such things as rent subsidies and the construction of housing projects is something that I don't know enough about to be able to comment on intelligently, so on this subject I'm going to pass.

The fundamental economic fact is that there isn't enough to go around. All of our lives are shortened by this fact.

The way to minimize this regrettable situation is to raise the general welfare — that is, make goods as plentiful and inexpensive as possible. This result is achieved by channeling our wealth into investment in productive facilities, not by siphoning it off in taxes to provide for general relief.

We must also face the fact that, once it's assured that the government will provide for unmet needs, at least some people are going to do less than their utmost to provide for themselves, which means that they're going to exploit the rest of us, because it's our taxes that's supporting them.

Government help programs should be monitored to be sure that they're being administered humanely. But the help provided should be minimal. Some degree of individual suffering is preferred to damage to the nation.

Given that government is necessary, taxation to support it is inevitable. The only open question is how taxation should be administered.

The general approach should be to get rid of the income, corporate and estate taxes. They discourage saving and investment. The question is: What form of tax should take their place?

My personal preference is one that I'm pretty sure would never find its way into implementation — a flat head-tax. Each year, the government would estimate what it's going to spend in the next fiscal year. This estimate would then be divided by the size of the population, and the quotient is the tax that each individual owes.

A flat head-tax is simple, straightforward, and easily administered. We could consider this tax to be our dues for membership in a society that's dedicated to maximizing the freedom for us to provide for our welfare in the manner that each of us sees in his own individual way.

Some consider a flat head tax regressive and, thus, unfair. It would let the rich off easy but be burdensome for the rest of us.

But this is an advantage. It reminds us that we should be keeping taxes to a minimum. And if all citizens share equally in paying taxes, the public will be united in its desire to keep taxes down.

Some people won't be able to pay a flat head tax. They're going to have to be excused. But as with any other form of welfare, exemptions should be monitored to assure that the necessity is real.

Another approach to taxation that might be more viable than a flat head tax is a progressive consumption tax. In general, the more that someone spends on consumption, the more that he's purchasing luxuries. And under a progressive consumption tax, the more someone indulges himself, the more disproportionately his tax bill would grow.

A progressive consumption tax is easily administered. At the end of the tax year, income is reported just as always. Also reported is savings. Income less savings is consumption. (F 76,77,78)

Another advantage of a consumption tax is that, in the event of a downturn, a temporary suspension of the consumption tax would encourage people to spend, because that's the only way to benefit from the suspension. Suspension of an income tax is less likely to stimulate spending, since many people will just save what they receive from the suspension. (F 83)

Sources

(F) Frank, Robert H. *"The Darwin Economy"* (Princeton U 2011)

CHAPTER SEVEN

# International Relations

Our foreign policy has been a work in progress. We expanded aggressively on the North American continent, and in the Spanish American war, we began an imperialist reach into the Caribbean and Pacific.

However, since then, we've backed away from territorial expansion. Since 1900, we've engaged in two world wars and several regional conflicts with no thought of increasing our territorial domain.

Nevertheless, we do maintain military bases all over the world. From large contingents in long-term bases to small units engaged in training, peacekeeping, special operations, and counterinsurgency activities, we maintain a military presence in 130 countries (2013) (N 141).

At the moment, we sit in the vanguard of the evolution of Western civilization. Until the end of the Cold War, our approach to foreign nations has been to wish them the benefits that we reap from our civilization.

As one of our more astute secretaries of state said, "[The US] goes not abroad, in search of monsters to destroy. She is the well-wisher to the freedom and independence of all. She is the champion and vindicator of her own. ... America ... well knows that by once enlisting under other banners than her own, were they even the banners of foreign independence, she would involve herself beyond the powers of extraction, in all the wars of interest and intrigue, of individual avarice, envy, and ambition, which assume the colors and usurp the standard of freedom. The fundamental maxim of her policy would insensibly change from liberty to force ... She might become dictatress of the world. She would be no longer the ruler of her own spirit." (John Quincy Adams)

Since the end of the Cold War, we've departed from this foreign policy. We started to think of ourselves as the world's policeman and began involving ourselves in the affairs of other nations. As a consequence, we've engaged in an addictive pursuit of chronic crisis management all over the world (U 261,296).

This has damaged us, both politically and economically (U 283). Attempting to police the world requires a globe-girdling web of military bases, which entangles us in alliances that we might not otherwise find desirable, creates security issues that would otherwise not exist (U 2), justifies covert operations (U 95,98), and runs up the military budget (U 65).

Our interventions in the affairs of other countries aren't justified in terms of national interest. Instead, they're cast as a moral imperative requiring us to step in and battle evil.

The results of this new foreign policy haven't worked out well. My feeling is that we need a more conservative foreign policy.

One of the most effective things that we can do to in the foreign policy area is to set a good example. This is the venerable Puritan concept of the city on the hill.

We believe in freedom. We have to behave in such a way that we exhibit our commitment to this belief. In addition to testifying to our beliefs, there are down to earth, practical reasons for respecting the rights of people at home.

For example, police brutality makes no sense. If we want the public to cooperate with the law, it must be above reproach. As another example, prison brutality doesn't improve the chances that, when a convict returns to civilian life, he'll become a law-abiding citizen. (S)

Internationally, as well as domestically, we must condemn torture and refrain from using it ourselves, something that we haven't been conscientious about recently. (H 111)

However, as committed as we are to our way of life, no matter how firmly the evidence seems to be that this way of life leads to a more wholesome, rewarding existence, and regardless of how tirelessly we work to promote our ideas, there are nations and peoples who not only disagree with us but are also determined to bring us down. In the last century, we fought two world wars because we were attacked without warning. We recently emerged from a 50 year struggle with Russia, which not only espoused a social, political and economic model opposed to ours but was willing to engage in any kind of action, short of outright war, to expand adoption of its life style until it circled the globe. Now, we live under the threat of attack by terrorist organizations.

In the face of such intransigence, we have no alternative but to maintain a military presence sufficient to protect ourselves. This is dangerous, since a deterrent force has the potential for metamorphosing into an aggressive one that can be used against either other nations or ourselves. Consequently, cautions are appropriate.

A deterrent force should be the minimum possible. Both fear of external force and the vested interest of career military officers and arms manufacturers tend to expand the national force beyond that required for deterrence.

All levels of command, both in the military and in national political life, should continually be reminded that their function is deterrence, not aggression.

History seems to indicate that, to protect itself against external violence, a country must have the military power to be able to say, "You do that, and we'll clobber you," and mean it. Such a policy is expensive, but it's cheaper than war.

As a result, it behooves us to always be prepared to go to war. What might be some of the ways for us to enhance our preparedness?

First of all, we should be pessimistic. At all times, we should be looking for trouble. Early warning can sometimes provide enough time to respond effectively before a situation metastasizes.

In general, the people to look out for aren't the wicked. It's the self-righteous, such as the Jacobins, Nazis, Bolsheviks, Ayatollahs and Islamists, who tend to cause the trouble.

Given a military potential sufficient to protect ourselves against external aggression, and given that, to make this potential effective, we must, on occasion, use it, it's in our interests to have as clear a guideline as possible as to when we should engage in military action and when we should refrain.

One of the most ancient and enduring principles of international relations is the concept of the *sovereignty of nations*, the right of each nation to do as it will within its borders. With one exception, we have no right to interfere with what another nation does. The exception is when that nation presents us with a clear and present danger.

We don't want other nations telling us what to do within our borders. Consequently, as a matter of principle, we shouldn't interfere with the internal matters of other nations. In addition to the ethics of the matter, there are practical reasons for keeping our nose out of other people's business.

Even if we have the power to do so without fear of retaliation, interfering in another nation's domestic matters is going to be resented, not only by the nation on which we impose our will, but even more importantly, by the other members of the congress of nations. We may be powerful, but our power isn't without limits and we need the support and cooperation of the international community to most effectively look after our interests.

At worst, involving ourselves in the internal working of other nations can lead to war, and war is destabilizing. It's elusive, untamed, costly, difficult to control, fraught with surprise, and sure to give rise to unintended consequences (B 160). As Churchill said, "The statesman who yields to war fever is no longer the master of policy, but the slave of unforeseeable and uncontrollable events." (B 157)

When we go to war, the best that we're going to be able to do is win. We're then faced with what to do after the war is won.

Clausewitz said that war is "an act of force to compel our enemy to do our will." Our enemy is doing something that we don't want him to do, and we go to war to stop him from doing it. Consequently, when it comes to war, the overall strategy has to be to *clear, hold and build.*

The war is the clearing operation, which is concerned with defeating the enemy and stopping him from doing what we don't want him to do.

But to see that the enemy continues to refrain from doing what we don't want him to do after the war is over, it's necessary to undertake a holding operation — garrisoning the cleared area with our or friendly troops that are charged with seeing to it that the enemy continues to behave. However, a holding operation can never be more than a short-term solution to the problem.

In the long run, holding is costly, dangerous (it fosters insurgency), and politically problematic (continued occupation ultimately comes to be seen by other nations as colonialism). The only lasting solution is to build a stable, healthy, indigenous political order that allows the local population to thrive in harmony with us, which requires a large investment in time and effort. (R 278,279)

Which says something about how hard we should think about the long-term before we contemplate injecting ourselves into a trouble spot. Before considering war, we should define goals precisely and check the price of a clear, hold and build operation before buying (R 285).

We've recently been witness to a number of internecine battles between groups within one country. The struggle in Ireland, the slaughter in Cambodia and Rwanda, and the conflict in the Balkans, Syria and Yemen are examples. Some of these contests take on the characteristic of genocide, and there are those who argue that such a development is sufficient cause for intervention.

Thus, from this point of view, it can be maintained that our intervention in Bosnia and Kosovo was right and that our failure to intervene in Rwanda is a blot on our escutcheon. I'm not so sure. Intervention may stop what's going on at the moment, but as we just got finished saying, what follows intervention is a costly holding and building operation to keep it from happening again.

One of the problems that we face today is international terrorism. The overall defense against terrorist attack is intelligence that detects and thwarts attacks before they occur and steps that deny, to terrorists, the resources that they need, such as financing. (H 166). In gathering intelligence, we need the help of other nations, and we need their cooperation in denying resources to terrorists. We can't do it by ourselves. (H 78)

It's not economically feasible for us to protect against all attacks. It would cost more than the damage that an attack would cause.

We have to confine ourselves to providing extensive security measures for hypersensitive targets (such as power and communications grids) and being satisfied with a lesser degree of security for the vastly larger number of targets available. Terrorists may take the position that, for attacks to achieve the proper fear level, they have to be against major targets, which gives us our best chance to defend ourselves.

However, if terrorists are satisfied with demonstrations, they can choose among the many lesser targets and achieve success and considerable destruction. The best that we can do in these situations is to optimize our rapid response to contain damage.

With all terrorist attacks, what we have to protect against is letting a successful attack create enough fear to cause us to reduce our commitment to our individual freedoms under the misconception that doing so will reduce the probability of such attacks. The reduction of our civil liberties that would be necessary to reduce this kind of terrorism to something near zero would be self-defeating and would concede the battle to the terrorists. (H 26)

We have to be resilient. When a terrorist attack occurs, we have to clean up the mess, bounce back, and continue the life that we know is productive and rewarding. Such a response demonstrates the futility of the attack.

The only effective attack that terrorists can carry out is the explosion of a nuclear device. That's why it's so important to reduce the existence of nuclear weapons and to securely lock up both the ones that remain and all stockpiles of weapons-grade nuclear material.

It's in everyone's interest to reduce the stockpile of nuclear weapons. One of the ways that we can promote this reduction is to set an example and eliminate our own stockpile.

Nuclear weapons are ineffective as deterrents, since using them is impossible. In addition, they're unnecessary.

Modern conventional weapons are adequate for deterrence. They're lethal and accurate. And they're credible — they can be used. (B 179)

We should make it clear that terrorism doesn't pay by capturing or killing terrorists. The primary weapon here is, once more, intelligence. And that means cooperating with the intelligence agencies of other countries.

If we again experience an attack on the order of 9/11, we should respond with a blow all out of proportion to the attack. We should bomb all of the terrorist camps of which we know until they're reduced to rubble without regard to whether the particular camp was or was not involved in the attack and without consideration for collateral damage. This is in keeping with the policy articulated by General Sherman on his march through Georgia and South Carolina. "We cannot change the hearts of the people of the South," he said, "But we can make war so terrible ... that generations would pass away before they would again appeal to it."

Afghanistan is a continuing problem. If we get out, the chances are that the Taliban will return. And they'll provide sanctuary for al Qaeda. That's a development that we can't permit. So we have to stay there. However, to the extent possible, we should limit our presence there.

ISIS has now become a matter for concern. Its extremism is unacceptable. I see no problem with our supplying intelligence and strategic support to the local forces fighting to wipe out ISIS, but the boots on the ground should be those of these local forces. When the clearing operation is complete, it should be the local forces who should be dealing with the holding and building operations to follow.

Then there's Israel. The Jewish people inspire admiration. For thousands of years, Western civilization has, at best, offered Jews second-class citizenship and, at worst, subjected them to persecution, sometimes severe and lethal.

Through it all, the Jews have retained their identity and excelled in all of the areas where they've been given the opportunity to do so. In the last half-century, they've forged a nation that has made the desert bloom, created a vibrant economy within a republican political organization, and developed a military that no Arab nation or coalition of Arab nations is willing to take on.

However, after having said that, it remains true that the Israeli-Arab conflict is a problem that defies solution. I sometimes imagine that all of the Israelis might emigrate to the US. We could even finance the trip.

We also pursue a foreign aid program. Unfortunately, a good bit of this foreign aid is in the form of military aid.

Better would be to help implement an incremental approach to improving the situation of other peoples. Worthwhile programs would be to promote family planning and literacy, both for men and for women. Particularly effective would be to help nations establish a rule of law that would make it possible for people to get clear title to property, especially real estate.

## Sources

(B) Bacevich, Andrew J. *The Limits of Power*

(H) Heymann, Philip B. *Terrorism, Freedom, and Security* (MIT Press 2003)

(N) Naim, Moises *The End of Power* (Perseus 2013)

(R) Rose, Gideon *How Wars End* (Simon & Schuster 2010)

(U) Unger, David C. *The Emergency State* (Penguin 2012)

# CHAPTER EIGHT

# Financial Industry Regulation

*Bubbles* are a characteristic of financial markets, which are inherently unstable. Unlike classic markets for consumption and production goods (where whenever the market becomes disrupted, the forces of supply and demand push it back into price equilibrium), in financial markets, incentives are perverse.

Instead of pushing toward the center, the inclination of incentives in financial markets is to push toward the tails. Whether the situation is good or bad, it tends to be pushed to excess.

In reaction to fear, depressions are intensified. And in reaction to greed, prices continue to be bid up until the bubble bursts. Investors call this phenomenon momentum.

When a new profit opportunity in the economy opens up, it's pursued by increased buying of the real and financial goods related to the opportunity. When this increase begins, demand for these goods tends to outstrip supply. The result is a price increase.

At this point, things can continue in a rational way. Or a sense of *euphoria*, fed by *greed*, can begin to build up and encourage *overtrading*, where the real goods related to the profit opportunity are bought for resale rather than for use and the financial goods related to the opportunity are purchased in anticipation of outsized capital gains resulting from market activity rather than for purposes of accumulating income and the more modest gains in capital accruing from increased productivity.

These goods are the *objects of overtrading*. Credit expands to fund and encourage the overtrading, and euphoria escalates into *mania*.

Eventually, the people involved in the overtrading start to recognize that a bubble is being created where more real goods than can be used have been purchased and more investment in financial goods have been made than can be supported by the existing economy.

This stage in the life of a bubble is what Hyman Minsky, in his paper "Financial Instability Revisited", prepared in 1964 for the Board of Governors of the Fed, called *distress* (H 95,99).

The bubble then bursts, and *panic* begins. The top of the market has been reached, and the price of the objects of overtrading begin to drop.

The panic then begins to feed on itself. Selling picks up, prices fall further, and loans are called. There's a *revulsion* with the objects of overtrading, people dump them as fast as they can, and they're no longer accepted as collateral for loans.

The *fear* that feeds the revulsion spreads from the overtraders to the population in general. Spending is reduced to bare necessities, which exacerbates the economic distress.

Sales fall off, inventories build up, plants close, firms fail, and unemployment spreads. Depression has arrived and continues until enough confidence in the economy is generated to dispel the fear feeding the depression.

(K)

The fundamental point is that bubbles aren't deliberately created. Instead, they're a byproduct of the human instinct to follow the herd. (M 403)

As disastrous as bubbles can be, economies eventually recover from them.

Bubbles occur all of the time. Most are short-lived and cause only minor, local disruption. Some are more damaging. Just recently, we've had a savings and loan bubble and a junk bond bubble in the 1980s, the Long-Term Capital Management bubble and a dot-com and telecommunications bubble in the 1990s, and a residential mortgage bubble in the 2000s.

The mother of all bubbles ushered in the Great Depression of 1929. Here the object of overtrading was stock, the source of credit expansion was the call loans that banks and corporations made to allow stock to be bought on margin, and the circumstances restoring confidence was success in the prosecution of the Second World War.

In the recent residential housing bubble, the object of overtrading was residential housing.

In the mid 1990s, housing prices began to increase at an unusual rate. Between 1997 and 2006, the value of real estate owned by US households went from $8.8 trillion to $21.9 trillion, an increase of about $125,000 for each household. During this time, the ratio of median home prices to median household income went from about 3 to 4.6. (C 237,238)

House buying is, characteristically, leveraged. Even if you put 20 percent down on a house, you borrow to leverage your investment by a factor of four.

And as happened in the real estate bubble, when you could put down even less, the leverage was intensified. (In some cases, the banks required as little as $3000 down, which you could borrow from elsewhere, in which case equity disappears and leverage becomes infinite.)

In this way, the foundation for a bubble was created. Once prices started to go up, people were willing to buy more expensive houses, since they believed that prices would continue to escalate. Banks could issue bigger mortgages, because the value of the collateral underlying them had increased. Demand for housing grew, and that forced up prices. The vicious cycle of price expansion that characterizes bubbles had been entered. (C 241)

The mortgages being offered became more exotic and risky — adjustable rate mortgages, mortgages with balloon payments at the end, 2/28 hybrids (relatively low rates for two years, after which the rate would float up to somewhere between 10 and 15 percent (C 258)), 80/20 piggyback loans in which a first mortgage covered most of the purchase price and a second mortgage covered the rest of the purchase price and the settlement costs (Fe 63), interest only mortgages, optional payment mortgages (where the mortgage holder could opt to make payments that were less than the accrued interest, so that as time passed, the principle amount increased (Bl 71)). Interest only and optional payment mortgages were introduced in 2003, when they accounted for six percent of the mortgages originated. In 2004, they made up for 25 percent, and in 2005, 29 percent. (Mr 276)

The government aided and abetted in the creation of these exotic mortgages. In 1980, it passed the Depository Institutions Deregulation and Monetary Control Act, which abolished state usury caps. Two years later came the Alternative Mortgage Transaction Parity Act, which made things like adjustable rate mortgages and mortgages with balloon payments legal and preempted state laws designed to prevent both these new kinds of mortgages and prepayment penalties. (Mc 29) Both of these pieces of legislation encouraged the extension of mortgages to people with smaller and less reliable incomes (Chi 63).

During this time, due diligence also relaxed. Instead of investigating a mortgage applicant's income, loan officers relied on the applicant's credit rating. The loan officer accepted, as the applicant's income, whatever the applicant told him.

The resulting stated-income loans came to be known as liar's loans. (C 241,242) Estimates are that, in 2004 and 2005, over a third of the mortgages issued were stated-income loans.

Subsequent investigation indicated that over 50 percent of stated-income loans were, in fact, liar's loans — the stated income was exaggerated. (C 244) One of the attractions of these mortgages and loan practices was that they allowed people to buy more house than they could afford, thus generating a larger income for the banks (C 243).

Some of these mortgages were directed at the subprime market. In the case of many mortgages, prime or subprime, the people who entered into these contracts either didn't know what they were getting into, or believed that prices in the housing market would continue rise and that, in a few years, they'd be able to refinance with better conditions, or planned to live in the house for only a few years and then sell and move on, or were out-and-out speculators intent on flipping the property (C 243,270).

One might consider banks engaging in such practices irresponsible, if not downright deceitful. But if bank A abstained, bank B down the street wouldn't, and then, bank A would miss out on all of that lucrative business. (C 246)

And besides, politicians wanted banks to make loans in the subprime market (C 253,254). So the vicious cycle was magnified.

In any case, banks didn't have to worry about their risky practices. They would originate the mortgage, collect their fees, and sell the mortgage to a securitization firm, and in this way, pass on the risk. Securitization has a long history.

The Federal National Mortgage Association (Fannie Mae) was created in 1938 during the Great Depression (Mr 12,13). It was an agency of the government and its role was to buy up mortgages that the Veterans Administration and the Federal Housing Administration had guaranteed, thus freeing up capital so that more government insured housing loans could be made.

In 1968, Ginnie Mae was split off from Fannie. Ginnie remained a government agency and continued the role of buying up government insured mortgages.

To further free up funds for mortgages, Fannie was allowed to buy "conventional" mortgages — mortgages issued by the banking industry that conformed to strict underwriting standards (30 year mortgages with a fixed rate issued to people with good credit who put up a 20 percent down payment) and not insured by the government. It became a kind of quasi government agency. It had a vaguely defined government mandate to promote housing, but at the same time, it issued stock and became a publicly traded corporation, first offering shares to the public in 1989. (Mc 6,7,38,39,Mr 13)

At about the same time that Ginnie split off from Fannie, Congress created Freddie Mac (the Federal Home Loan Mortgage Corporation), which was designed to perform the same function for the S&L industry that Fannie was doing for the banking industry. Until 1979, Freddie was owned by the S&Ls and was overseen by the Federal Home Loan Bank Board, which regulated the S&Ls.

Freddie then joined Fannie by becoming a quasi-federal agency cum publicly traded company. In this way, Fannie and Freddie became known as government sponsored enterprises, or GSEs. (Mc 6,7)

These GSEs had an implicit government guarantee. There was no legal requirement for the government to come to the rescue of a GSE that got into financial trouble, but because the GSEs were government sponsored organizations, creditors assumed that the government stood behind the GSEs. As a result, GSEs were able to borrow at a lower rate than was available to other borrowers.

In 1970, Ginnie Mae began gathering the mortgages that it had purchased into pools and selling shares in the pools to the public. These were pass-through securities. As the mortgage payments flowed into a pool, they'd be distributed, on a pro rata basis, to the shareholders.

A year later, Freddie Mac did the same thing with conventional mortgages and guaranteed the principal and interest — if a mortgage owner defaulted, Freddie would make the payments to the pool itself. (Mc 7,8)

Forming a pool of debt obligations, such as mortgages, and then issuing shares of the pool was known as securitization of the debt.

Soon, Freddie started using Wall Street to market its securities. Wall Street contributed the idea of dividing up the mortgage securities into tranches, securities with varying kinds of risk designed to appeal to different classes of investors, thus making the offerings more broadly attractive.

For example, you could make available what were known as stripped securities. Here one class of investors would receive nothing but the interest payments and another class just the principal payments. (Mc 7,8)

In 1983, Larry Fink and First Boston put together the first collateralized mortgage obligation (CMO). It had three new, radically different tranches, a short-term five-year debt instrument, a medium-term 12-year debt instrument, and a long-term 30-year debt instrument. The mortgages making up the pool that backed up this CMO came from Freddie Mac. (Mc 13)

In 1984, with the help of Lewis Ranieri, the government passed the Secondary Mortgage Market Enhancement Act (SMMEA). It exempted CMOs from state blue-sky laws restricting the issue of new financial products. (Mc 13,14)

Mortgage origination wasn't confined to banks. Independent mortgage originators, such as Countrywide, Long Beach, and Ameriquest, also got into the act.

Unlike banks, which could draw on customer deposits to finance mortgages, the independent mortgage originators needed funds to carry on their business. This they got in the form of so-called warehouse loans made to them by investment banks, which would then buy up the mortgages, created by the independent mortgage originators, to be packaged in CMOs. (Mc 134,Mr 52,96)

The next step in the progression was the development of collateralized debt obligations (CDOs). Here a securitization organization would buy up a collection of CMO tranches, combine them into a pool, and then slice up the cash flow from the pool into payments on securities called CDOs (C 260). For any one pool, there were typically several classes, or tranches, of CDOs, each with different risk-return characteristics (C 261,262,271). There were even CDOs-squared, where the pool was made up of tranches of CDOs.

Once a firm had originated a CDO offering, it became necessary to sell the securities to investors. Buyers of CDOs didn't do due diligence. They depended on Moody's, Standard & Poor's, and Fitch to evaluate the quality of the instruments. (C 257,262)

These credit rating agencies had been designated by the government as Nationally Recognized Statistical Rating Organizations (NRSROs). SMMEA allowed investors who weren't supposed to take much risk, such as pension funds and insurance companies, to invest in securities that the NRSROs rated highly, even if they weren't guaranteed by a GSE. (Mc 8,9,14)

These agencies were paid by the CDO originators to evaluate and rate their CDOs. The CDO originators would shop around among the agencies for their ratings.

The better the rating that an agency gave, the more likely it was that the agency would get the rating job. This created competition among the agencies to provide the highest ratings. (C 262,263) The vicious cycle was ratcheted up another notch.

Then there were credit default swaps (CDSs). CDSs are the equivalent of credit insurance.

A CDS takes on the risk that a debt obligation, such as a CDO, will lose value, in which case, the CDS will offset the loss (Lo 52). In return, the CDS receives a kind of insurance premium in the form of a share of the income stream of debt instrument. (C 280)

However, CDSs differ from traditional insurance in two ways. For one, CDSs aren't regulated, there's no obligation to build up a reserve against claims, and in fact, no reserves were accumulated (C 282).

And secondly, there's no insurable interest requirement. You can pay the income stream called for by a CDS, and if the security protected by the CDS defaults, you receive the appropriate compensation, even if you never owned the security. (C 281)

According to the Bank for International Settlements, by June of 2007, there were CDSs on $42.6 trillion of debt (C 281,282). About 80 percent of these CDSs were naked — the holders of the CDSs didn't hold the underlying security (Bl 67).

As another variation on CDOs, a pool of CDSs would be formed to serve as the basis for a so-called synthetic CDO.

Financing this boom was money pouring into CDOs from all over the world (Chi 19 Mau 102). And from November 2001 to February 2005, the Fed kept the federal funds rate below 2.5 percent (C 223), making the cost of credit relatively cheap.

But the financial community not only created these new financial products, it also invested in them. Low interest rates encouraged the carry trade. A firm would borrow to buy CDOs that returned a higher rate than what it cost to borrow the money. In addition, not all CDO tranches were equally marketable, and to keep up the volume of CDOs being issued and the profits that they brought in, originators would hold onto the less marketable tranches themselves (C 273,274).

Banks, in particular, found that holding CDOs was desirable. The Basel rules, established by the Basel Committee on Banking Supervision, a group formed to establish global bank capital requirements, considered mortgage backed instruments to be less risky than commercial loans, even though, as events later demonstrated, the opposite was the case.

The riskier a bank's holdings, the more capital it had to hold. Consequently, according to the Basel rules, a bank could reduce the capital that it had to hold by preferring CDOs to commercial loans. (Mc 59,60) And the less capital a bank had to hold, the more capital it had for other investment opportunities.

Banks enhanced their leverage through the use of off balance sheet units known as Special Investment Vehicles (SIVs). The Basel rules allowed for these units, subject to the requirement that the duration of their credit lines be less than year.

If an SIV met this requirement, then the bank didn't have to hold any capital against the SIV. (Mc 60) Consequently, banks would park the CDOs that they owned in an SIV, which was financed by short-term borrowing. In this way, neither the CDOs nor the short-term borrowing appeared on the bank's books, which allowed them to appear to be in better financial shape than they were, and on the basis of this appearance, they were able to enhance their borrowing.

Also augmenting the ability of large financial institutions to borrow was the idea that they were "too big to fail" — that because their failure would cause such disruption in the financial markets, the government would have no choice but to bail them out. As a result, creditors were more willing to lend to large firms than they were to the small, just as Fannie Mae and Freddy Mac were able, because of an implicit government guarantee, to borrow money at a lower rate than could other financial institutions.

A study indicated that, before the bubble, big financial firms could borrow at a rate 78 basis points less than that available to small firms. Because of this significant advantage, the large firms could ramp up their leverage even further together with the attendant risk.

So the party spun on. Any organization that didn't participate fell behind its competitors. As Charles Prince, the CEO of Citigroup, said, " … as long as the music is playing you've got to get up and dance." (C 12,296)

What was happening was the construction of a tower of financial assets consisting of floor after floor of derivatives all financed by debt. The foundation for the tower was made up of real assets — residential housing and the land on which the houses sat.

On the first floor were mortgages based on and deriving their value from the housing on which they were taken out. Next were CMOs, deriving their value from the mortgages that backed them up.

CDOs derived their value from the CMO tranches that backed them up. CDOs-squared derived their value from the CDO tranches that backed them up.

CDSs piggybacked on these debt instruments. And synthetic CDOs derived their value from the CDSs that backed them up.

This tower of derivatives held as long as its foundation remained solid. But once people began to fail to make their mortgage payments, the foundation started to crumble, and ultimately, the tower collapsed. (Ch 238,239)

In the summer of 2006, the Case-Shiller index of housing prices peaked (L 95), and the skin of the bubble was beginning to show strain. Between September 2007 and September 2008, house prices fell 32 percent (C 311).

Between August 2007 and October 2008, according to Realty Trac, 936,439 homes were foreclosed on (C 312). Firms began to write off bad loans and go bankrupt. (C 297)

In June 2007, Bears Stearns was forced to spend $3.2 billion to bail out two of its hedge funds because of exposure to investments in subprime mortgages (H 51,65). In July, the German bank IKB collapsed when two of its funds, Rhineland and Rhinebridge, faced a severe funding crisis (H 51). The funds had purchased long-term mortgage-backed securities with short-term debt (H 66).

On August 9, 2007, BNP Paribas froze withdrawals from three of its subprime mortgage funds because of "a complete evaporation of liquidity" in the market (H 68,141). Fearing that the move would halt interbank lending, the world's central bankers, led by the European Central Bank's Jean-Claude Trichet, pumped billions of dollars into global money markets. (Fr 141)

By the middle of August 2007, trading in many mortgage backed securities had come to a halt, and the lack of a market left firms holding paper, so-called toxic assets, that couldn't be traded and on which a value could no longer be placed. As a result, the solvency of firms became unknown, and to avoid extending credit to a firm that might possibly be bankrupt, banks refused to make loans. The credit crunch had begun. (C 302,303,319)

The crunch was particularly onerous when it came to short-term financing. Financial firms ran on large amounts of short-term debt.

As long as these firms could roll over this debt, there was no problem. But if their creditors decided to no longer participate in this rollover, they quickly found themselves unable to operate and faced the certainty of going bankrupt. (C 315)

On March 13, 2008, Bear Sterns was in this position. It had just $2 billion left in its cash reserves, not enough to meet the next day's obligations.

The next day, the Fed agreed to provide Bear with temporary financing, to the tune of $13 billion, and by March 16, had arranged for J. P. Morgan Chase to acquire Bear for $10 a share. (C 316 Bl 105) (A year before, Bear was selling at over $150 a share (C 315).)

As an incentive to J. P. Morgan to enter this deal, the Fed agreed to put $30 billion of Bear's assets in a stand-alone entity. Morgan would absorb the first $1 billion of any losses in the entity, with the Fed compensating Morgan for any further losses (C 319 Mc 347 T 221).

The Fed rescued Bear from bankruptcy because of what it thought was the counterparty problem. If Bear reneged on its obligations, then the counterparties to which it owed these obligations wouldn't be receiving the funds that they were expecting, which would put strains on them in meeting their obligations.

If these strains forced these counterparties into bankruptcy, they, in turn, wouldn't meet their obligations, and their counterparties would be put under strain, and so on, the effects of Bear's bankruptcy cascading through the financial community. Bear had more than 5000 counterparties. (C 318,319,342)

On September 7, 2008, the government took control of Fannie Mae and Freddie Mac by putting them under conservatorship (B 77,79). Since then, the government has poured more than a hundred billion dollars into them to keep them solvent (Mc 363).

It was then Lehman Brothers' turn to become illiquid. The Fed decided to let Lehman go bankrupt, which it did on September 13, 2008. (C 324)

The same weekend in which Lehman declared bankruptcy, Merrill Lynch agreed to be acquired by Bank of America (B 111). To make this deal stand up, the government ultimately poured $45 billion into Bank of America (B 155).

Just two days after Lehman's bankruptcy, it became clear that AIG, which had sold CDSs on about $400 billion in debt, was heading toward bankruptcy. (C 325) On September 16, 2008, the Fed extended $85 billion to AIG to keep it afloat, in return for which the Fed, through the acquisition of convertible preferred stock, became the putative owner of 79.9 percent of AIG. (Bl 136 C 327 328 T 239) Ultimately, between the Fed and the Treasury Department, the government would pour a total of $182 billion into AIG (B 123 Mc 358).

One of Lehman's counterparties was the Reserve Primary Fund, a big money market fund and the country's oldest (T 236). It was left holding $785 million of Lehman's short-term debt, on which it was unable to collect (T 236).

On September 16, 2008, Reserve Primary informed its customers that they would no longer be able to withdraw cash from their accounts, because it didn't have enough to pay them all. Its net asset value had fallen below a dollar a share. The buck had been broken.

In the next few days, $150 billion were withdrawn from other money market funds. (C 327) On September 18, 2008, a second money market mutual fund, Putnam Prime, was forced to close (Lo 23).

On September 19, 2008, the Treasury announced that all of the existing funds in money market accounts would be guaranteed. To prevent people from withdrawing funds from bank accounts and moving the money to money market accounts, the guarantee wasn't extended to any new money deposited in a money market account after September 19. (Lo 229)

On September 21, 2008, Goldman Sachs and Morgan Stanley changed their status from investment banks to bank holding companies, which brought them under the regulation of the Fed, but more importantly, gave them access to the Fed's discount window for emergency short-term funds (B 130,131).

After the initial cash infusion into AIG, Ben Bernanke, the Fed's chairman, decided that he had had enough. He told Hank Paulson, the Treasury Secretary, that what the Fed was doing wasn't its role and that the problem should be turned over to Congress to be dealt with democratically. On October 8, Congress passed the Troubled Asset Relief Program (TARP), which authorized the Treasury Department to spend up to $700 billion to deal with the problem. (C 328,329)

The fall in house prices and the increase in foreclosures forced households to cut back dramatically on consumer spending (Mi 38,40,42,45,50,51,71). During the last three months of 2008, spending on durable goods fell 22 percent on an annualized basis. GNP fell at an annualized rate of more than 6 percent.

As demand fell off, firms laid off workers. By June 2009, unemployment had reached 9.5 percent. (C 332)

As of 2015, things seem to have stabilized, and there are some indications that a recovery may have begun. But the situation remains problematic.

What will pull the economy out of the depression isn't yet clear. The real estate bubble was more severe than the dot com bubble but less traumatic than the 1929 bubble. Instead of requiring a dramatic event like World War II to pull the economy out of the current depression, a gradual return of confidence, such as occurred after the dot com bubble, may be enough to do the job.

Most people are convinced that the massive intervention of the government into the economy was necessary to keep the panic from spinning out of control into a full fledged, drastic depression. I'm not so sure.

Deposits are an integral part of a nation's payment system (Mi 124), which is essential, since it's the payment system that makes trade, other than barter, possible. Here it's important to recognize that deposits in money market funds and whatever other mechanisms people and organizations use to make payments are just as much a part of the nation's payment system as are deposits in a traditional bank.

To keep terminology simple in the following discussion, when we use the term, deposits, we're going to be referring to payments into whatever mechanism people and organizations use to make payments, whether it's a traditional bank, a money market fund, or whatever. Also, we're going to refer to all of these mechanisms as banks.

To preserve the integrity of the payment system, it's essential that, when a depositor makes a deposit, he's assured that his money is safe — that anytime that he wants to, he can withdraw his deposit and the funds will be there to meet the withdrawal.

Banks have to make money to stay in existence. They make some of their money by charging fees for their services. They make the rest of their money by keeping a fraction of the deposits, which they've received, in reserve to meet any demands for deposit withdrawal and investing the rest of the deposits. This is called intermediation, because the banks serve as intermediaries — it's through them that many small short-term loans (a deposit in a bank is a loan to the bank) get converted into fewer larger long-term loans.

The fundamental point of intermediation is that a bank's investments tie up its funds in commitments that are time dependent. Unlike a depositor, who can withdraw his deposit any time that he wants, a bank has access to the funds that it has tied up in its investments only when the investments come due at some time in the future.

Barring outside intervention, this business operation of intermediation, in which banks engage, leaves them open to the following danger. If a bank experiences an unusually large demand for deposit withdrawal all at one time, it may not have sufficient reserves to meet all of the demands. This throws the bank into bankruptcy, which ties up all of the funds still on deposit at the time of the bankruptcy.

Depositors don't want their deposits tied up in a bankrupt bank. Consequently, when it looks as if a bank may become illiquid (have insufficient reserves to meet all demands for deposit withdrawal), they rush to withdraw their deposits even if they don't need the money. This is a bank run, and it will drive any bank, no matter how solvent, into bankruptcy.

Moreover, when a run on a bank begins, it's contagious. It will spread to other banks. Ultimately, such a development can bring down the whole banking system and the payment system with it.

Consequently, the government has an unquestioned obligation to see that, no matter what, money to meet any deposit withdrawal is available (Mi 127). The government action in this situation is two-part.

If the bank, that has insufficient reserves to meet all demands for deposit withdrawal, is solvent (that is, it has sufficient assets to cover its liabilities), then the government advances sufficient money to the bank for it to meet all demands for deposit withdrawal. Since the bank is solvent, when enough of the bank's investments come due to return the bank to liquidity, it will pay back to the government with interest whatever money the government made available to it.

On the other hand, if the bank is insolvent, then the FDIC steps in, depositors get their money back, and the bank's shareholders and creditors are wiped out (Mi 125,126).

Beyond that, I'm short on details. But it seems to be clear that preserving the nation's payment system didn't require the massive bailout given to the financial system, where financial institutions, which received government support, were required to settle with their counterparties 100 cents on the dollar.

As Luigi Zingales, a professor at the University of Chicago's Booth School of Business, has pointed out, when Paulson went to Congress and argued that, if TARP wasn't passed, the world as we knew it would end, he was right to the extent that the financial world in which he lived and worked would end. But, as Zingales argued, "… Henry Paulson's world is not the world most Americans live in — or even the world in which our economy as whole exists." (Br 261,272)

Our response to the bursting of the residential real estate bubble has increased the instability of the financial market. The institutional incentives for taking unreasonable risks has just become more concentrated in even larger firms that are "too big to fail".

This inclination toward unreasonable risk is known as moral hazard, a term borrowed from the insurance industry. For example, if your house is insured against fire, the probability that it will burn down is increased.

This doesn't mean that you deliberately set your house on fire. It's just that, since you're protected from the financial damage that would result from having your house go up in flames, you may unconsciously become somewhat more careless about how you handle inflammables. As another example, there's evidence that the introduction of seat belts and airbags in cars has encouraged drivers to behave more dangerously (Ha 188).

The same is true in the financial industry. When the residential real estate bubble burst, thousands of people working on Wall Street lost their jobs and savings. This was tragic.

But the government didn't bail out financial firms to preserve the jobs and savings of the firms' employees. It bailed out the firms so that their creditors could walk away with at least some of their skin. When the government bailed out Bear Sterns, the GSEs, and AIG, they were required to meet their obligations 100 cents on the dollar (Bl 138). The object of the bailout was to prevent the financial world from cratering.

Given this implicit government guarantee that, if large financial firms get into trouble, they'll be bailed out, the firms become more willing to take risks, an inclination that seems particularly likely, given the human propensity to succumb to greed. If the risk pays off, the firms profit handsomely. And if a bet fails and threatens a firm's solvency, no problem — the government will come to the rescue.

Creditors don't want their debtors to take unnecessary risks. They want their debtors to be around when it becomes time to pay off the debt. But if the government guarantees debt, which it's increasingly doing, creditors become inclined to relax their vigilance, with the result that debtors will begin to entertain more risk than may be healthy. (Mo 43,47)

In addition to all of these other reasons why the financial firms shouldn't have been bailed out, the bailout violates the moral principle that people should live with the consequences of their actions. That so many didn't, at the same time that they caused such irreparable harm to so many other, completely innocent people, justifiably fills most people with disgust, throws the government into disrepute, and may have caused more harm to the fibers that hold our nation together than any damage that could have come to our economic situation by allowing failed financial firms to go bankrupt.

So, to channel Lenin, the question is, "What is to be done?" (C 339) Industrial safety experts regard complexity (being made up of many separate, interacting parts (S 368)) and tight coupling as making inevitable failures more likely to be catastrophic (Ha 216).

Applying this thinking to the financial industry, it seems to me that commercial banks, investment banks, insurance companies, mutual funds, hedge funds, private equity, proprietary trading, and debt securitization should all be separate firms walled off from one another and doing only what is called for by their specialty, whether they're operating domestically or internationally. This would reduce systemic risk (tight coupling) and keep firms small enough to fail (less complexity).

Access to government deposit insurance and last resort lending should be restricted to the banks that make up the payment system. All other financial institutions would be on their own. In particular, this means no government guarantees for debt securitizers (i. e., no Fannie Mae, no Freddie Mac).

Mutual funds, hedge funds, private equity, proprietary trading, and debt securitizers should be prohibited from issuing stock. This means that they would have to be privately funded, probably by the formation of partnerships, which would cut down on excessive risk taking.

Purchase of a CDS without owning the bond being insured should be prohibited. Buying a CDS in anticipation that the bond is going to default is similar to selling a stock short. But there's an essential difference.

Before you can short a stock, it has to be in your possession. If you don't already own it, you have to borrow it before you can short it. It's the manifestation of insurable interest in the stock world.

Accounting tricks, such as setting up SIVs, shouldn't be allowed.

Reward systems should be more long-term oriented. Instead of awarding a trader with a large bonus when he has a good year, because it's not easy to claw back the money when he follows with a bad year, bonuses should be based on longer term, such as five year, performance. (R 164)

Rating agencies should be legally liable for the quality of the ratings that they issue (Bl 81).

Finally, any firm, that gets into so much trouble that it's unable to recover, must be allowed to fail.

The debt problem also has to be addressed. We need to encourage savings and reduce consumption.

Government policies that encourage borrowing, such as the deduction of mortgage interest payments from taxable income, should be repealed. Taxation should depend less on income taxes, which discourage saving (any earnings on savings is taxable income), and more on consumption. The benefits of Social Security and Medicare should be scaled back. (Chi 207,208,209 F 76,77,78)

On a private level, excessive leverage has to be prohibited. It aggravates the business cycle, being pushed up during vibrant economic (boom?) times and worsening the downturn when it comes. There should be a limit on leverage, a limit that becomes more restrictive during economic expansions (less leverage requires holding more equity for each dollar borrowed) and less restrictive during downturns (reducing the equity required for each dollar borrowed and making it easier for firms to weather the setback). (Chi 213)

With the exception of a wave of the hand at contingency plans for winding down financial institutions, the 2300 page Wall Street Reform and Consumer Protection Act enacted by the government on July 21, 2010, which was designed to regulate the financial industry, (Mc 358) does none of the things that we've just listed. It didn't even resuscitate Glass Steagall.

Instead, this so-called Dodd-Frank bill continues to favor sprawling megabanks whose complexity often brings tax advantages and are seen as better credit risks (Ha 204). The "too big to fail" problem has not only not been addressed, it has just gotten bigger.

More generally, concentration should be centered on seeing that the financial community is doing what it's supposed to be doing (allocating resources effectively) and not on awarding individuals excessive income (M 404).

Eventually, the economy will recover from this most recent bubble. Will we then have another bubble?

As it now stands, another bubble is a near certainty. When? Who knows? But they seem to be coming more frequently.

What will the next object of overtrading be? It's anyone's guess.

<u>Appendix</u>

Here's an example of how a risky investment can get a triple A rating (S 26,27). Imagine a pool of mortgages on which you're going to issue a CMO. There are five mortgages in the pool, each of which has a five percent possibility of going into default.

You set up the CMO so that it consists of five tranches, A, B, C, D, and E. If one of the five mortgages goes into default, then tranch E doesn't pay out.

If two mortgages go into default, then tranches D and E don't pay out. And so on, until it takes a default on all five mortgages for tranch A to fail to pay out.

Now, if there's no correlation between the possibility that one of the mortgages might go into default and the possibility that any of the other mortgages might also go into default (that is, if these possibilities are independent of each other, such that the reason why one mortgage might go into default is different from the reason why any of the other four mortgages might go into default), then the probability that tranch A will fail to pay out is five percent raised to the fifth power, which is one chance in 3,200,000, which certainly qualifies the tranch for a triple A rating.

But if there's perfect correlation between the possibilities of the mortgages going into default (that is, the reason why one mortgage might go into default is the same reason why the other mortgages might also go into default), then if one mortgage goes into default, it's certain that the other four mortgages will also go into default. In this case, tranch A is just as risky as tranch E, or any of the other tranches. In the case of all tranches, the possibility that the tranch may not pay out is five percent, which doesn't qualify any of them for a triple A rating.

In the case of the recent residential housing bubble, the situation was characterized more by the second of the above scenarios than by the first, but the rating agencies based their ratings on the first scenario.

Sources

(B) Bartiromo, Maria *The Weekend That Changed Wall Street* (Penguin 2010)

(Bl) Blinder, Alan S. *After the Music Stopped* (Penguin 2013)

(C) Cassidy, John *How Markets Fail* (Farrar, Straus and Giroux 2009)

(Ch) Chang, Ha-Joon *23 Things They Don't Tell You about Capitalism* (Bloomsbury 2010)

(Chi) Chinn, Menzie D. and Frieden, Jeffery A. *Lost Decades* (Norton 2011)

(Fe) Ferguson, Charle H. *Predator Nation*(Random House 2012)

(F) Frank, Robert H. *The Darwin Economy*(Princeton U 2011)

(Fr) Freeland, Chrystia *Plutocrats*(Penguin 2012)

(H) Hancock, Matthew and Zahani, Nadhim *Masters of Nothing* (Biteback Publishing 2013)

(Ha) Harford, Tim *Adapt* (Farrar, Straus and Giroux 2011)

(K) Kindleberger, Charles P. *Manias, Panics, and Crashes*

(L) Lewis, Michael *The Big Short* (Norton 2010)

(Lo) Lowenstein, Roger *The End of Wall Street* ({Penguin 2010)

(M) Madrick, Jeff *Age of Greed* (Knopf 2011)

(Mau) Mauldin, John *Endgame* (Wiley 2011)

(Mc) McLean, Bethany and Nocera, Joe *All the Devils Are Here* (Penguin 2010)

(Mi) Mian, Atif and Sufi, Amir *House of Debt* (U of Chicago 2014)

(Mo) Moyo, Dambisa *How the West Was Lost* (Farrar, Straus and Giroux 2011).

(Mr) Morgenson, Gretchen and Rosner, Joshua *Reckless Endangerment* (Henry Holt 2011)

(R) Rajan, Raghram G. *Fault Lines* (Princeton U 2010)

(S) Silver, Nate *The Signal and the Noise* (Penguin 2012)

(T) Tett, Gillian *Fool's Gold* (Simon & Schuster 2009)

# CHAPTER NINE

# Energy

In their book, *Revolutions That Made the Earth*, Tim Lenton and Andrew Watson propose that, in the history of the Earth, there have been four events that have been difficult enough to achieve, have happened only once, and have had significant enough consequences to be considered revolutionary.

1.  The genetic code (DNA) (the origin of life)
2.  Oxygenic photosynthesis (the oxygenation of the Earth) (the only revolution not involving information transmission)
3.  The eukaryote cell (the basis for the development of complex, multi-cellular life)
4.  Language, which decoupled information transmission from reproduction

These revolutions have caused disruption on a global scale. Oxygenation triggered climate instability that lasted tens of millions of years before the Earth established a new stable state.

The first two information transmission revolutions created new life forms demanding greater use of energy, which in turn, dumped waste products on the Earth. These disruptions were stabilized through recycling — the waste products of one organism became the food of another and a disastrous accumulation of waste was avoided. This recycling was accomplished through blind evolution.

The language revolution has produced a civilization that's making even greater energy demands and, as a result, is once more polluting the Earth with waste products.

It was with the language revolution that we became a significant factor in the development of the earth.

In his book, *A Farewell to Alms*, Gregory Clark presents a grand theory of economics. As he says, it's a simple theory — from

100,000 BC until 1800 there was no change in the general standard of living (C 1,371). Then the Industrial Revolution occurred.

It's not that no productivity improvements were made before the Industrial Revolution (C 9,31) There were, but population increase kept pace with increasing productivity, and there was no increase in the general standard of living.

Clark points out that, throughout history, there has been an elite that lived better than others. But this elite was small, and when he talks about the general standard of living, he's not talking about the elite. He's talking about the mass of people. (C 8)

It was with the Industrial Revolution, with the harnessing of the combustion of carbon-based fuel to generate energy, that production began to outstrip population growth and an increase in the general standard of living was experienced.

This dependence on carbon-based fuel combustion to generate energy has resulted in the creation of a number of questions. Is the Earth warming up? If it is, is it a matter of concern? And if it's of concern, what's causing it and is what's causing it anything over which we have control?

So, is the Earth warming up? Not everyone thinks so. But here's some data.

1. In the last half century (1950-2000), the average temperature in the Northern Hemisphere has been higher than it has been for any 50-year period during the previous 1300 years (Cl 42). The Earth's temperature is about 1.3 degrees Fahrenheit higher than it was in 1900 (Cl 5,41,85). In the past 50 years, the average temperature rose twice as fast as it did in the previous 50 years (Cl 41). Between 1979 and 2005, the average temperature rose 0.8 degrees F, over half of the 20th century's overall warming (Cl 86). There are four major organizations that build estimates of global temperatures from thermometer readings around the globe — NASA, the US National Weather Service, and the meteorological offices of England and Japan. All four show a clear long-term warming trend, especially since the 1950s. (S 393,394,395)

2.  The growing season is defined as the period between the last frost of Spring and the first frost of Fall. During the 20th century, the growing season in the continental US has lengthened by an average of two weeks. (Cl 98)
3.  In the 1980s, there were about 14 percent more record highs than lows. In the 1990s, it was 36 percent. And in the 2000s, it was 50 percent. (Cl 88)
4.  The glaciers are shrinking. Since 1850, the Alps have lost about half of their ice. There was a slow decline in glaciers between 1850 and 1950, followed by a short period of growth. But since 1970, glaciers have been shrinking at an accelerated pace. (Cl 89) One recent study puts the shrinkage at 105 billion tons of ice per year (Cl 92).
5.  In 2009, the oceans were about eight inches higher than they were in 1880 (Cl 5,84). From 1961 to 2009, the average rate at which the sea level rose was about 0.07 inches a year. From 1993 to 2009, the rate was 0.12 inches a year, approaching double the rate. (Cl 84)

All of the above indicates that the Earth is warming up. And outside of maintaining that the above information isn't definitive, there doesn't seem to be any data that would argue otherwise. Concluding that global warming is a fact seems to be reasonable, even if it's not greeted with a rousing acclaim.

So, even if the Earth is warming, would it create problems for us? Here are some of the things that will happen if the world heats up.

1.  The sea level will rise (F 181). Sea ice, similar to what covers the Arctic Ocean in the winter, isn't a problem. It's already floating, and if it melts, the sea level will remain the same. It's the massive ice sheets that cover land that are the threat. When they melt or when icebergs break off from the glaciers, sea level rises. The result will be damage, possibly significant, to port cities, on which much of civilization depends.
2.  The world will become more tropical, which will bring with it the spread of tropical diseases (such as malaria, ebola, elephantiasis,

schistosomiasis (infestation by blood flukes), leprosy), rampant intestinal parasites, poisonous spiders and centipedes, and new and vicious kinds of ants (W 176,188).

3. The oceans will warm up. When water heats up, it expands, which contributes to a rising sea level. But more importantly, warming oceans will result in more volatile weather — there will be more intense tropical storms (hurricanes and typhoons), more frequent flooding, dry areas will become drier, and drought is a possibility, all of which could compromise agriculture as well as causing other destruction (G).

So perhaps we can agree that global warming would be a problem. In fact, I doubt that I even have to press it. As near as I can tell, almost everyone agrees that global warming is a threat.

So if the world is warming up and it's a problem, the third question is: What's causing this warming and what can we do about it?

Now we begin to get some real difference of opinion. First, let's look at some things on which people agree.

The Earth gets its heat from the Sun, mostly in the form of visual light rays. In conformance with the second law of thermodynamics, what heat the Earth absorbs it radiates back into the atmosphere. But this radiation is in the form of infrared rays. (Go)

There are gases, called greenhouse gases, in the atmosphere that allow the visual light from the Sun to pass unobstructed to the Earth. But these greenhouse gases reflect part of the Earth's infrared radiation back onto the Earth.

It's this reflection that keeps the Earth warm. If it weren't for this greenhouse effect, the Earth's temperature would be about zero degrees Fahrenheit, all the water on the Earth would freeze, and the Earth would turn into a giant snowball. (Go)

The most common greenhouse "gas" is water vapor. The warmer the Earth is, the more water evaporates and the more vapor the atmosphere can hold.

The second most common greenhouse gas is $CO_2$. Once in the atmosphere, $CO_2$ can stay there for a long while without breaking down. Its half-life has been estimated to be about 30 years (S 392).

The third most common greenhouse gas is methane. Methane is 21 times more efficient at trapping heat than $CO_2$, but it breaks down quickly.

The fourth most common greenhouse gas is nitrous oxide. There then follows a host of other chemical gases, many containing chlorine and fluorine.

Many of these gases are more efficient at trapping heat than $CO_2$. Some are tens of thousands times more efficient. But they're rare.

Natural processes send more than 700 billions tons of $CO_2$ into the atmosphere every year. The carbon-based fuel that we burn adds about 30 billion more. That's only a four percent addition, but it upsets the balance.

Without our contribution, there has been an equilibrium, natural processes removing $CO_2$ from the atmosphere at the same rate as they add it. Now, each year, more and more $CO_2$ accumulates in the atmosphere. (Cl 54) There's more $CO_2$ in the air now than there has been for at least 650,000 years (Cl 82).

There's a 1500 year cycle to the Earth's temperature, where the temperature varies about 4 degrees Centigrade from peak to trough (Si v,xv). Ice cores and seabed sediments testify to this 1500 year cycle for the past 900,000 years (Si xii,6,29,128). The cycle is linked to small changes in the Sun's irradiance (Si 2), which is from where the solar wind comes.

The more cosmic rays enter the earth's atmosphere, the more they ionize the air. The ionized air seeds the growth of low lying clouds, which tend to reflect the Sun's light rays back away from the Earth, and there's a cooling trend.

When the solar wind increases, it creates more of a shield around the Earth against cosmic rays, and as a result, fewer low lying clouds are formed and the Earth's temperature increases. In contrast, when the solar wind abates, cooling occurs. (Si 192,193,194)

The changes in the Sun's irradiance follow a 1500-year cycle (Si 191), which is why the Earth's climate cycles every 1500 years. And there's little that we can do about it (Si 233).

And now the contention begins.

The minority opinion is that, within the context of this temperature cycle, the amount of $CO_2$ in the air is irrelevant. In addition, each added molecule of $CO_2$ in the air has a reduced ability to trap heat. Therefore, as the $CO_2$ level increases, the increasing effectiveness of the heat trap tails off. (Si 36)

Historically, warmer weather has moved in tandem with rising $CO_2$ levels in the air, but the rise in $CO_2$ lagged the warmer weather by about 800 years. This is because, as ocean temperature rises, it can hold less and less $CO_2$, so more of it is released into the air. (Si 11,37)

The majority opinion maintains that global warming is the result of the buildup of greenhouse gases in the atmosphere and that, the greater the buildup, the more the Earth will warm. If you take into consideration how common a greenhouse gas is, how efficient it is at containing heat, how long it lasts, and what control we have over it, then if we want to contain global warming, it's clear that we should be concentrating on reducing $CO_2$ emission as much as possible (Cl 33-36).

So, here we are, in the classic layman's position. For our information, we depend on experts. And when the experts disagree, what are we to do?

In such situations, the standard approach is to just suspend judgment and wait for the experts to sort it out. But in the case of global warming, if the majority experts are right, then we're facing a growing, significant problem that, if nothing is done about it, will create a situation where what would at one time have been an effective countermeasure is no longer adequate.

What others would do in this case, I don't know. But as for me, I think that we have no choice but to go with the majority opinion.

So, to summarize: In my opinion, global warming exists, it's a problem, the primary culprit is the amount of $CO_2$ in the atmosphere, and it's within the realm of possibility for us to do something about it. So:

Global warming is … well … a global problem. That means that it requires a global solution.

There is no global government. That means that the problem of global warming has to be solved through the cooperative efforts of the world's nations.

How this cooperation will come about I haven't the foggiest. For myself, I find solace in the belief that, if something has to be done, then sooner or later, it will be done.

If we could agree on a program for addressing the global warming problem, it might constitute a first step toward an international solution to the problem, because we could then enter into what would be, hopefully, a constructive discussion on how to implement the agreed on program.

I do have some thoughts on what would constitute such a program. And it's an outline of this program to which I'd like to address myself in the remainder of this chapter.

To the extent possible, we have to abandon the use of carbon-based fuel.

We should power our industry with electricity and drive electric cars. Ships can be driven with nuclear energy.

Unless there's some dramatic breakthrough, planes will probably have to be powered with carbon-based energy. But we can minimize the need for flight by using communications technology.

We currently produce a lot of electricity to be used in the residential and commercial sectors of the economy, primarily to provide what's called HVAC — heat, ventilation, and air conditioning (Y 628). We're going to have to produce even more electricity to drive our industry and cars. From where is all of this electricity to come?

It can't come from the coal, oil and gas fired power plants that we currently have, because they're $CO_2$ producers. They have to be phased out.

Renewables (hydro, wind and solar) have been suggested as possible electricity generators.

Hydro is a nonstarter. Most of it is generated by building dams, which is environmentally undesirable (Y 714).

A disadvantage of electricity as a source of power is that there's no way to store it in volume. Since to run our plants, commercial facilities, residences, and cars, we need electricity to be available

24/7, this means that we must have the ability to constantly generate electricity. In other words, our electricity generating facilities must be sustainable.

Wind and solar power electricity generation are environmentally friendly and should be pursued. But they're not sustainable. You can't run a windmill when there's no wind or collect sunlight when the sun isn't shining, which is, at least, half of the time. (Y 585,589)

At some point, nuclear fusion may become a power source, but it's unlikely. Nuclear fusion is what goes on inside the Sun or any other star, and controlling it is a formidable problem. As has been said, nuclear fusion may be the energy of the future, and it probably always will be.

That leaves nuclear fission. There are two things that concern people with respect to nuclear fission.

One concern is fear of an accident.

The atomic power industry is intensely interested in safety. It appreciates that one bad accident could be the end of the industry. (Note the reaction to the damage to atomic energy plants caused by the tsunami in Japan.) So it takes steps to see that accidents don't happen.

Borrowing a concept from the airlines industry, where when crises occur, instant and competent action is required, but where reality provides little opportunity to practice in real life situations, an atomic energy plant has a simulation room that duplicates the plant's control center and where all kinds of complications in plant operation can be simulated. Every few weeks, all the operators in the real control center are required to practice handling emergencies in the simulation room, the same way that pilots practice handling emergencies in plane simulators. (T)

Atomic energy generation apes the airlines industry in other aspects of safety. There's continuous equipment maintenance, and when an accident does occur, it's investigated intensively to establish what has to be done to prevent similar accidents from happening in the future.

The other concern that people have about nuclear fission is the sequestering of the atomic waste produced by atomic energy plants.

One alternative that has been proposed is to stick with carbon-based fuel to generate electricity and capture and sequester the carbon dioxide.

The idea is to liquefy the captured gas and transport it by pipeline to a site where it can be buried in a secure underground geological formation. (Y 401) The approach is expensive and complex, both technically and politically (Y 402).

Comparatively, the challenge of sequestering atomic waste is "beautifully small". (L 404). It's primarily a NIMBY problem, which should be amenable to economic incentives.

If want to wean ourselves away from carbon-based fuel, we could either tax carbon when it comes out of the ground or institute a cap and trade program. Either would confine the use of carbon-based fuel to the more extreme situations where all of the other alternatives are either technologically unattainable or prohibitively expensive. And if the program originally instituted doesn't sufficiently reduce the use of carbon-based fuel, then all that's necessary is to ratchet up the program.

Another proposed solution to generating too much greenhouse gases through the use of carbon-based fuel is to become more efficient in using energy and, as a consequence, reduce the amount of gases produced. Efficiency is good, and we should pursue it. But as far as reducing the use of energy is concerned, efficiency is an illusion.

Until the industrial revolution, the only sources of energy were muscle (both of man and animal), wind and water. This limitation placed an iron ceiling on the extent to which social development could occur. It was only with the advent of a new method of capturing energy, the burning of carbon-based fuel, that social development was able to break through the hitherto unbreechable barrier. (M 382 ,491,492,493,499,515,537,560)

As a result, today, energy use permeates our culture. The fundamental characteristics of modern life are mechanical production, heat, light, cooling and mobility (Y 666). All require energy (Y 712).

Efficiency simply means that you get to do what you want to do with the use of fewer resources. But that just frees those resources to be used for other purposes, and those other uses inevitably involve the use of more energy. Efficiency, in and of itself, does nothing to reduce energy use. (O 147,152,246)

If we want to reduce energy use, then we have to be frugal — use less of everything, because almost everything involves the use of energy. We have only one Earth, and ultimately, its resources are limited. We Westerners are currently too profligate, and at the moment, we're just encouraging the rest of the world to emulate us.

In addition to cutting our greenhouse emissions back to near zero, there are other things that we can do to prevent global warming. One is to create a blanket of sulfur dioxide in the stratosphere to block out some of the sun's rays (Le 193-200). That's what supervolcanic explosions do, and the result is a drop in temperature (Le 189,190). What's needed is to run a tube up into to the air via a balloon and pump sulfur dioxide through the tube into the air.

Another way to prevent global warming is to increase cloud cover. For three days after 9/11, there were no commercial flights and, consequently, no contrails. During those three days, ground temperature was two degrees higher than would otherwise be expected.

It takes three things to make a cloud — ascending air, water vapor, and solid particles known as cloud condensation nuclei. In contrails, exhaust particles serve as the nuclei. Over land, dust particles do the job.

Over oceans, where clouds are sparser, salt-rich spray could serve as nuclei. What you have to do is get the spray a few yards above the sea, which can be done by running specially designed speedboats (electric, of course) through the ocean, and nature will do the rest. (Le 201,202)

Sources

(C) Clark, Gregory *A Farewell to Alms* (Princeton U 2007)
(Cl) *Global Weirdness* by Climate Central, a nonprofit, nonpartisan science and journalism organization (Random House 2012)
(F) Flannery, Tim *The Weather Makers* (Atlantic Monthly 2005)

(G) Private communication with Mark D. Gildersleeve, president of WSI, a weather service firm, on 12/7/12

(Go) Goodstein, David *Out of Gas* (Norton 2004)

(L) Lenton, Tim and Watson, Andrew *Revolutions That Made the Earth* (Oxford U 2011)

(Le) Levitt, Steven D. and Dubner, Stephen J. *Superfreakonomics* (Harper Collins 2009)

(M) Morris, Ian *Why the West Rules — For Now* (Farrar, Straus and Giroux 2010)

(O) Owen, David *Conundrum* (Penguin 2011)

(S) Silver, Nate *The Signal and the Noise* (Penguin 2012)

(Si) Singer, S. Fred and Avery, Dennis T. *Unstoppable Global Warming* (Rowman & Littlefield 2007)

(T) Talk given by Michael Twomey, an officer of Entergy, which manages Indian Point, among other nuclear facilities, to the Darien (CT) Senior Men's Association on 3/28/12

(W) Ward, Peter D. *Under a Green Sky* (Smithsonian 2007)

(Y) Yergin, Daniel *The Quest* (Penguin 2011)

# CHAPTER TEN

# Employment

Recently, even if you ignore the impact of the Great Recession, employment isn't working out in the way that we'd like. The reason is that our expectations have become out of joint with what's going on. The world has changed, but our expectations haven't changed with it.

We matured in the post WW II era, and our concept of what jobs for US workers should be comes from that experience. It was the halcyon years for US workers.

The US emerged from the war with the only undestroyed production system. The unions would say, "We want more."

And management would say, "Sure. No problem. We'll just raise prices." And they could get away with it, because there were no competitors to place restraints on manufacturing's pricing policies.

The US worker had a guaranteed job, a defined benefit pension plan, lifetime medical coverage, and a wage sufficient to support the ownership a car and a house on a quarter acre plot in a middle class neighborhood. That's the job that we want for US workers today.

But our perception of what jobs are available has been distorted by this experience. It was the exception rather than the rule.

It was a onetime situation. It's gone. And it will probably never come again.

What we now have is a global market for labor. It's the West and the Rest.

And at the moment, the Rest will work for less. So that's where the jobs go.

Moreover, automation has been eating away at the jobs that are available.

The countervailing force in this situation seems to be a better-educated workforce.

CHAPTER ELEVEN

# Education

The object of education is to produce adults who derive satisfaction out of leading productive lives. This education is two part: character development and academic achievement. And there are two major players involved in this education: parents or their stand-in caregivers and the schools.

For a child to be able to get the optimum benefit out of his education, he must have a nutritional diet, both during the time that he's in the womb and afterward. On that basis, character and achievement can be built.

## CHARACTER DEVELOPMENT

The brain is where learning occurs. It's a marvelously complex organ about which I know little. But for the purpose of discussing education, I believe that the brain can be thought of as consisting of a number of functional areas: the basal area, the sensory system, the speech area, the prefrontal cortex, and the limbic system.

### The Basal Area

The basal area of the brain, located in the upper part of the brain stem and cerebellum, is responsible for the basic, automatic functions of the body, such as heartbeat, breathing, temperature control, and digestion. It operates with amazing efficiency without the need for education.

### The Sensory System

Another part of the brain is concerned with the senses. For example, the occipital lobe, located at the back of the brain, is responsible for vision, and the temporal lobes, located above the ears, for hearing.

Basically, your child's sensory system will develop without assistance, but its function can be enhanced by a broad exposure to sensation. (Sc 58) So, talk to your baby, sing to him, bounce him to music and poetry, read to him, point out to him the wonders of sight, sound and smell to be found in the world, play with him, and embrace and fondle him.

When it comes to developing your child's sensory areas, the real thing is required. Screen images won't do. A screen image of a puppy doesn't provide any of the sensory stimuli that come from seeing, hearing, feeling and smelling the real thing. (St 173,174)

## The Speech Area

The speech area, located forward from the temporal lobes, is responsible for language production. Your child has an inborn propensity for speech, but it won't develop without exposure to language being used around and directed toward him.

And there's a window during which this exposure to speech must take place. Infants, who are raised without such exposure, lose the ability to develop speech and become, forever after, unable to communicate verbally.

As long as you do your part, your child will learn to speak by himself. Your job is to talk to him … a lot and right from the moment that he's born. Starting before he's born is even better.

And listen to your child with understanding when he talks to you (Ma 1). He won't be interested in talking if no one listens to him.

Talk to your child about what the two of you are doing, about what you're doing, about what you see, about what you feel. Point things out and name them. Identify the attributes of things and name them. (St 215,224)

It doesn't matter what's said. It's a numbers game. A child builds up a vocabulary by hearing and using words (H 62).

The more words that a child hears, the higher his IQ, independent of socioeconomic status. (St 218) But the words have to be spoken fluently in a positive tone and within the context of a conversation.

Of course, at first, your baby isn't going to be able to talk to you. But if you pause in your conversation when it would normally be the time for the other person to talk, your baby will soon get the idea.

And as soon as he can make sounds, he'll start responding. (St 227) (When your child is born, he can cry, but his larynx hasn't yet dropped and he can't make any speech sounds.)

At first, you have to speak in parentese, because this is what a baby can process. Speak slowly, enunciate with emphasis, speak in a high pitch, and elongate vowels. As your child matures, you can switch to more normal speech.

Parentese isn't baby talk. It's regular speech modified as described above. (St 228)

## The Prefrontal Cortex

The prefrontal cortex, located behind the forehead, is where reasoning and the executive functions of the brain reside. The prefrontal cortex has much to do with both character development and academic achievement and is a primary focus of education.

But the functions of the prefrontal cortex don't kick in until between the ages of five and seven, each child developing on his own timetable as it were (E 122). It's only then that your child reaches the age of reason.

Until a child reaches the age of reason, any kind of academic instruction is not only a waste of time but may also have a negative impact on the effectiveness of subsequent education (E 123). Despite the fact that all of the clinical evidence supports this contention, nursery schools emphasizing academic instruction continue to spring up and thrive. (E 97,98) People seem to feel that, if they don't expose their children to such instruction, they'll handicap their children in the competition of life.

They say such things as, "Tiger Wood's father started teaching Tiger golf at age three and look what Tiger has accomplished." The important point here is to not let the exceptional child cloud what happens in general.

Most children aren't exceptional. And if one is, it will soon become clear. Only then does special treatment become productive.

By the time that children are seven or eight, the only difference between children who spent their years in nurseries that were rigidly academic and those who came from laid back, play-based ones is that those in the first group were more anxious and less creative (Ho 59). The child who's going to benefit from school isn't the one who arrives knowing the alphabet. It's the one who knows how to share, empathize, and follow instructions (Ho 59).

The age of reason begins when the child is able to grasp the idea that something can be two things at one time. For example, a child is confused when he sees his nursery school teacher in the supermarket. How can one person be both a teacher and a shopper? (E 124)

The sure test that a child has reached the age of reason is when he can draw, or copy, a diamond. This task requires that the pencil, crayon, what have you, be moved both horizontally and vertically at the same time, and that's a problem for someone who can't conceive of doing two things at once. (E 141,142)

Since a child doesn't reach the age of reason until some time between the ages of five and seven, trying to teach him how to read and write at the age of five isn't developmentally appropriate. However, if a five-year-old is going to learn how to read and write, then when he enters kindergarten, he has to be able to distinguish words, syllables and phonemes in the spoken language, and he has to be able to hold a pencil and make shapes with it. These are the academic achievements with which preK education is concerned.

The rest of preK education has to do with developing a healthy, active, nurtured brain. (St xiii) The child who's going to advance in elementary school is the one who can deal with separation from his parents, develop independence, learn how to get familiar with the idea of being a member of a group, exercise self-discipline, share, empathize, make friends, pay attention, and follow directions.

The development of the prefrontal cortex isn't complete until high school and beyond (up to age 25, according to neurologists (P 129)).

This is a clue as to how much you can trust your children to figure out things for themselves. In other words, don't spare the advice.

## IQ

IQ stands for Intelligence Quotient (N 5). The name, IQ, derives from the history of IQ testing.

Originally, IQ tests were developed for school children and were designed to determine a child's mental age. His mental age was then divided by his chronological age, which gave a quotient, his "intelligence" quotient.

As in percentages, this IQ quotient was then multiplied by 100 to avoid having to deal with decimal points. Thus, if a ten year old tested at a mental age of 10, his IQ was 100, at a mental age of 12, his IQ was 120, at 8, his IQ was 80, and so on.

IQ is no longer a quotient. Instead, it's just a score. (B 34) IQ tests are developed on the basis of the assumption that whatever they're measuring is normally distributed and are structured so that a score of 100 represents the mean of the distribution with a standard deviation of around 15.

The mean plus or minus one standard deviation is considered to be the "normal" range for IQ. Anything above or below the normal range is considered abnormal, either abnormally gifted or abnormally deficient. (N 5)

An interesting aspect of keeping mean IQ at an arbitrary value of 100 is that, as the years pass, it's necessary to make IQ tests more and more difficult (N 44). The almost inevitable conclusion is that IQ testing is measuring something that can be learned.

As far as what we call intelligence itself is concerned, there seems to be two types.

One type is called fluid intelligence. It has to do with solving novel, abstract problems, ones to which your accumulation of real-world information has little to contribute. A simple example would be, given a series of numbers, determine what the next number in the series is.

Fluid intelligence involves the use of what are called the "executive functions" of the prefrontal cortex, which include (N 7):

1. Working memory: Solving abstract problems usually involves taking a series of steps, and working memory is the ability to maintain in your mind information developed in previous steps while you concentrate on the next step in developing other information relevant to the solution to the problem
2. Attentional control: The ability to concentrate on only those aspects of the problem that are relevant to the current step in the problem solution, and once that step has been taken, to be able to shift attention to the aspects relevant to the next step in the solution
3. Inhibitory control: The ability to ignore aspects of the problem situation that are irrelevant to its solution

The other type of what we call intelligence is known as crystallized intelligence, which is the store of information that you've built up about the nature of the world and the procedures that you've learned that help you make inferences about the world (N 9).

The part of IQ tests that tries to get at fluid intelligence is called Performance Testing. The part that concentrates on crystallized intelligence is centered on information, vocabulary, comprehension, identification of similarities, and math. (N 9)

From all of this it should be obvious that, just like all other aspects of human behavior, while some of us may be more inclined biologically to a given level of performance than others, there's nothing immutable about it — performance can be taught and improved on through practice.

On the other hand, we're not completely independent of our biology. The part of the brain involved in the executive functions of fluid intelligence are the prefrontal cortex and the anterior cingulate (N 9). Severe damage to the prefrontal cortex results in performance of fluid intelligence at the level of mentally retarded people even though crystallized intelligence may be unimpaired (N 9).

Both fluid and crystallized intelligence develop rapidly in early life. Fluid intelligence then begins to taper off while crystallized intelligence continues to grow. So mathematicians and scientists usually make their contributions early in life while the output of historians may continue to improve throughout adulthood.

Both types of intelligence suffer decline as the brain ages. The prefrontal cortex begins to deteriorate before the other parts of the brain. (N 10,11)

Academic success increases the probability of occupational success, but it's only one factor (N 17,55). A good IQ score increases the probability of academic success, but again, it's only one factor. There's suggestive evidence that self-discipline (the ability to postpone reward) predicts academic achievement better than IQ (B 133). Conventional IQ tests predict only about ten percent of the reasons why a child will be successful in school or in the workplace.

Going to school tends to increase your IQ score (N 42). This makes sense, since IQ tests consist primarily of questions of an academic nature (Ma 15).

Certain ethnic groups seem to excel academically as well as occupationally. One such group is Asians (N 154).

However, Asian superiority apparently comes more from sweat than high IQ (N 154). In fact, Asians tend to score slightly lower on IQ tests than Americans or Europeans (N 156).

The school year is significantly longer in Asia than it is in the US (155). Asians work on homework about three and one half hours a day (N 158).

Asian culture exerts pressure on children to perform academically. For thousands of years, Asian culture has emphasized respect for elders, and what the elders have been and still are interested in is academic achievement. (N 159,160,161) Asians are accustomed to constructive criticism, which US students tend to resist, and Asians are encouraged to persist in the face of failure (N 159).

Jews, another ethnic group who've excelled academically and occupationally, exhibit similar characteristics: respect for elders and emphasis on educational achievement (180). Once more, it seems that occupational success is more a matter of persistence than it is of IQ (181).

In sum, IQ tests appear to measure something associated with occupational success. But perhaps even more important is persistence in the face of failure and a willingness to take on new challenges.

## The Limbic System

From day one of your child's life, the limbic system of his brain is in operation (St 23). The limbic system is what has enabled us and our vertebrae cousins to survive for 500 million years. It controls the basic functions that provide for the preservation of the species, commonly known as the four Fs — fight, flight, food and sex.

The fight or flight function throws you into a state of stress (S 11,12,39,80). Here is, perhaps, the quintessential example of stress.

A lion is chasing a zebra across the savanna. If the zebra doesn't run faster than the lion, he's going to be eaten. If the lion doesn't run faster than the zebra, he's going to go hungry. So their bodies gear up for maximum running ability.

Glucose and the simplest forms of proteins and fats come pouring out of the fat cells, liver, and muscles of the animals. Heart rate, blood pressure, and breathing rate increase, all to transport those nutrients and oxygen at maximum speed to the running muscles.

Those body functions, involved in more long-term concerns, shut down — digestion is inhibited, tissue growth and repair are curtailed, sperm generation stops, and the immune system ceases operation. Why waste all that energy on these long-term concerns when the pressing need at the moment is to see that those running muscles get all of the energy that the body can generate?

The perception of pain becomes blunted, so that, if an animal runs into something, the injury doesn't interfere with the project of the moment — keeping up a maximum rate of speed. The bladder and bowels evacuate. Why carry around all that extra weight when you're running for your life? (S 11,12,39,80)

In short, the lion and the zebra are under stress, and stress is all about preparing the body for a major expenditure of energy in physical activity — fight or flight (S 33,401). When lack of vigilance could mean that you'd become someone else's dinner, stress was important.

Today, the threat that you could become prey has, pretty much, disappeared. But don't expect a body reaction that has been essential for 500 million years to extinguish any time soon.

So, when we experience discomfort, stress sets in. We recognize some of the effects of stress — we begin to sweat, our skin grows clammy, we get a queasy feeling in our stomach, our mouth becomes dry, our heart beat quickens, and we start breathing faster.

And a lot of other things that we don't sense also occur. For example, our blood pressure goes up, our immune system shuts down, our sense of pain is deadened, glucose levels rise, and adrenaline and cortisol course through our bloodstream.

And this system isn't selective. It doesn't analyze the threat and determine which of the body's many responses are appropriate. Regardless of the threat, it just mobilizes the whole defense system. (T 12,13)

It would be nice if we could just avoid stressful situations, and to the extent that it's possible, that's a good idea. But the fact of the matter is that stress situations, like the Biblical poor, are always with us.

So total avoidance of stress isn't an option. We have to adopt some other approach.

And fortunately, there is one. It's managing stress.

When you undergo stress, the object is to return the body's defense mechanism to its pacific state as soon as possible. When you experience stress, you have to talk yourself down from the high level to which your body's stress reaction has raised you — you have to calm yourself.

In the first years of your child's life, he's going to experience a lot of discomfort. That means that he's going to undergo a lot of stress.

Your child has to learn to manage his stress. In later life, children who haven't learned how to manage stress exhibit a characteristic collection of maladaptive behavior.

When they get to school, they find it harder to concentrate, harder to sit still, and harder to follow directions (T 17).

When children enter adolescence, they become more sensation seeking and more emotionally reactive at the same time as their cognitive control system, which doesn't completely mature until the mid 20s, is still in an immature state. As a consequence, it's not uncommon for adolescents to make poor judgments. When this potential for getting into trouble is compounded by an inability to manage stress, the consequences can be catastrophic. (T 21,22)

If these people are lucky enough to get through adolescence, then in later life, they are fated for tragic outcomes — failed careers, broken relationships, addiction, and poor health (T 34).

The first step in teaching your child to manage stress is to provide him with an environment in which everything unfolds in a consistent way. Feeding, bathing, sleeping, naptime, getting dressed, etc. all occur on a schedule that's the same everyday. (St 115,148,154,161,G 185). This consistency tells your child that his world is predicable, stable, and therefore, safe (St 13,J 116).

But that's just a beginning. What's essential is a caregiver.

There can be more than one caregiver. But there has to be at least one person on which the child can absolutely rely 24/7 for consistent, predictable and loving care. (St 135)

Note consistent: It has to be the same caretakers, day after day. (St 135) Forming a strong bond with caretakers is the cornerstone of child development (Ho 45).

For better or worse, a nurturing relationship with caregivers in early infancy is generally referred to as mothering, regardless of how feminists might object and also regardless of the fact that a father can provide just as much mothering as can a mother. (T 28)

Mothering involves making the interactions between you and your child enjoyable and as frequent as possible. The most interesting thing to your infant is your face. So put in front of him, maintain eye contact, and interact with him. (Ho 44) Be responsive. Be predictable. Touch. Read. Get down on the floor and play with your baby. Talk to your child. Be attentive and responsive to your child's moods. Providing your child with a secure, nurturing relationship fosters in your child the development of a powerful buffer against the damage that stress can cause (T 32,33,34,37,182,195).

In the beginning, when your child experiences stress, he's not going to be able to tell you what's wrong. Instead, he's going to misbehave. (J 133)

When your child acts up, it's because he's in distress (M 117,195). An angry child is a child who's scared, disconnected and hurting (M 120).

When your child is under the power of a strong emotion, what he doesn't need is a lecture. What he needs is some understanding. (J 237)

An upset child needs to be held, embraced, caressed, and assured that everything is all right. This calms him down at the same time as it teaches him how to calm himself down. (T 182 L 4,43,91)

Your child may resist you physically, but don't give up. Keep soothing him. (M 99)

The most likely result of such a crisis is that your child will experience a meltdown — he end up in tears and clinging to you. Continue to sooth him. He's releasing the emotions that caused his distress in the first place. (M 99,104,191)

No matter what your child's behavior, no matter how disobedient he has been, no matter how defiant, no matter what damage he has caused, you must show him that you're on his side and that you're never going to abandon him (M xxi). That's what unconditional love means. The less his behavior "deserves" your love, the more essential it is for you to be there for him (M 14,35,119).

You can't spoil your baby. It'll be years before he develops the mental wherewithal to manipulate you. (St 151)

When things go wrong, someone has to act like an adult. That someone isn't going to be your child. (M 5) He's acting like a child because he is a child (M 14).

Stay calm. When you become anxious, fearful, upset, or angry, you're raising the anxiety level of your child. You're stressing him out, and that's not good. (M xxi,4)

In addition, you're not serving as a good role model. How do you expect your child to learn to control his emotions if you don't control yours? (M 17)

When your child misbehaves, stop whatever you're doing, give him your attention, try to figure out what it is that your child is feeling, and reflect that feeling back on him in words — "Oh, you're so angry. Maybe it's because (whatever)." (J 138)

Try to help your child to name his feelings. "Oh, you're so mad. Is it because I was doing the dishes and couldn't play Legos with you right away?" (Si 6) "You seem to be upset. Is it because Johnny cancelled your play date?"

Notice that you don't tell your child what he's feeling. You're just making suggestions. It's up to your child to determine what his feelings are. If your child can name his feelings, he's already taken the first step toward controlling them (D 177 Si 50,129). Your role is to be an understanding mirror to your child's feelings, so that he's in a position to do his best to tell you what's troubling him (D 175).

Be tentative in suggesting what may be troubling your child. It's not up to you to tell your child what's troubling him. He knows what's troubling him. The object is to let your child know that he's being heard, understood and accepted. (J 143)

Once again, notice the word "accepted". We all experience distress when things go wrong or when they don't work out in the way that we want them to. The difference between you and your child is that you've learned how to deal with your negative emotions, but they overwhelm your child.

Your child is entitled to his feelings, and you should never imply that it's bad for him to have them. Having feelings is human.

You don't want to give your child the impression that it's wrong to have negative emotions. You want him to develop the ability to understand these emotions, accept them for what they are, and develop the ability to deal with them. (J 152)

What your child has to learn to do is to recognize and control his feelings and not just give in to them. It's OK to be so mad at something that you'd like to destroy it. It's actually destroying it that's not OK. (Si 175)

When calming the situation, never belittle your child's feelings. They're his feelings, he's feeling them, they're neither good nor bad, you should accept that he's having them, and you should make clear that having them is OK (Si 129).

If you belittle your child's feelings ("You're just tired." "Stop fussing." "It's not a big deal." (Si 243)), he's going to start questioning their validity and begin to doubt his ability to accurately observe and comprehend what's going on inside of him. This will leave him confused, full of self-doubt, and disconnected from his feelings. As he grows into an adult, he may doubt his subjective experience and, at times, have a hard time knowing what he wants. (Si 178)

The more often you use words to express feelings, the more your child will begin to understand his feelings. They will become easier to accept, and he'll become more capable of letting go and moving past them. (J 145)

Your child is totally dependent on you. Every time that you yell at him, every time that you punish him, whether it's a slap on the behind or an isolating time out, every time that you turn way from him in disgust, every time that you deliberately ignore him, every time that you arbitrarily say, "No," opens up, for your child, a void between him and you. When he feels that you aren't there to support him, that is, for him, just about the ultimate in a stressful situation.

Giving your child the impression that your love is conditional on his good behavior opens up, for your child, the potential abyss that he may be abandoned by you (M 204,205). Maybe the world isn't such a safe place after all.

Maybe caregivers aren't as trustworthy and reliable as would be liked. Maybe it's better to be cautious about the world and to be distrustful of people. An insecure child who's constantly monitoring his environment to see whether he's in harm's way isn't going to have a lot of time for learning things (St 33,34,71,133).

Besides teaching your child how to manage stress, mothering has a biological effect on child development. The prefrontal cortex has substantial interconnections with the limbic system, making the prefrontal cortex heavily involved in stress.

During emotional arousal, the operation of the prefrontal cortex is reduced, and continued stress may result in permanently reduced prefrontal cortex activity. (N 11,12) The result is that infants, who grow up with a lack of mothering, suffer from a prefrontal cortex with reduced executive function ability, such as working memory and dealing with confusing situations and information. (T 17,18,20,28)

The way that a child develops a rich vocabulary is by hearing a rich vocabulary being used. So to equip a child with a good vocabulary, what you have to do is see to it that the child's parents have a good vocabulary — a near impossibility. (T 41)

But in contrast, giving a child's parents lessons in mothering is relatively straightforward. Mary Dozier, a psychologist at the University of Delaware, has developed an intervention, which she calls Attachment and Biobehavioral Catch-Up (ABC).

Paul Tough, the author of *How Children Succeed*, observed a session of this intervention conducted by Anita Stewart-Montgomery, an employee of Catholic Charities, which runs the intervention program sponsored by the Ounce of Prevention Fund, a Chicago-based philanthropy. Anita was working with Jacqui, a 16-year-old single mother, and her eight-month-old daughter, Makayla.

Anita was with Jacqui and Makayla for one purpose only — to work with Jacqui's mothering skills. All of the other disadvantages, under which Jacqui and Makayla operated, were ignored.

So Anita paid no attention to the furniture with the sharp corners, the noise and smell of cigarette smoke in the apartment, and the abandoned lot next door in a rough neighborhood. Instead, Anita concentrated on working with Jacqui and Makalya, as they played together, and encouraged Jacqui to be more attentive, warm and calm in responding to Makalya's cues.

Experience with ABC indicates significant improvement in secure attachment among children after just ten home visits. (T 39,40,41)

The rest of the good news is that, even if a child has missed out on good mothering when he was an infant, it's still not too late to develop self-control. The prefrontal cortex is more responsive to intervention than other parts of the brain, and it stays flexible well into adolescence and early adulthood.

In addition, the executive functions of the prefrontal cortex are more malleable than other cognitive skills. (T 21,48) The brain is plastic and has the ability to reorganize itself. (St 21,22)

A nonprofit organization called Youth Advocate Programs (YAP) runs an intensive mentoring program paid for by the Chicago public school system. It focuses on "ultra-high risk" students in high school and, at least in the case of one child on whom Tough reports, the attention provided by the child's YAP advocate has had a significant positive effect in turning around the child's prospects. (T 22,23,43-48)

As Maria Robinson famously said, "Nobody can go back and start a new beginning, but anyone can start today and make a new ending." (M 252)

The bad news is that stress isn't going to go away any time soon. When we have to perform, we tend to get anxious and start thinking about all of the bad things that will happen if we choke up and fail (D 220).

In particular, many people experience test anxiety (D 224). When we become anxious, our limbic system takes over, our prefrontal cortex shuts down, and all of the skills that we need to do well on a test become unavailable to us (D 221).

When we tense up, we have to relax (D 221). And the sooner our children learn how to relax, the better off that they are.

There's a two-step process for achieving relaxation (D 220). First, you take a deep breath through your nose. Make it as big as you can and push it all the way down into your belly. Hold your breath for a few seconds. Then, blow the breath out through your mouth really hard. (D 222)

And second, while you're taking your deep breath, say something positive to yourself. Like "I know this stuff. I can do this." (D 224,225)

Whenever you get anxious in a performance situation, use this two-step technique to relax yourself. And teach this technique to your child.

When a child is brought up in a consistent, predictable environment in which he can count unqualifiedly on the support, care and love of a caregiver 24 hours each day, he'll have built up a firm conviction that his world is a predicable and emotionally safe place and can be relaxed, alert, and ready to have fun learning about the world around him (Sm 199). He's then ready to take on the development of other essential character traits — resiliency, optimism, motivation, reliability, responsibility, ethics, and social intelligence.

## Resiliency

Resiliency is the ability to deal with failure. (T 84,85,162,183) It's probably fair to say that resilience is the most essential ingredient for success in life (P 64).

When it comes to resiliency, unstructured play has a role to play. Don't over schedule your child's extracurricular activities.

Elementary school children should have, at most, three extracurricular activities, one social (e. g., scouting, church activities), one physical (e. g., Little League, dance school), and one artistic (e. g., piano lessons, drawing). You should leave time for unstructured play, where your child can figure what to do on his own. (Ho ch 8)

Unstructured play allows the child to investigate how the world works, use this perception of the world to predict how things (that he's going to try) will work out, improve this perception on the basis of the feedback that he gets from failure, and learn how to tolerate failure. (W 26,27,39,Gro 131)

The way that a child learns is by exploring. If every time that he turns around, he hears, "No," his natural inclination to explore is inhibited. (M 156)

So, do everything that you can to avoid saying, "No." (M 195) When your child is an infant, to the extent possible, baby-proof your home.

Get the breakables and dangerous things out of your child's reach. Then let him explore. (M 156,210)

Your child is going to put things in his mouth. If it's not dangerous, then let him do it.

If your child wants to take the pots and pans out of the cupboard and spread then around the room, that's OK. (M 156,210) When he's done, you can make it a game to have him help you put them all back.

Pulling down the Christmas tree is out — someone could get hurt. Taking ornaments off of the tree and rearranging them is OK.

There can be only one dessert a day. But if your child wants it for breakfast, that's OK. If he wants to wear polka dots with stripes, that's OK.

Giving your child the freedom to explore and express himself should continue as he grows. You can't let your child make disastrous decisions, but for those things that aren't crucial, let him be independent, even if what he chooses, such as his clothes or music, doesn't appeal to you. A child's peers have considerable influence over things like dress, music and recreation, but he'll continue to respect his parents' values (Le 130).

Get your child outside. If your neighborhood is safe and your child has demonstrated an adequate capacity to be responsible (comes when called, follows directions, and can cross the street safely), by nine, your child should be able to navigate the neighborhood. He has to be given the opportunity to learn how to live in the world on his own.

The world is a dangerous place, but within reason, a child benefits by being exposed to it (Ho 240). Stranger danger doesn't fit the statistics. Predators are overwhelmingly people whom the child already knows — parents, relatives, family friends. (Ho 248)

Activity is important. It brings the child into contact with the world, which he needs to do to develop an effective character.

Some children are naturally active — you can't keep them off of their bikes, skates, etc. But other children need to learn to be active.

Parents can encourage their child to be active by being active themselves and encouraging their child to be active with them. A child shouldn't be encouraged to be sedentary. Driving a child to school when it's close enough for him to walk is an example of encouraging him to be sedentary and not active. (E 61)

Physical activity is important. Children are calmer, happier and more able to focus after being physically active. (D 115) Every day, your child should get thirty or 40 minutes of vigorous exercise (D 129).

The advantaged child can be exposed to a serious handicap. His parents may insist on him having a high level of academic achievement, which brings forth harsh criticism when the level isn't attained, while often being so involved in other things that they have little time to give him a feeling of emotional attachment or the supervision and guidance that are required to develop the requisite coping skills. The result is that the advantaged child often experiences intense feelings of distress, shame and hopelessness. (T 82,83)

Encourage your child's creativity (W ch 6). Keep toys basic and to a minimum.

LEGOs are good. Sand, water, clay, paint and blocks are ideal. Electronic toys amuse but don't encourage imagination.

For example, one parent gave her child, for his birthday, a cardboard box, a six-foot stick, a four-foot one, and two pieces of rope. Another year, she took him to a hardware store, gave him $25, and let him buy whatever he wanted.

Don't immediately jump in and help your child with his problems. Give him a chance to work them out on his own. (Le 221)

Don't protect your child from failure. In life, failure is inevitable.

You must give your child the opportunity to make a bad choice that may not turn out well (D 166). If the weather forecast says that it's going to be hot today and your child comes down for breakfast dressed in a turtleneck, you can point out to him that, if he goes out in a turtleneck, he's going to be uncomfortably hot, but if decides to not take your advice, then let him find out for himself that, on a hot day, wearing a turtleneck is a bad choice. If your child isn't given the opportunity to choose between options, he isn't going to learn that good choices result in desirable consequences and that bad choices lead to undesirable ones. (D 14,15,17,18,33).

To build the character to be able to withstand some shocks, a child has to experience some discomfort — some hardships, deprivations, and challenges where there's a real possibility of failure. (T 83,84,85,86,183,Po 66,Sm 121) On the other hand, continuous, devastating failure is going to kill interest (Sm 128).

In general, make sure that, when your child undertakes a task, there's a reasonable chance that he'll be able to handle it. Just also see to it that failure is a possibility. Your role is to help, not to rescue.

Your child is going to make mistakes. Your job is to help him see his mistakes as opportunities to think things through and develop more productive alternatives (M 157). People who experience nothing but a series of easy successes tend to give up at the first sign of difficulty (Le 237,238).

Your child needs to be resourceful. Introduce some necessity into his life (e. g., have him prepare his own lunch). Tell your child about the everyday problems that you've had to face and how you went about contending with them.

Don't do things for your child that he can do for himself. Give him the opportunity to learn how to do things for himself. (L 2,Gro 279) Encourage your child's autonomy (Mi 59)

When your child becomes old enough to do something for himself, stop doing it for him. Instead, teach him how to do it himself. (J 38,Gro 269) Show patience, offer step-by-step instruction, and give him the time to work it out for himself (Ma 72). If you continue to do things for your child after he has become capable of doing them himself, you're robbing him of the opportunity to develop self-reliance (Gro 110).

From an early age, have your child contribute to the family's welfare. He should have chores to do. (G 185) As he grows, his ability to carry out chores grows, and he should be given more challenging chores for which he's responsible (Gro 267). Having family responsibilities contributes to his sense of self-worth and confidence (L 165,Gro 187).

When your child fails, don't let him shift the responsibility. Others, indeed, may be partially responsible. But your child has to learn to take the responsibility for his own life.

It's in the area of managing failure and dealing with obstacles that the disadvantaged child has an edge on his advantaged counterpart. By the time that the disadvantaged child reaches college age, he has seen a lot of failure and has had to surmount numerous obstacles.

As a consequence, if the disadvantaged child gets to college, the chances are good that he'll finish and graduate. Being entitled is something that has never occurred to him. Everything that he has gotten he has had to work for. (D 245)

The advantaged child, on the other hand, is overindulged, has had the way smoothed for him, and if he gets into trouble, his parents bail him out. He develops a sense of entitlement — things should come to him just because he is. As a result, when he gets to college or goes to work and faces, by himself, an environment where he's expected to work independently on more difficult assignments, he's often overwhelmed by the pressure and drops out. (Ma 71)

Entitlement kills enthusiasm. If a child wants for nothing, then there's nothing for which to strive.

Enthusiasm comes from achieving goals. Encourage persistence and responsibility.

Your child shouldn't feel that he's automatically entitled to anything. His approach should be that, if he wants something, he has to work to get it. (D 102)

Nudge your child toward doing well what he likes to do. Most of that has to do with effort and persistence (Le 33).

The more competent your child is, the more confidence he'll have. Both competence and confidence are built out of the hundreds of small, successive successes leading to the attainment of a goal. (Le 227,228)

Don't hover. Leave your child to his own devices. What interests your child is something that he, not you, will determine (En 160).

Your role is to act as a coach. Encourage. Make suggestions.

Give assistance only if asked, and keep it to a minimum. It's your child's activity, not yours. (M 213) You can advise and supervise, but he's the one who should do the job, experience the mistakes, and learn from them (Mc 77,L 9).

Instill in your child the idea that to be good at what interests him requires hard work — a conscientious application of effort to achieve a high standard of performance in goal oriented activity. The key word here is effort. What you should do is praise effort and go easy on praising achievement. The focus should be on process rather than on outcome. (D 36,188 En 153,154,162,165,166 Ho 204 M 231)

Don't praise indiscriminately. Telling someone that he's good by itself does nothing to encourage effort (Le 230,231,232). Empty praise can actually be damaging to self-esteem (Ma 205).

Praise should be descriptive. Describe to your child what he's done to please you, tell him why it pleases you, and relate what he's done to the relevant desirable quality, such as a show of respect, cooperation, generosity, etc. (J 42,59,60). What he's done to earn your praise can be an achievement, a step toward achievement or any other kind of improvement, or even not doing what's not desirable (J 44).

When complementing your child's performance, say things like, "I'm impressed with your performance," instead of things like "I'm proud of your performance." When you say, "I'm proud of your performance," you're claiming some of the credit for your child's performance. (Mc 70)

The child who thinks of himself as hardworking will, after having mastered a skill, look for other opportunities to broaden his experience. (N 188,189) So, don't tell children that they're smart. Instead, praise hard work.

It's particularly important to praise your child when he tries something new. And it's the fact that he has tried something new that should be praised, to the exclusion of how well he carried out the new behavior.

It's not how well he did the new thing that's important. What's important is that he tried something new. Trying new things is what you want to encourage, so that's what you want to praise. (D 37)

Once a child becomes convinced that he's gifted, he wants to retain the status that comes from being gifted. He avoids taking the chances that might lead to accomplishment, because he fears failure, which would demonstrate that he's not as gifted as he believes himself to be. (Ro 42)

Such a child talks about the big things that he's going to do, but he doesn't do them. (Ro 28) He prefers to continue to do the things at which he's good and retain his status. He tends to not achieve much in the way of accomplishment (Ma 20).

The child who qualifies for potential success is the one who tries, experiences the inevitable failures, sees the failures as lessons on how to improve, and tries again. Instead of going for the big hit, he concentrates on the incremental steps that lead to accomplishment. (Ro 28) He has what's known as grit — consistency of interests and perseverance over time (Ro 47).

The incremental approach has a second advantage. It produces small wins. Each win produces a shot of testosterone, which makes the winner less anxious, more motivated, and more willing to put up with hardship. (Ro 62,63,Ma 207)

In general, rewards are counterproductive. They encourage children to engage in activities for the sake of the reward rather than for the activity itself, to the point where the children sometimes resort to cheating in order to win the prize. (M 232)

Schools tend to rely on extrinsic incentives, such as grades, rather than on intrinsic rewards, such as entertainment, enjoyment and satisfaction. (W 57) They penalize failure and, consequently, don't encourage risk taking (W 113).

Our schools are turning out students who perform well on tests and who are wily but who are superficial and indifferent learners (Le xiii,Gro 149). They become adept at image management, but their external successes are superficial and meaningless, even to them (Le xxv). This results from the schools' narrow definition of success, which consists mostly of academic awards and sports trophies (Le xiii,xv).

Encourage your child to work just outside of his comfort zone. When he takes that extra step (e. g., crossing the street by himself), you're going to feel anxious. Don't display it.

Children need someone who takes them seriously, believes in their abilities, and challenges them to improve themselves (T 120,121).

If your child chooses to do something, such as play the guitar, encourage him. For example, you could suggest that you'd be willing to finance some preliminary lessons for him.

But let your child decide how he wants to approach the activity. If his enthusiasm wanes, don't be disappointed. Part of growing up is experimenting with activities to see how they fit. If on the other hand, his interest deepens, then is the time to point out that the road to improvement is to practice and that practice is most effective when done under the supervision of a coach. (Le 199,200 Ma 67)

When your child is engaged in an activity, unless absolutely necessary, don't interrupt him. He's working on something.

Interrupting your child when he's doing something implies that what he's doing isn't important. And it interferes with his concentration and the building of his attention span. (M 211)

A child dawdles because he's looking at the world with fresh eyes. He's seeing things for the first time and has to absorb them. (E 98) It's hard for adults to believe that, initially, a child doesn't even know that dropped objects fall — it's something that he has to learn for himself (E 101).

Don't put your child under pressure to perform (Show Grandpa what you can do). Your child does what he does for the fun of it, and putting pressure on him takes away from the fun and discourages further development. (E 70)

Don't demonstrate dysfunctional responses (such as taking a drink) in response to stress. (Le 192,193,194)

Optimism

Optimism is an outgrowth of resiliency, at the same time as it feeds back and strengthens resiliency. Optimism is the feeling that what you do has an effect on your life.

Optimism is the faith that you can handle life as it comes to you, that despite setbacks, you're good enough to overcome them. (M 202,203) It's the conviction that, when you lose, it's just an incident. It doesn't make you a loser. (P 65)

Optimism is seeing yourself as an agent rather than as a victim. It's one of the key factors in a person's ability to be resilient — to bounce back after failure. (Le 232,233,235)

Optimism is the belief that your current conditions aren't your destiny, that they can be changed (T 165). Pessimists see failure as a general, unchanging, personal experience (I'm no good, and there's nothing that I can do about it.) Optimists see failures as specific, short-term and limited — things from which it's possible to recover and go on. (T 54)

The difference is between conceiving of losing as something that happens to you rather than as something that you are (T 116). Or to put it another way, the difference is between seeing failure as an action rather than as an identity (P 38,144).

Optimists think that, basically, things are all right, and when something goes wrong, it was a fluke. Pessimists think that, basically, things are in bad shape, and when something turns out to be good, it was a fluke. (En 209,210,221) Encourage your child to think of disappointments as specific, temporary, fixable things (En 230).

Pessimism is a formula for failure. People, who believe that they've been born to an inferior role and that there's nothing that they can do about it, turn out to be failures. (Ro 29,49) It's a self-fulfilling prophecy.

Belief that you have no control over your life pumps cortisol into your blood stream that, in high doses, shrinks brain cells and their connections, which impairs memory and problem solving ability (Ro 161). You may become listless, unmotivated, anxious, and overly concerned with risk (Ro 203).

## Motivation

Motivation is the determination to keep on working toward a goal, even when there's no external reward involved (T 64,69), the willingness to work hard at a task, even if it's dull, simply because it has to be done to achieve the desired goal (T 73).

Motivation begins with an interest in something. Unstructured play has a lot to do with developing interests.

Some children will pursue an interest on their own. But more generally, parents can help in this area.

Find out what interests your child and encourage him to pursue his interest, until he has achieved accomplishment often enough that the motivation to continue is internalized (Ro 27). He can then set rules for himself (such as good work habits, time management, and promptness), so that behavior can be channeled toward desired ends (T 93,94,153).

Which may explain why children of successful parents often don't succeed themselves. For successful people, time is money. So they work long hours to maximize income, ostensibly to provide a better life for their children. (Ro 14)

But the parenting disappears. Without developed motivation, the children's attitude is, "Why bother? I'm going to be rich anyhow." (Ro 26) Researchers have determined that richer adolescents are more anxious and depressed and use more cigarettes, alcohol, marijuana, and other illegal drugs than their less well off peers (Ro 13).

Ability, by itself, doesn't lead to success. No matter how naturally gifted a child is, if he doesn't have the motivation to work on developing his skill, he'll never be topflight. (D 234)

## Reliability

A reliable person has integrity. You can trust him. (T 162)

If you want your child to be trustworthy, then you have to model trustworthiness. If you promise your child something, you have to make sure that you deliver on your promise. That's why it's important to be careful about what you promise.

For example, if you promise to do something with your child and are then called away on business, so that you can't deliver on your promise, what that means to your child is that you've failed him — what you did was more important than delivering on your promise to him. In the longer view, that may, indeed, be the case. But it's important that your child be aware of such contingencies ahead of time.

You should make clear to your child up front that your work is what puts food on the table and that he should understand that, when you agree to do something with him, there's always the outside possibility that your work responsibilities may interfere. Other contingencies, such as an illness in the family, are also things about which it's important for you to see that your child has preknowledge. (J 229,230)

If you want a respectful child, treat him with respect. If you don't want your child to interrupt you, don't interrupt him (D 183).

Show that you value your child's ability to go against the crowd (e. g., "A lot of kids cheat, but I don't think that it's right"). (Le 223,224,J 220)

<u>Responsibility</u>

A responsible person gets done what he has committed to do on time.

To be responsible, a person has to be organized, have good work habits, and be able to manage his time, so that when the time comes to deliver, he's ready to do it.

One aspect of being organized is to keep your possessions in order (D 141). A place for everything and everything in its place.

After you've finished doing something, put the things that you used to accomplish the task back where they belong. Then, whenever you want something, you know where to find it and can avoid wasting the time that you'd otherwise have to spend looking for it.

At the beginning, you can work with your child in putting his things away. But over time, you should encourage your child to understand that putting his things away is his responsibility.

Another aspect of being organized is having a schedule. Your child should have a daily schedule for when he's to get up, when he's to be in school, when he's going to exercise, when he's going to fit in any other activities to which he's committed, when he's going to do his chores, when his homework time is to begin, when he's going to spend time with his family, when he's going to do his school-independent reading, and when he's to go to bed.

Once your child's schedule has been set up, he should adhere to it. Consistency and repetition are the keys to establishing a good work ethic (D 23).

Without a schedule, your child won't develop the ability to manage his time (D 142). Children don't come with an inborn ability to understand how long it takes to do things (D 136). Working out a schedule and then working with the schedule helps him develop this ability.

In addition to things that take place daily, there are longer-term tasks, such as preparing a term paper, for which your child will be responsible. You should help him use his developing time management skills to judge how much time a longer-term task is likely to take and setting aside enough time in his schedule to complete it on time. (D 146)

Having a schedule to follow will allow your child to focus on the task at hand to the exclusion of distractions (D 229).

Help your child develop a good work ethic. Let your child know that, when you personally work hard on a project, you get a feeling of accomplishment and pride.

Children with a full schedule of schoolwork, sports, chores, and family activities don't have time to get into trouble (D 118). Tired children are good children.

You have to not take responsibility for things that your child can control (D 188). It's important to let your child experience the consequences of his actions. If you rescue him so that the consequences don't occur, he's not going to learn to be responsible for his own behavior. (D 147)

For example, if your child has finished a project for school and, on the day that the project is due, he forgets it and goes to school without taking it with him, he may call you from school and ask you to bring the project to school for him. Don't do it.

If he doesn't turn his project in on time, he may get his grade reduced for turning it in late. But that's the consequence of not seeing to it that he remembers to bring in the project when it's due. He has to learn that getting his project in on time is his responsibility, not yours. (D 26)

Ethics

To raise an ethical child, the first step is to teach values — sound guidelines on what's the right thing to do (Ki 1). There are five fundamental values — be honest (don't lie, be transparent and open, and show candor), be responsible (accountable, dutiful, obedient, loyal), be respectful, be fair (be just and treat people equally), and have compassion (warmth, affection, care, kindness, empathy, love, mercy).

You don't have to be self-conscious about promoting these values. They're recognized the world over as the characteristics of a good person. And their opposite defines what constitutes an unethical person — one who's dishonest, irresponsible, disrespectful, unfair, and/or lacking in compassion. (Ki 1,35,47,50,51,53,87)

There's no bad time to promote values — talking about them in general, discussing how you apply them to your own circumstances, and exhibiting them in your own behavior. But it's particularly important during the young years (birth through age four, particularly ages three and four), when the child is forming the principles on which he's going to base his behavior (Ki ch 2).

One way to decide if something is right or wrong is by applying four tests (Ki 84,85).

1.  Is it legal?
2.  Does it abide by the rules?
3.  Does it smell? This is, perhaps, the most fundamental test. It has been maintained that all of our sense of morality derives from the physical repugnance that certain actions arise in us. (Is it a shitty thing to do?)
4.  Would you like to see what you're contemplating doing described in the lead headline of the local newspaper?

The second step in raising an ethical child is to instruct him on how to make wise decisions in situations in which values conflict (Ki 1). These situations generally resolve themselves into one or more of the following — truth versus loyalty (what do I do about a friend who's cheating?), what's good for the individual versus what's good for the community, justice versus mercy, and what's good in the short term versus what's good for the long term (Ki 2).

Here it's important for the child to recognize that these situations exist and that, in such cases, a choice has to be made in terms of which is better. If the child fails to appreciate this fact, then when facing such dilemmas, he may just decide that the values that he's been taught don't make sense and might just as well be ignored (Ki 23).

Again, there's no time when it isn't right to be concerned with ethical dilemmas, but children tend to first run up against these conflicts between the ages of five and nine (Ki ch 3). Sometimes, although not always, a middle way can be found.

For example, a mother who found his son's friend stuffing his pockets with cookies from her pantry said, "You don't have to do that. You can always have as many as you want.", making it clear that what the boy was doing was wrong at the same time as she demonstrated her loyalty to her son and his friend.

Finally, it's necessary to summon the moral courage to take the action that you've decided is right even though it constitutes a threat to yourself (Ki 1,2). For children, this challenge generally develops in their later years, as they become, more and more, independent (Ki chs 4,5,6).

## Social Intelligence

Social intelligence is the ability to navigate through day-to-day human interactions (T 59) and knowing how to seek help (T 161). It's about managing your own feelings and understanding other people's feelings (M 93,94).

Family life is a staging area in which your child learns how people relate to each other (Le 58). Eat as a family, so your child can see how people interact on a day-to-day basis (D 62 Ho 175).

Establish strong, positive family relations, in which you and your child can speak freely with each other. Do things together. (D 130)

During elementary school, children begin learning how to cultivate and sustain reciprocal relationships (Le 50).

A person's approach to other people is, pretty much, wired in. In particular, if you have a shy child, you aren't going to be able to get him to overcome his shyness.

But once more, biology isn't destiny. You may not be able to change your nature, but you can shape it. You can guide your shy child in more sociable ways by teaching him the behavior that will allow him to get along with people, things that come naturally to more gregarious people. (102)

Reading

As has been truly said, until grade three, children learn to read. After that, they read to learn.

Reading easily and with comprehension is the essential prerequisite to learning. If you can't read, you can't get anywhere academically. (D 124)

Good readers are children who read a lot. (D 124) See to it that your child reads, at least, one hour a day. He can read anything that he wants, as long as it isn't assigned school reading. (D 141)

This reading habit is one that should be worked on from the time that your child is born. Read to your child every day (Bo xxiii), even before birth.

In utero, your child can hear you, and when he's born, he'll recognize your voice (Bo 2). Your child will always enjoy the sound of your voice, but he has to get to be about four months old before he'll be able to see the pages in the book and feel them. (St 241)

When you read to your child, the reading should be a dialogue. Draw your child into the process.

Ask him to point out in the illustrations what the text is talking about. If for example, the subject is a balloon and your child can't find the balloon, point to the balloon and ask him, "Is that a balloon or a dirty sneaker?" (Bo 112)

Ask him about how the characters in the story feel. (St 250). Ask him to guess what happens next (Bo xxv). After reading the book, ask him to tell you the story (Bo xxvii).

When you read to your child, he should be encouraged to discuss what he's heard (H 29), and when in the reading, an unusual word is encountered, your child should discuss the word's meaning and, with your cooperation, develop a definition (H 65,66). A child who's consistently read to comes to kindergarten with a vocabulary 50 percent larger than one who's put in front of TV children shows, no matter how purportedly educational they claim to be.

A child who isn't asked known-answer questions, such as "Where's the balloon in the picture?" before he goes to school isn't prepared for such questions when the teacher asks them. His reaction often is, "If the teacher doesn't know that, then I sure don't." (N 113)

Stories with rhyme and rhythm particularly appeal to children, as Dr. Seuss well knew. Songs also fit into this category (St 243).

The most important thing in teaching a child to read is that he have been read 1000 books before teaching begins.

As you read to your child, point to the words that you're reading, so that he gets the idea that there's a relation between the words that he hears and the squiggles that he sees on the page. It's not uncommon for a child, who's read to every day, to by the age of three or four, spontaneously start reading on his own.

One way to encourage your child to read is to read yourself. It's that simple. (D 124)

Media Use

Media use is the use of any electronic device with a screen — smart phone, tablet, computer, game console, or TV.

After 45 minutes of daily media use, children's grades begin to drop. After three hours, the drop is rapid. (D 84) At five hours, a child's risk of getting Fs is twice as great as that of a child whose daily media use is a maximum of 15 minutes. (D 70)

After one and a half hours of daily TV watching, children's grades begin to decline rapidly. After four hours, children are virtually certain to get Fs. (D 72)

Children who game more than 90 minutes a day are twice as likely to have social problems — difficulty making friends, inability to join other children in play, and inability to effectively communicate their feelings and needs. They also exhibit a fear of trying new things. (D 63) A dedicated gamer is nine times more likely to get a failing grade in both English and math (D 64).

204 THINGS EVERYONE SHOULD KNOW

Children who use media more than two hours a day have double the trouble being able to focus than do children who use media less than two hours a day (D 227).

Getting enough sleep is essential for your child. He should get eight hours of sleep every night (D 129), and to see that he gets it, he should have a regular bedtime to which he adheres (D 141).

An increase or decrease of just 30 minutes of sleep can have a dramatic impact on your child's mood, ability to concentrate, grade level, and energy. One of the top causes of sleep deprivation is overuse of media (D 56,57,87).

Keep all media out of your child's bedroom (D 58 G 181,185).

Limit media use (G 182). Provide alternatives.

Family dinners should be media free (D 62). And that means you, parent, as well as your child. Children who eat with their family play 50 percent fewer video games (D 64).

Do things as a family. Children who regularly play board games with their parents are half as likely to play video games. (D 64)

When something is watched on TV, do it as a family, so that it's a social, rather than a solitary, event.

Chores, volunteer activities, and participating in sports or other activities, such as playing in a musical group, are all alternatives to media use (D 76).

Media should be used creatively rather than in consumption. Learning to touch type, creating word documents, developing PowerPoint presentations, and making videos are some examples of how to use media creatively. (D 76,80,90)

Don't buy your child a smart phone. Owning a smart phone is a responsibility, and if your child wants one, he should buy it himself. (D 84)

On the other hand, you should pay your child's smart phone bill. He should contract with you rather than with the phone company. In this contract, you spell out when and how his smart phone can be used — for example, no smart phone use during homework time. (D 83,84)

## Setting Limits

Expectations are important. There are things that we just don't do. We don't steal. We don't lie. We don't cheat. And there are behaviors that we do practice. We're polite. We treat each other with courtesy, respect and consideration. We do each other favors.

In general, there's no need to make any special effort to inculcate expectations. Everyone knows what's expected. If on a day-to-day basis, you behave as expected, then with your guidance, so will your child. (M 151,154)

However, because the development of your child's prefrontal cortex won't be complete until he's in the early 20s, his ability to make sound judgments on the spot may not be all that we'd like. Therefore, it's important to minimize the situations where a poor call can have serious consequences. Here, there's a need for a firm guardrail, and that's where setting limits comes in.

There are things that are serious no-nos, and violating these limits carries consequences. If you go out into the street, you spend the rest of the day inside. If you get home after curfew, you're grounded for the weekend. If you take your friends for a joyride in your car, you lose your car keys for a month.

Set up these limits in cooperation with your child. If he can participate in determining why certain situations call for limits, what these limits should be, and what consequences should follow when the limits are breached, he's more likely to see why the limits are necessary and why they must be respected.

Of course, you can't abdicate your parental responsibility. If your child can't be persuaded that a certain limit is reasonable, then you have to take charge. In such a case, just calmly lay now the rules and the consequences of disobeying the rules, make clear that it's up to the child to decide whether he wants to conform or pay the consequences, and end the conversation (Mc 77). This encourages self-discipline. (Le 213,214)

Don't be too rigid about consequences. When a limit has been violated, the goal isn't to see that the consequences are carried out. The goal is to see that the violation doesn't occur again.

Your child knows when he has been in violation of a limit, and if in retrospect, he can see that he's made a bad mistake that he doesn't want to make again, that may be enough. Children are inclined to try to live up to the expectations of someone who has faith in them (L 138).

When it comes to a repentant child, carrying out the consequences may not be necessary. In fact, under such circumstances, carrying out the consequences may be counterproductive. Only when violation is repeated is adherence to consequences essential.

After your child has breached a limit and paid the resulting consequence, give him another chance. It demonstrates that you have faith in his ability to follow rules.

Set a curfew and when phone calls are required and see to it that these expectations are met. Verify that parents will be home when your child goes to parties. (Le 165).

Respect your child's need for privacy. But don't back off from monitoring your child's activities. You need to keep him out of trouble — know where your child is, what he's doing, whom he's with, and when he'll be home. (Le 180,K 128)

Keep a sense of perspective. Try not to interfere. Advise when you can, but command only when you must. (Le 144)

Wait up until your child comes home. Knowing that, when he comes home, your child is going to have look you in the eye, talk to you, and kiss you goodnight is going to keep uppermost in his mind, while he's out, exactly what your expectations are with respect to things such as substance abuse or any other limit violation. (C 232,233)

Discipline

Your effectiveness as a disciplinarian is enhanced if your child wants to please you. Children have an inborn desire to please their parents, but this desire is intensified if your child is convinced that you like him.

Children know that their parents love them, but they also want to be liked. They want the knowledge that their parents enjoy having them around and interacting with them.

So do things with your child. It's not the big events, such as going to the circus or the professional ball club game, that are so important. They're nice.

But what counts is the day-to-day activities centered around the home, such as playing games or doing household chores together, which is one of the many reasons why eating meals together is so important. Have conversations with your child and take what he says seriously. (J 111)

Typically, desirable behavior isn't what consumes a parent's interest. When your child is doing what you want him to do, both you and your child are enjoying the situation, and that enjoyment is enough to see that the behavior continues.

What causes concern is behavior that parents find undesirable. They'd like to see their children not engage in undesirable behavior.

When misbehavior occurs, it's then time for discipline. The word, discipline, comes from the Latin disciplina, which means "to teach". (You can remember that, because a disciple is a student.) So an instance of misbehavior constitutes an opportunity to teach your child the value of inhibiting impulses, managing angry feelings, considering the impact of his behavior on others, and all of the other good things that will pay off for him, you, and the world, over and over again as he progresses through life. (Si xvi,xvii)

When the time to discipline has come, it's essential that your child be convinced that, no matter what he's done wrong, you're unqualifiedly on his side (Si xxii).

When your child has done something wrong, it's frequently because he can't control himself. After all, your child is a work in progress, and it's understandable that, from time to time, he's going to go off of the rails. In such circumstances, he's typically going to be in a highly emotional state.

In general, whenever your child is upset, it's not the time to try and reason with him. He's under the control of his limbic system and his prefrontal cortex isn't engaged, so reason isn't going to come through.

The first step in dealing with a child in the thrall of an emotional upset is to calm things down. Only after calm has been restored is it possible to investigate what went wrong and what you and your child should do about it. (M 151,176,195 Si xxiii)

So wait until both you and your child have calmed down before taking any further steps in disciplining him. Wait just as long as is necessary, even if it's a day or two. When the time has come and you bring up the subject of the misbehavior, you don't have to worry about whether your child will remember what you're talking about. He'll remember. Count on it.

Even so, don't broach the subject until both you and your child have the time to discuss it. The discussion of a disciplinary matter isn't something that should be rushed.

Once things have calmed down, it's time for your child to figure out what he did wrong and what he should have done instead, so that he's better prepared the next time a similar situation arises. Actually, this isn't usually too difficult.

The chances are that your child already knows what he did wrong and what he should have done. The difficult part is getting your child to explicitly acknowledge what went wrong and what he should have done.

There are several techniques for working with your child to elicit such acknowledgement. Here are some of them. They can be used individually or in combination.

1.  Don't worry about what your child did. Instead, concentrate on what he should have done. (Si 194,196) Ask him what he should have done. See to it that he tells you what he should have done rather than you telling him what he should have done. You don't have to tell him, because if you've established clear rules that have been consistently enforced, he already knows. (J 77,216,L 137) If your child tells you that he doesn't know what he should have done, ask him to make a guess. If he tells you that he really doesn't know, tell him that that's OK, but that he does have to

guess. Hold your ground and wait just as long as it takes for him to make his guess. The chances are that his guess will be pretty close to what he should have done, if not right on. Children know more than they're sometimes willing to let on. (J 92,93) The object of the exercise is that your child is describing what his behavior should be, rather than being lectured to, and the lesson will be more meaningful.

2. Describe, don't preach. To a toddler, you might say, "Oh, oh. You're throwing the cards. That makes it hard to play the game". To an older child, you might say, "Whoops. I see that the dirty dishes are still on the table." "Looks like Johnny would like a turn at the swing." is better than "You need to share." (Si 179,180) The idea is to draw your child's attention to the situation and then leave it up to him to figure out what the right thing to do is. If you've been diligent about inculcating the rules of good behavior, it's not going to be hard for your child to figure out what to do. Once more, the object is to get your child to determine what should be done, rather than you telling him what should be done. That helps develop the internal compass that will last him a lifetime. (Si 180)

3. You can try a "do-over". For example, if your child has been disrespectful to you, you can say, "Boy. That didn't come out very well. Would you like to try again?" (151)

4. Give your child a choice: You can play in the communal sandbox, but you can't throw sand. If you throw sand, you're going to have to come out of the sandbox for a wait period before you can go back in. (L 137)

If despite your best efforts, your child just won't cooperate with you in your disciplinary action, then you have no alternative to telling him what he did wrong and what he should have done. But keep it short.

The longer you talk, the less likely it is that your message will get through. Quietly tell your child, in as few words as possible, what he did wrong and what he should do in the future, and then move on. (Si 175)

Emphasize that, when your child transgressed, he violated things in which the family believes. He has stepped outside of the family circle. Make clear how important it is to you to have him back in accord with the family. (M 197)

In any case, punishment is out (M 148). It's both a clear demonstration to your child that you're not on his side and a breakdown in your relationship with your child.

Punishment creates a more fearful child at the same time as it erodes your ability to influence him. (M 56,150) A child that grows up in fear becomes hyper-vigilant and distrustful (M 95,105).

And this is true not only for physical punishment (spanking or slapping). Putting your child on time out or sending him to his room indicate, to your child, that you're separating yourself from him and leaving him to fend for himself. (M 56,148)

Punishment in any form triggers your child's fear of abandonment and causes him to question his trust in you (M 174).

Administering punishment whenever misbehavior occurs solves nothing. A regimen of punishment will produce a devious and defiant child who's going to be increasingly badly behaved.

The breakdown in your child's confidence and trust in you is going to make it more and more difficult for you to get him to listen to you. (M 182) It's more important to develop your child's ability to control his own emotions than it is to exercise the control that's necessary to attain short-term compliance (M xxi,xxii).

Developing Desired Behavior

The more that you build up a positive relationship with your child, the more that he'll want to please you and to follow your advice. (M 40,41)

The way to extinguish undesirable behavior is to decide what behavior you'd like to see instead of the undesirable behavior that's occurring and develop the desired behavior. Getting your child to develop desired behavior is a matter of training. So, before you begin to develop your child's behavior, be sure that you have the time to devote to effective training. (J 178)

For example, suppose that your child isn't doing his homework. Concentrating on what he isn't doing isn't going to help much.

You can nag. But the more that you remind him that he should be doing his homework, the less likely it is that he'll develop the ability to do his homework on his own. (vii)

You can punish him for not doing his homework. But this isn't going to be effective.

Over the long-term, punishment is just going to cause your child to be even less interested in homework. Which means that, to get any effect at all, you're going to have to keep on escalating the amount of punishment in a never-ending vicious cycle. (K 80,81)

Instead of concentrating on what your child isn't doing, you should focus on getting him to do what you want him to do, which is to do his homework. So, when you decide to begin the project, you start by suggesting that it's time for him to do his homework. Make clear that it doesn't have to be for long — to begin with, just five minutes will do.

And let him know that you're going to help (K 150). If it's math and he's having trouble with an exercise, you can help him develop an approach to solving the problem. If it's reading, you can share — he reads a sentence, then you read a sentence, and so on.

Be calm and polite in your approach. Show your child that it's him in which you're interested. (K 5)

In these circumstances, at the end of five minutes, it's unlikely that your child will have done nothing. However little it is, it's a start, and that's what you want. You now have something with which to begin.

So at the end of five minutes, compliment your child on the effort that he put in. Show him that you're pleased.

Tell your child exactly what he did that pleased you. Give him a pat on the back, or a light punch on the shoulder. (K 65,75)

If it's looks as if it might be appropriate, you can challenge him. You can ask him if he thinks that he can put in another five minutes. (K 39)

As the days pass, the time for homework is extended, you do less and less, and your child does more and more. But don't rush it.

You don't want to overwhelm your child just when he's beginning to develop the behavior for which you're looking. (K 32,63)

The recommended time to devote to homework is ten minutes per grade. So if your child is in first grade, the appropriate amount of time for him to devote to homework is ten minutes. If he's a senior in high school, the amount is two hours (10x12). (D 99,129)

Once your child has worked up to the recommended time for his homework, he should be allowed to quit, even if he's not done (D 100). If he's worked conscientiously, incomplete homework is his teacher's problem, not yours.

If your child wants to work on his homework for more than the recommended time, that's OK, as long as it doesn't cut into his other activities. He should go to bed on time, he should eat with his family, he should do his school-independent reading, and he should engage in his athletic activity. (D 98)

Neglecting these other activities in order to concentrate on getting homework done is a bad idea. Without a balanced approach to life, emotional problems develop and social skills decline, with the result that academic performance actually falls off. (D 101,102)

A definite time should be set to begin homework every day. And there should be a definite place, free of distractions, where it's to be done (D 212).

The kitchen or dining room table is an ideal location for doing homework. There's adequate space for your child to set out his work. And you'll be nearby but not interacting, just to be sure that everything is going well. (D 212)

The time set aside for homework should be observed every day. If your child finishes his homework before the time is up, he doesn't leave the homework location until the time is up.

The time left over after homework is done is to be devoted to reading. There should always be plenty of reading material around to satisfy this purpose. (D 100) And this reading time shouldn't count toward your child's school-independent reading (D 101).

The idea is that there's no point in your child rushing through his homework to get it done so that he can do something else. He's there for the allotted time, so he might as well concentrate on his homework. (D 108)

Never ask your child to do something more than once. Repeated requests just give your child the impression that there's no need to respond the first time that you ask. (J 175) Here's how to train your child to respond when asked.

The first thing to do is to go and stand where child is. Don't yell out the request from another room or up the stairs. Going to where your child is and standing both emphasize that what's on your mind is serious. (J 179)

The next step is to wait until your child stops what he's doing and gives you his attention. How long this will take depends on your child. Some children are very aware of what's going on around them and will quickly respond to your presence. Some are less willing to disengage from their activity. (J 180)

In any case, you just have to wait until you have your child's attention. You're only going to make your request once, so you want your child focused on what you're saying before you begin.

Eventually, an adult standing silently close by will get the attention of most children. If all else fails, you can get your child's attention by commenting positively on what he's doing, for example, by saying, "Boy, you're really concentrating on that (whatever)." (J 181)

When you're sure that you've got your child's attention, smile and, in a clear, calm, friendly voice, make your request. (J 182)

Chances are that your child will comply. If he doesn't, just wait. (J 187)

If after you've waited a while, your child still doesn't respond, what you've now got is misbehavior, and you should behave accordingly. See the above section on discipline.

When you ask your child to do something, what you want him to do is stop doing whatever he's doing and do what you've asked him to do. Your child has a natural inclination to please you and wants to do what you've asked him to do. However, he may be doing something that he doesn't want to stop so that he can do what you've asked him to do.

That your child is absorbed in what he's doing is positive and an attitude that you want to encourage. As we've said, interrupting what your child is doing is telling him that what he's doing isn't important.

So don't interrupt your child's activities with requests unless there's no alternative. That will underline the idea that what you're asking for is important.

And it will give your child the assurance that you consider his activities to be important and are interrupting because something needs to be done. For example, if it's time to wash hands and come to the table for dinner, then that's it and other things have to be set aside.

If there's a situation in which you have to say no to your child, try to do it with a conditional yes. For example, if you and your child are at Grandma's, it's time to go, and your child wants more time with Grandma, instead of just killing the idea, you can say, "Sure, you can have more time with Grandma, but not now — now it's time to go. Maybe we can come to Grandma's again on Saturday. Would that work for you, Grandma?" (Si 190). If your child buys in, he's expanding his ability to tolerate disappointment and practice delayed gratification (Si 192).

Compliance is about following other people's rules, which in general, is a desirable trait in itself. But it's not self-control. Self-control is developing, fortifying and internalizing your own rules. (Le 220)

If a child is to give up something, it has to be in the pursuit of a greater goal. That he should do something because you say so doesn't cut it.

You have to give a child an overriding reason for doing something. He's then able to internalize what's to be done, and it becomes part of his self-control. (Le 222)

Don't tolerate disrespect. But put up with irritability, crabbiness and moodiness. (Le 128,129) When you consider what children, particularly middle and high school children, have to put up with on a day-to-day basis with no choice in the matter, crankiness becomes understandable (P 121).

Children expend enormous amounts of psychic energy on trying to fit in and not draw negative attention to themselves. They save their worst selves for those that love them, particularly their parents. (P 123)

So when your child comes home from school and is irritable and sulky, you can say, "Okay. It's all right to be upset and grouchy. It's normal for a teen to act that way. We can live with it." Such a reaction may disarm your child and reduce his grumpiness. (K 165,168)

There are several basic skills that, if you and your child are to live an enjoyable, rewarding life, your child has to master. Here are some, accompanied by techniques that the science of child development says are the most effective ways to develop the desired behavior.

## Sleeping by Himself

Christine Gross-Loh, who has approached the subject of parenting by looking at the way in which it's carried out in various parts of the world, observes that, in contrast to what we, in the US, practice, in the rest of the world, parents and children sleep together for years before the children begin to sleep alone. She reports that children who sleep by themselves from the start do sleep through the night and wean earlier than those who co-sleep. However, those who co-sleep ultimately become more independent than solitary sleepers in that they dress themselves and work out problems with playmates by themselves earlier than do solitary sleepers. (Gro 25)

I don't know what you think, but as for me, I'm not interested in sharing my bed with my children. If you agree with me, then one of the first skills that your child must learn is to sleep by himself. By the time that he's a few months old, he's ready to learn this skill. (L 21)

Going to sleep should be a routine, something that happens at the same time every day, so that it comes to be what's expected (L 24,29). You should have a pre-bedtime routine, including cuddling and rocking, to quiet down your child and induce drowsiness, but he's the one who should sooth himself to sleep (L 29). (You can sooth him to sleep. But that's not teaching him to go to sleep by himself.)

The pre-bedtime routine should be just that, a routine — every night, same time, same length of time, same number of stories or songs. This isn't playtime. It's sleep preparation time. (L 36)

Here's the Ferber (Richard Ferber, director of the Center for Pediatric Sleep Disorders at Boston's Children's Hospital) Method for teaching your child how to sleep.

When you decide to start the training (at about two months), after the pre-bedtime routine, put your, hopefully by now drowsy, child in his crib in his room, say goodnight, and then immediately, leave. If he begins to cry and hasn't stopped at the end of five minutes, go back into the room and comfort him by patting and talking to him. But don't pick him up.

Stay for no more than two or three minutes. Then once more, say goodnight and leave.

Don't sneak sway. Let your child see you leave.

If your child continues to cry, this time, wait ten minutes before returning to comfort him. Continue in this way, adding five minutes to each consecutive wait period, until he falls asleep.

On the second night, the procedure is the same as it was on the first night, except that the initial waiting period is ten minutes. Third night, ditto, but now the initial waiting period is 15 minutes. And so on, adding five minutes to the initial waiting period each successive night, until your child goes to sleep on his own when he's put to bed. (L 28-31)

Under no circumstances does your child sleep anywhere but in his own bed. No matter how many times he shows up at your bedside, you calmly walk, not carry, him back to his own bed. (L 44,45)

## Not Sucking His Thumb

Before the age of four, trying to break a thumb sucking habit is pretty hopeless. When the time comes to break the habit, lecturing isn't going to do much good. Instead, your child has to decide that he doesn't want to suck his thumb.

So give him a choice. He can suck his thumb, but he has to go to his room to do it. Thumb sucking in public isn't acceptable. Your child can now choose between sucking his thumb and enjoying your company. (L 60)

You can use the same approach to breaking habits such as toting around a security blanket (L 61).

## Eating

The solution to the battle over food is to not engage. Instead, divide the responsibility.

You decide of what meals are going to consist and when they're going to be served. Your child decides if he's going to eat and, if he does, what he's going to eat and how much of it he's going to eat (Be 311,321,327,328).

You just have to trust your child. He'll eat what he needs when he needs it.

Children's intake can vary widely from to day, which is scary, and what your child eats eagerly one day, he'll decisively refuse the next. You just have to put up with it. Besides, what he's telling you is that he likes variety, which you should encourage.

Your child may turn down a food as many as 15 times, but if you just keep serving it, the chances are that he'll finally end up eating and enjoying it. (Be 311,324,325) One technique for getting him to try something is to take the broccoli, for example, and say, "This is my broccoli." Then pause, and finally say, "But I'm willing to share. Want to try some?" (Be 325,326)

Forcing your child to eat when he doesn't want to disconnects him from his body signals. Forcing him to eat things that he doesn't want to will frighten him because he has lost control. (Be 310)

Eat as a family. You're your child's model. He wants to eat what you eat in the way that you eat it. So you not only need to serve your child a balanced meal, you have to eat one yourself. (Be 315,316,325)

Developing what we consider to be polite eating habits is a messy and sometimes disgusting procedure. You have to just let it happen.

First of all, you're not going to be able to feed your baby any solid food until he's ready for it. That's not going to be until he's at least four months old.

He has to be able to sit up in a high chair. He has to be able to hold his head up. The tongue thrust reflex has to have become extinguished (when born, a child will reflexively push out anything that gets in his mouth, a life protecting reflex.).

When you start presenting your baby with spoonfuls of food, open your mouth, so that he gets the idea of what to do (Be 323). After all, he's never seen a spoon before.

As time passes, your child will decide that he wants to feed himself. That's good, that's what you want him to do, so you have to let him do it.

First, he'll probably just grab a handful of food and jam it toward his mouth. Pretty messy, but you have to put up with it.

Eventually, he'll start picking up pieces of food with his thumb and forefinger, which indicates that he's beginning to develop motor skills. Finally, he'll start using utensils.

He'll chew food and then spit it out. Probably, he wants to see what it looks like.

That's pretty gross, but if you leave the masticated food on his plate, the chances are that he'll get around to eating it. That's really gross, but if you leave him alone, he'll outgrow the activity.

Ultimately, you'll end up with a child who eats politely. But more importantly, you'll have one with no hang-ups over food. (Be 325,326)

If your child misuses a food item, just quietly remove it for a short period. For example, if your child insists on throwing his food on the floor, take the food away from him for one minute for each year of his age, tell him why you took the food away and tell him what food is for, then when the time is up, give his food back to him. (L 82)

## Toilet Training

First of all, you can't expect your child to go potty until he's capable of doing so. He has to be able to walk well, pull down his pants and underpants, remember where the potty is, get interested in how other people go to the bathroom, and become familiar with and lose any fear that he has of sitting on the potty (L 100,101).

Even then, you can't decide when your child is going to start going to the potty. That's a decision that he has to make.

You can show your child what it's all about and introduce him to the potty, but don't pressure him. (L 99) Instead, wait until he gives you a clue that he's ready to begin, like asking to wear underwear or telling you that he needs a diaper change or that he needs to go (102).

If your child can handle using the toilet during the day but has trouble at night, let him wear a diaper at night until he's ready to transit (L 110). Otherwise, once you commit to underpants, stick with it.

Remember: consistency. Flipping back and forth between underpants and diapers just confuses your child. (L 105)

## Summary

When it comes to developing character, it's never too late. Character issues are ones that are easily verbalized, and parents (or in their absence, a mentor) can work with the child to develop the necessary traits, no matter what the child's age.

KIPP (the Knowledge Is Power Program, the charter school system that has had such remarkable success in educating children from disadvantaged neighborhoods) has a character report card, on which is listed a number of character attributes on which each student is marked. On this card, the student can see where he has done well, where he could use improvement, and over time, what improvement he has made. (T 98)

The best that parents can do is to provide their children with a loving relationship, a bar set high enough to give them something to reach for, and a sense of being understood and valued for themselves (Le 34). In raising a child, assume little, wait to see the particulars of the child, concentrate on character and values, provide opportunities, and let the child develop naturally into his unique self (Le 38).

In general, make as few assumptions as you can about what's driving your child's behavior. Don't assume that he has the same issues that you do. (Le 274).

See your child clearly. Try to find out how he sees things. (Le 275) If you can see your child clearly, love him unconditionally, set limits when necessary, hold fast to a core set of good values, and serve as a positive role model, you'll be able to withstand the inevitable squalls of parenthood (Le 244,Mi 210,225).

## ACADEMIC ACHIEVEMENT

For our society to operate at peak efficiency, we want it to be peopled by citizens that are equipped to work effectively in our economic system and be responsible in their political activity. And since, if there's any purpose to life, it's to enjoy a rewarding one, we also want our people to be in a position to do just that. For all of these reasons, providing everyone with a quality education is essential.

### Curriculum

In the past 50 years, the world has changed. But our schools haven't. (Wag xxi,xxii)

As a consequence, our schools are concentrating on the wrong things. It's no longer necessary, and in a number of cases, was never appropriate, to commit a lot of information to memory.

You don't have to have the details at your fingertips. These days you can easily look them up. What's important is to know where to find what you need and to be able to evaluate the reliability of data and figure out what those details imply.

You don't need to know the rules of grammar. What you do need to be able to do is speak effectively and write documents that communicate. (Wag 111)

Tony Wagner, the author of *The Global Achievement Gap*, thinks that it's still necessary to commit the multiplication table to memory. I wouldn't even go that far.

It's important to understand what multiplication is. But a calculator will do the operation for you more accurately and easily than you can by using the multiplication table.

However, there are essentials that do need to be committed to memory. For example, you need to know the alphabet and how to count.

A lot of what's taught in schools is determined by what colleges require for admission.

Colleges insist that applicants for admission have to have studied math up to, at least, Algebra II. So students struggle with quadratic equations. With the exception of the very few who are going to concentrate in the area, the need to be able to know how to solve a quadratic equation almost never arises. But frequently, we're faced with the need to understand statistics, probabilities and logic, subjects on which schools spend almost no time. (Wag 296)

Colleges require exposure to a foreign language. So students contend with vocabulary and declensions. Here I stand way out in left field.

It's my feeling that most of time spent on trying to learn a foreign language is wasted. For those who have a flair and interest in the subject, I think that knowledge of a foreign language is great, and I admire, applaud and envy the skill. But for most of us, studying a foreign language demands the investment of a lot of time and effort with little payoff.

Being fluent in a foreign language is great for casual relationships, which are nice and, in diplomatic matters, almost an essential. It's always convenient, and sometimes useful, to be able to catch the nuances of what people are saying in their own language. But when it comes to critical communications, it's more reliable to use an experienced translator than to depend on your own language skill.

Then there's finance. Almost every day, most of us manage money. How to finance big-ticket purchases is a question that frequently arises. More and more, the conversion from defined benefit to defined contribution retirement plans places the responsibility for managing an employee's pension investments in his own hands. Yet schools provide little guidance in these matters. (Wag 296)

Schools shy away from contention. Yet where is it more important to be able to marshal facts, draw valid conclusions, and argue persuasively?

What the teacher thinks isn't important. It's what the students think that counts.

The teacher shouldn't be expressing his own opinions, no matter how well grounded. Any effort to do so smacks of indoctrination, the polar opposite of inquiry. The job of the teacher is to ask questions and hone his students' ability to grapple with thorny issues.

Teacher Performance

Academic education is like any other human activity — it responds to incentives (Gr 221). One of the reasons why we have difficulty with the performance of our school systems is because some of its incentives are perverse.

The quality of the teacher is a major factor in student academic achievement (Gr 61, T 159). But teachers don't get rewarded for being good at teaching and penalized for being poor at it (Gr 218).

A teacher's command of his subject, as measured by their scores on skill tests, makes a substantial positive contribution to their teaching ability. Reward for superior performance in this area? Zippo.

There's some indication that holding an advanced degree in his subject contributes to teacher effectiveness. Reward? Again, zippo.

Instead, teachers get paid for being certified, getting a masters degree in education, and accumulating years of teaching (Gr 219). There's little indication that certification has any correlation with teacher quality, and the influence of a masters degree in education is nil (Gr 63).

Forty two percent of public school teachers have masters degrees in education (Gr 64). Is that a response to an incentive, or what?

During his first few years of teaching, a teacher's skill typically increases, but after that, the contribution of added years of experience is, at best, minimal. (Gr 66).

The best teachers consistently come from organizations such as Teach for America and TeachNOLA rather than from teacher colleges (Me 178). These organizations select academic overachievers directly out of college, run them through a summer boot camp to train them in what will be expected of them, and put them in the classroom. However, after completing their two-year commitment stint, most of these teachers leave for a different career (Me 179,180).

So while it looks like we're getting better at selecting teachers, we haven't done as well in teacher retention. The challenge now is to make teaching a more desirable job, an honorable calling, and a well-respected profession (Me 38,180)

A quality teacher is an essential. But to produce, he has to be given the autonomy to run his class in the way that he sees as effective, rather than being tied down by micromanagement and mountains of regulations on what he can and can't do (Gro 194,R 143,325,Ma 133). And the school has to back up his decisions.

Principal Performance

If we want principals to run schools that educate, then we have to give them the opportunity to manage their schools — to hire, evaluate, train and, if necessary, fire teachers, to arrange for all of the ancillary services of their schools (such as bus schedules, lunch programs, text availability, prompt response to teacher human-resource problems, and whatever else it takes to make their schools effective), and manage their budgets (Kl xvii,23,163,236). When it comes to the qualifications for a principal, familiarity with education helps, but management and leadership skills are essential. (Kl 164)

Once empowered, principals should be held accountable for the performance of their schools as indicated by the performance of their students (Kl xvii). Poor student performance should call for an evaluation to determine if training and coaching can improve principal performance. If it can't or if the principal doesn't respond to such aid, he should be dismissed. An ineffective principal is a guarantee of a failing school and can't be tolerated. (Kl 23,164)

Fundamental to school superintendent success is his ability to select, develop and support effective principals. They're his front-line team, and he should keep in direct contact with them, so that they can keep him abreast of what's going on in their schools. There should be no bureaucracy insulating him from them. (Kl 184)

Other Considerations

More time for learning has to be created. (Wa 175,178,179,195) There must be adequate time for class work. But there must also be time for tutoring or whatever is necessary to meet a faltering student's needs. There must also be time for students with special interests to pursue projects under the guidance of mentors drawn from the community, industry and universities. We no longer live in an agricultural society, and children are no longer needed early in the afternoon and all summer to work on the family farm (Wa 204).

Social promotion is out. It doesn't contribute to self-esteem. If after best efforts on the part of the student, teachers and school, a student hasn't, by the end of the school year, shown mastery of the material, promoting him to the next grade is just going to make his learning conditions that much more impossible. (Kl xviii) Achievement, rather than social promotion, is what contributes to self-esteem (Kl 54).

The school must be safe and violence free, so that the students can concentrate on learning. There can be no drugs, weapons, or gang activity in the school.

Instead of picking on other students, children in a school should learn that they're part of a team dedicated to helping each other. For the benefit of both the bully and his victims, any instances of taunting, harassing, ridiculing or bullying have to dealt with immediately. (Wa 180,219)

In addition to the academic subjects, school is the occasion for the development of the work habits, discipline, character, and sense of personal responsibility that will carry over into work and society (Wa 218).

Parental involvement is important. But first comes student performance. When parents see that the school is making a difference in their children's learning, they'll begin to support the school. (Wa 173)

Private Schools

Private schools are an alternative to public schools.

At present, private schools consistently outperform public ones. The myth here is that it's unreasonable to expect public schools to perform as well as private ones, because private ones are awash with money, can be selective in whom they admit, and can expel under-performing students.

This is the Exeter Myth. When we think of private schools, we think of the elite ones. But they're unrepresentative.

Catholic schools educate 48.6 percent of private school students. Other private religious schools educate another 35.7 percent.

The vast majority of private school students attend schools where tuition is less than half of the per-pupil spending in public schools. Most private schools accept most comers. Eighty eight percent of those who apply are accepted. And the expulsion rate in private schools is lower than it is in public schools.

It's sometimes argued that, since the parents who send their children to private schools place greater emphasis on education than those who send their children to public schools, the quality of the students in private schools is higher, and that's what accounts for the superiority of the private schools.

Well, to some extent, maybe so, but the significant distinction between private and public schools is that a private school is run by a headmaster, who's in charge of, among other things, hiring and firing, while a public school is part of a bureaucracy. This lends credence to the idea that a principal has to be given the administrative independence to make decisions for his school without having to consult with an unwieldy bureaucracy or having to follow a set of complicated rules. (Wa 76,180,181,193)

Charter Schools

Another alternative to the bureaucratically run public school is the charter school. The charter school is a public school. Its advantage is that it has greater administrative and regulatory freedom and, consequently, has the potential for implementing policies that result in effective teaching (Wa 192).

But the charter school, in and of itself, is no panacea. Only 17 percent of charter schools produce results significantly better than comparable public schools (Wa 58).

However, there are charter schools that perform as well, or better than, private schools. Some are KIPP, YES (which stands for "Youth Engaged in Service", which reflects the vision of students returning with college degrees to make a positive difference in their neighborhoods), North Star Academy in Newark (T 188), and Success Academy, Achievement First, and Uncommon Schools in New York City (Kl xiii,230).

Here are the problems that a charter school faces. Its student body is made up of children from low-income communities and are, on average, two to three years behind in reading skills by the time that they reach fourth grade.

In the absence of a charter school, half of these children won't graduate from high school. Those who do graduate will read and do math, on average, at the level of eighth graders in high-income areas.

The fundamental problem that these children face is that there's nothing in their life to indicate that they can achieve academic success and that this will lead to success in life (Ko 9). Given these circumstances, schools in under-resourced areas that do no more than fulfill the traditional mandate of public schools (present material for the students to absorb) won't be successful in educating their students (Ko 10).

The characteristic of successful charter schools is high expectations (Wa 175,178). No child gets a watered down course of study. Every student is required to take demanding classes in the core subjects — English, math, science and history. And advanced study is always available. (Wa 217)

The fundamental principle is, "No excuses," a motto of the KIPP schools (Wa 47). There's no excuse for a principal to not run an effective school. There's no excuse for a teacher to not run an effective class. There's no excuse for a student to not perform. If a principal or a teacher is producing, not results, but excuses, then the wrong person is in the position (Wa 190).

The approach is pragmatic. Ideology isn't allowed to get in the way. The object is to get results. If that's not being done, you do "Whatever it takes", a motto of Harlem Children's Zone, to get it done (Gro 205).

If a child has a transportation problem, it has to be solved. If a child is so hungry that he can't concentrate, he has to be fed. If a child has a medical problem, it has to be addressed (Wa 196,197). Since these factors influencing education vary by locality, it's important that decision-making with respect to schools be local (Wa 100 R 61,69,70).

If a child is falling behind, he's tutored until he catches up. If a class tests poorly on a given subject, the lesson plan is adjusted and the topic is tackled again until the children get it.

If a teacher or principal is doing less than an effective job, he's coached (Gro 197). If that doesn't work, he's let go ... immediately. No waiting for the end of the school year or after a protracted hearing. Children can't afford a lousy teacher or principal. The children's needs are more important than job security. (Wa 55,56,98,99,181,194,199,218)

The KIPP School in the South Bronx, founded by Mike Feinberg and Dave Levin, is a successful charter school. It's a public middle school.

Enrollment is based on a lottery from those who apply. Half of the students are black. The rest are Hispanic. Three quarters of the students come from single-family homes. Ninety percent qualify for free or reduced lunch. Ninety percent of its graduates get scholarships to private or parochial schools. (Gl 250,251,267)

School begins at 7:25. It ends at five. There's a three-week summer school. Homework typically takes three hours.

Students wear a uniform. They have to dress neatly (e. g., no shirttails hanging out).

Discipline is in (movement between classes is quiet and done in orderly, single-file rows). When addressed, students practice SSLANT — smile, sit up, listen, ask questions, nod when spoken to, and track with your eyes. There's a lot of talk about grit and self-control. (G1 250,251,257-261)

As you may have already noted, these successful charter schools seem to live by mottos. The slogan of Rafe Esquith, the renowned Los Angeles teacher, was "Work Hard, Be Nice", which was adopted by Feinberg and Levin for KIPP (Co 141). Other mottos are: Be prompt, polite and prepared. And HEART (honor, excellence, absolute determination, responsibility, teamwork).

Fixing our school system is a monumental job. There are about 50 million students in our schools. If half of them need the kind of intensive care offered by good charter schools because these students lack the supplemental support that more affluent families can provide, then we have to find 1.5 million teachers and some 47,500 principals with the talent, dedication, perseverance and drive exhibited by their counterparts in these successful charters. (Br 2,427)

## Standardized Testing

The single most important factor in effective education is the teacher (Wa 206). In a school year, a good teacher will teach a year and a half's worth of material, at the same time that a poor teacher will cover a half-year of material.

A good teacher in a bad school is better than a bad teacher in a good school. Teacher effects are stronger than class size effects. (G2 318).

So it becomes imperative to be able to identify good teachers. Certification, number of education degrees, and years of experience have little correlation with effective teaching. And a checklist of characteristics that will distinguish between good and bad teachers has yet to be devised.

The only sure indication of a good teacher is the quality of his product. A good teacher is one that produces results — consistent development of educated students. (Wa 83,84)

That's why frequent, standardized testing is important. It's the benchmark for success.

Standardized testing tells the teacher how each student is doing, so that if remedial action is necessary, it can be tailored to the difficulty. It also tells each teacher how he's doing. And the test results for the whole school keep the principal, parents, and the school superintendent up to date on how the principal's school is doing.

Teacher and principal performance are a direct function of student performance, and their jobs should depend on it (Wa 94,175,179,195,204). If principals know that they're going to be penalized if their schools don't perform, school performance improves. (Gr ch 10).

Critics of standardized testing don't have compelling arguments.

Students who score well on standardized tests go on to make more money than poor scorers (Gr 126).

That standardized testing takes emphasis away from such things as critical thinking is an opinion, not an empirical finding. However, basic literary and numeracy do count, and since many children don't seem to have these skills, maybe concentrating on reading and arithmetic, before moving on to analytical skills, may be the proper approach. (Gr 126)

That the cost of standardized testing drains significant funds from attaining other school objectives is a myth. If a school isn't already developing the skills required to pass a skills test, then directing money toward the development of such skills is just allocating funds according to the appropriate priorities.

Standardized testing is objected to because, it's said, standardized testing results in a teaching style where students are drilled on the test material so that they'll be prepared to do well on the test. As Tony Wagner, the author of the book *Creating Innovators*, says, "Who wants to go through the crap of all of that rote work and memorization just to pass some dumb test?" (W 145) I certainly agree.

But drilling isn't the way to teach. Learning can and should be fun. After all, we're wired to learn.

As people keep pointing out, when children come to school, they couldn't be more enthusiastic. But over the years, the schools beat the enthusiasm out of the children.

Math is problem solving, and if presented property should appeal to any engaged child. History is the story of mankind, the greatest story ever told, and if presented as such, should be fascinating.

English has two goals. One is to learn to express yourself, orally and in writing. That's something that everyone wants to do, and once more, if presented properly, it should be engaging.

But no grammar or vocabulary drill. Grammar and vocabulary are picked up during use. Drill does nothing to improve in these areas and is deadly dull.

The other goal of English is to savor great literature, which can't be anything but fun. But please, no "great master works", such as *David Copperfield*, or wimpy poetry, such as Walt Whitman, which just bore children out of their gourd. Enjoyment of literature depends on, among other things, being able to read with comprehension, which is one of the first responsibilities of a school system and, unfortunately, one that school systems frequently fail to meet.

Science is somewhat different. It's about how the world works, and consequently, has an inherent interest, but it's difficult.

Here tracking is probably the way to go. Some children eat up science, and they should be put on a fast track so that they don't become bored. But for the majority, a more measured, sensitive approach is probably more appropriate.

If subjects are taught in an interesting way that appeals to students' interests, the students will learn enough (and much, much more) to pass any standardized test with flying colors without even thinking about it. The test will be a nonevent. If the teacher is doing his job of teaching his students the subject, teaching to the test is unnecessary and decidedly beside the point.

Most subjects are amenable to standardized testing. Writing is an exception.

When using standardized test results to determine student, teacher and school performance, test results shouldn't be measured against an arbitrary benchmark, because students vary. Student test results should be measured against prior performance on tests. If a student, teacher or school is starting at a low performance level but test results show that steady progress is being made, then education is occurring, which is all that can be asked for. (Kl 203)

Miscellany

Just spending more money on schools doesn't improve their performance. In the past 30 years (2005), spending on schools, measured in inflation-adjusted dollars, has doubled. During this period, the National Assessment of Education Program (NAEP) has been measuring student outcomes, and for 12th grade students, the end product of the educational system, NAEP scores have been flat. (Gr 10)

To determine whether there are barriers that prevent large numbers of students from going to college, Jay P. Greene, the author of *Education Myths*, set up a three stage screen to determine whether a student was college ready — that is, capable of performing in college. The first screen was a high school diploma. The second was the completion of four years of English, three of math, and two each of natural science, social science, and foreign language. The third was at least a basic level of proficiency on the NAEP reading test.

When Greene applied this screen, he found that the college ready population is about the same as the number of students who entered college. Actually, the college ready population was somewhat smaller. Moreover, this balance holds for both the white and black populations.

So, financial restraints and prejudice aren't keeping the black students out, and affirmative action isn't keeping the white students out. What's keeping them all out is a lousy K-12 education. (Gr ch 9)

Sources

(B) Barry, Scott *Ungifted* (Perseus 2013)
(Be) Berman, Jenn *Superbaby* (Sterling 2010)
(Bo) Boog, Jason *Born Reading* (Simon & Schuster 2014)
(Br) Brill, Steven *Class Warfare* (Simon & Schuster 2011)

(C) Califano, Jr., Joseph A. *How To Raise a Drug-Free Kid* (Simon & Schuster 2009)

(Co) Coyle, Daniel *The Talent Code* (Random House 2009)

(D) Donaldson-Pressman, Stephanie, Jackson, Rebecca and Pressman, Robert M. *The Learning Habit* (Penguin Random House 2014)

(E) Elkind, David *The Power of Play* (Perseus 2007)

(En) Engel, Susan *Red Flags or Red Herrings?* (Simon & Schuster 2011)

(G1) Gladwell, Malcolm *Outliers* (Little Brown 2008)

(G2) Gladwell, Malcolm *What the Dog Saw* (Little Brown 2009)

(G) Gnaulati, Enrico *Back to Normal* (Beacon 2013)

(Gr) Greene, Jay P. *Education Myths* (Rowman & Littlefield 2005)

(Gro) Gross-Loh, Christine *Parenting without Borders* (Penguin 2013)

(H) Hirsch, Jr., E. D. *The Knowledge Deficit* (Houghton Mifflin 2006)

(Ho) Honore, Carl *Under Pressure* (HarperCollins 2009)

(J) Janis-Norton, Noel *Calmer, Easier, Happier Parenting* (Penguin 2013)

(K) Kazdin, Alan E. *The Everyday Parenting Toolkit* (Houghton Mifflin 2013)

(Ki) Kidder, Rushworth M. *Good Kids, Tough Choices* (Wiley 2010)

(Kl) Klein, Joel *Lessons of Hope* (HarperCollins 2014)

(Ko) Kopp, Wendy *A Chance To Make History* (Perseus 2011)

(L) Levine, Alanna *Raising a Self-Reliant Child* (Random House 2013)

(Le) Levine, Madeline *Teach Your Children Well* (HarperCollins 2012)

(M) Markham, Laura *Peaceful Parent, Happy Kids* (Penguin 2012)

(Ma) Matthews, Dona and Foster, Joanne *Beyond Intelligence* (Anansi 2014)

(Mc) McNerney, Neil *Homework* (Integrated Publishing 2011)

(Me) Merrow, John *The Influence of Teachers* (Learning Matters 2011)

(Mi) Mischel, Walter *The Marshmallow Test* (Hachete 2014)

(N) Nisbett, Richard E. *Intelligence and How to Get It* (Norton 2009)

(Ou) Ouchi, William G. *Making Schools Work* (Simon & Schuster 2003)

(P) Porter, Susan Eva *Bully Nation* (Paragon House 2013)

(R) Ravitch, Diane *Reign of Error* (Knopf 2013)

(Ro) Robertson, Ian H. *The Winner Effect* (St. Martin's Press 2012)

(S) Sapolsky, Robert M. *Why Zebras Don't Get Ulcers* (Henry Holt 2004)

(Sc) Schoen, Marc *Your Survival Instinct Is Killing You* (Penguin 2013)

(Si) Siegel, Daniel J. and Bryson, Tina Payne *No-Drama Discipline* (Penguin Random House 2014)

(Sm) Smoller, Jordan *The Other Side of Normal* (HarperCollins 2013)

(St) Stamm, Jill *"right from the Start* (Penguin 2007)

(T) Tough, Paul *How Children Succeed* (Houghton Mifflin Harcourt 2012)

(W) Wagner, Tony *Creating Innovators* (Simon & Schuster 2012)

(Wag) Wagner, Tony *The Global Achievement Gap* (Perseus 2008,2010,2014)

(Wa) – *Waiting for Superman* (Perseus 2010)

# CHAPTER TWELVE

# Drugs

To me, it's so obvious that drugs should be legalized that I can't understand what all of the fuss is about. Require a license for its sale, sure. But make a pure, safe product available at a reasonable price.

One of the first victims of an uncritical war on drugs is the facts. The standard myth is that anti-drug laws were passed in response to the devastation caused by a wave of addiction.

Such isn't the case. Anti-drug laws were passed to legitimate the harassment of groups of which the nation didn't approve.

Opium prohibition was directed against the Chinese. Concern with cocaine use arose when it was perceived (mistakenly, it turned out) that cocaine was particularly attractive to blacks. The outlawing of marijuana was aimed at Hispanics.

Perhaps the worst misrepresentation of all is the idea that drug users constitute an undifferentiated group. Again, this isn't the case.

Many drug users are chippers, people who use drugs for recreational purposes only. These people pursue normal lives with commitments to family, work and community.

These people just happen to have integrated drug use into their recreational activities. Given that drug use is illegal, it's almost impossible to gather statistics on this use, but it's not beyond the realm of possibility that chippers constitute the majority of users. They pose no more of a social problem than do recreational users of alcohol.

Then there are those who are self-destructive. They make up a second group of drug users.

Self-destructive people misuse drugs. They misuse alcohol.

And these people don't confine themselves to substance abuse in pursuing their own destruction. They also engage in reckless driving, gambling, sexual promiscuity, and defaulting on gambling debts or on money due to suppliers.

No law against drugs is likely to change this behavior.

The third class of drug users is addicts. Addiction is life destroying, and many addicts recognize this, regret the loss of all the other aspects of their lives, and voluntarily quit.

The remaining group of addicts seems to be those who seek to avoid personal responsibility. They do this by submitting their lives to the dominance of their drugs.

The groups that seem to be most successful in curing these addicts are religiously based organizations. The implication is clear. The cured trade in submission to drugs for submission to Christ.

I'm not in favor of either, but if you have to have a master, Christ is the lesser evil.

If we were to legalize drugs, we'd cut down on violence in the streets, reduce our prison population, stop destabilizing Central and South American countries, and dry up a major source of terrorist financing.

The black market for drugs is the purest form of unfettered free-market capitalism. The rules are Darwinian.

With each failure to stamp out drug traffic, the authorities respond by tightening the screws. As a consequence, drug dealing becomes more risky, which results in an increase in both the cost of buying drugs and the payoff for dealing in them.

Being illegal, drug dealers have no access to the court system to resolve their differences. The alternative is violence, which results in the elimination of the more conservative players, leaving the market in the hands of barbarians who will stop at nothing. (G)

One only has to look at Mexico to see what forcing the demand for drugs into illegal channels has done to the stability of Central and South American countries. The Shining Path got its first foothold by providing protection for coca growers from the attempt of Peruvian forces, under our pressure, to wipe out coca production (N 25). If by some miracle, we were successful in driving drug production out of one country, we'd just push the industry into neighboring countries. (K)

How we can pursue our drug wars in the light of our experience with Prohibition boggles the mind. Repeal of Prohibition didn't eliminate the catastrophe of alcoholism, but it did destroy the base of black-market alcohol-supplying organizations that became so powerful that they could corrupt the police and compromise local government. It also gave the millions, who use alcohol for recreational purposes only, a product, made cheaper by legal competition, that they can use without fear of poisoning themselves and without having to break the law.

The point of legalizing drugs is that it will remove the cost of the criminal activity now associated with the underground production and distribution of drugs. In addition, with an open market, we can begin to realistically assess and take steps to reduce the use of drugs, just as we now do with respect to alcohol and tobacco use.

The most successful antidrug crusade in history was the one waged against tobacco over the last thirty years (2010), a campaign that avoided prohibition altogether. The tool was education, and it proved far more formidable than coercion. Temperance originally involved an extended educational effort, and alcohol consumption was on the wane when the crusaders took the fateful step of passing Prohibition.

A study in northern California from 1985 to 1987 revealed that fear of arrest was number six on the reasons for not using drugs. It seems that the real reason that most people stay away from drugs, alcohol and tobacco included, isn't criminal sanctions but common sense — concern for jobs, families, friends, the ingredients of a normal identity. (G)

The argument against drug legalization is that it will increase both drug addition and child access to drugs. Did the repeal of Prohibition increase alcoholism? And how many beer pushers have you found lately hanging around the playground? (G)

There's also concern expressed about who's going to pay for the all of the medical and social problems of drug addicts if drug prohibition is removed. Does anyone think that, because drugs are currently prohibited, these problems don't now exist? We have to pay these costs regardless.

## Sources

(G) Gray, Mike *Drug Crazy*
(K) Kissinger, Henry *Does America Need a Foreign Policy?*
(N) Napoleoni, Loretta *Modern Jihad* (Pluto 2003)

# CHAPTER THIRTEEN

# Immigration

Give me your tired, your poor,
Your huddled masses yearning to breathe free,
The wretched refuse of your teeming shore.
Send these, the homeless, tempest-tossed to me,
I lift my lamp beside the golden door.

What more is there to say?
Let them in. And let their children go to school.
But no welfare benefits (unemployment insurance, food stamps,
Medicaid, etc.) until they become citizens.

Sources

Lazarus, Emma *The New Colossus*

# CHAPTER FOURTEEN

# Community

If the postal service were a private enterprise, we wouldn't expect it to deliver mail to everyone's doorstep. In fact, not even the present postal service does this.

You can see the collections of mailboxes at the entrances to cul-de-sacs that testify to the absence of doorstep postal delivery. And there are communities where, if you want postal service, you must rent a post office box, because there's no local mail delivery. With a private postal service, we could expect even worse delivery service.

Under such conditions, what's a person to do? One alternative is for each of us, who doesn't live in an area having local mail delivery, to trek to the post office more or less once a day to see what mail we might have.

Or we could get together with our neighbors and form a kind of association where we take turns going to the post office to collect the mail for all of us. Or we might form an even larger group and hire someone to do this postal collection for us. By creating such an association, we'd be taking a step toward forming a *community*, a collection of people with common interests who live in a common geographical location.

If road building were a private enterprise, we'd still have the turnpikes and lesser arteries connecting communities, because building such highways would pay. However, we'd never get local street systems.

If we want local streets, and we do, we'd have to build them ourselves. And we'd have to build them in a cooperative way, since they'd service our community generally.

We might be able to maintain local postal delivery on a pretty informal basis, but for road building and maintenance, a more formal organization is almost inevitable. If someone doesn't want to pay for his share of postal delivery, his postal delivery can be discontinued.

But if somebody doesn't want to pay for his share of road building and maintenance, it's pretty hard to keep him off of the streets.

A more formal organization, with the ability to apply sanctions against those who don't pay their dues, is required. Thus, communities incorporate themselves — that is, they form municipalities.

Once a municipality is formed, other community services may come into being. Local police protection is an example. A fire fighting company is another. So is a local public library and a local public school system.

Here we see that, for life to go on, a single structure isn't sufficient. A hierarchy of structures with distinguishing features is required. We haven't yet mentioned the first of these, which is the family.

The family is a frankly communist structure. Each member of a family contributes to the unit according to his abilities, and each member is provided for according to his needs.

The able child, who can fend for himself and progress on his own, is provided with the minimum of help and may even be required to contribute to the family resources. At the same time, the physically or emotionally disabled child has resources lavished on him up to or beyond the limit of the family to provide. And we wouldn't have it any other way.

When we get to community, we start to formalize relationships. But these formal structures are in the background and are resorted to only when extreme measures become required.

Most pressure within the community is of the moral kind. Unacceptable behavior is avoided because people like us don't do such things. It's a comfortable way to live, and again, we wouldn't have it any other way.

But there's a limit on how large a community can be before the moral tendons that bind it together become stretched beyond their ability to do their job. It doesn't take long to reach this limit. Studies indicate that this limit lies at somewhere around 150 community members (G 179 ff).

Beyond that, moral suasion begins to break down. We begin to resort to formal rules enforced by some kind of rudimentary governmental structure.

By the time that we get to communities of 5000 to 10,000 thousand people, we're electing a representative governing group with an executive who may be called a mayor or first selectman and employing a paid, full-time police force.

And at the national, state and, perhaps, county level, we're looking at a democratically elected government, abiding by the rule of law and confining its activities to the essential activities that a market system is unable to provide.

Community has ambiguous appeal. Yes, it's nice to live with people who know and are concerned for you. It's a warm and comfortable feeling.

But on the other hand, these people, who are your familiar friends and support, are also the same people who know all about you and who won't hesitate to criticize you if you wander from the moral precepts undergirding the community. You never have to stand by yourself, but you also have little privacy. You receive strong support in your every endeavor, just as long as you don't depart from what's expected.

For a model example of a community, think of a church or a small town. Is this what you want? Or would you sometimes prefer the anonymity and freedom to act that goes with a more atomistic life style? Perhaps a little of both would be what you'd prefer.

# CHAPTER FIFTEEN

# Managing Your Money

## Getting the Money To Invest

Before you can invest, you have to have money to invest. A few of us may be fortunate enough to come into money. But most of us have to earn the money to which we have access. And it's out of savings from that earned income that our investment money comes.

Perhaps the most effective way to save money is to fix on a specific amount of money that you're going to save each pay period. Then treat that amount the same way that you treat a utility bill. Each time that it comes due, which is every payday, you have to pay the "savings bill" before spending your pay on other things.

A second way to save money is to not buy things on time. When you buy something on time, you're paying someone else for the use of their money, when what you should be doing is getting other people to pay you for using your money.

For example, suppose that you're going to buy a $20,000 car. Suppose further that you're going to finance this purchase at an interest rate of six percent a year for three years. You would then be paying $608.44 a month for 36 months, for a total of $21,903.84 — $20,000 for the car and $1903.84 in interest.

If instead, each month, you deposited $608.44 in a saving account that paid an interest rate of four percent a year (unfortunately, the financial industry will always charge you more for using its money than it will pay you for it to use yours), at the end of three years, you would have accumulated $23,231.19. You could then buy the car for $20,000 and have $3231.19 left over to add to your savings. And you wouldn't have experienced the interest cost of $1903.84 for financing the purchase, which is a drain on your savings.

A third way to way to save is to avoid unnecessary expenses. Here I can only speak from my own experience.

I'm a penny-pincher and proud of it. (Actually, I prefer to be called frugal.)

I pick up pennies that I find lying in the street. (I really do. But of course, that's just a habit. I don't maintain that it makes any difference as far as my wealth, such that it is, is concerned.)

But I don't have a TV, a cell phone, or Internet service. I don't buy candy bars, bags of nuts, soft drinks, or drinks at a bar. (After a round of tennis, I'll join my colleagues for lunch and a beer. When I take my lady to dinner, I do have a beer. And no matter what my lady orders for an entree, I don't flinch. I may be a skinflint, but I do believe in being sociable.)

I don't buy newspapers or magazines. Although I'm an inveterate reader, I don't buy books. (I borrow books from the library.) I don't go to the movies, and I don't go on trips.

I don't claim to be principled with respect to any of these things. It's just the fallout of choices that I've made.

I don't have a TV, because if I did, I wouldn't do anything but sit and watch movies all day long, and I don't want to do that. I have no self-control. The only way for me to avoid succumbing to marathon movie watching is to not have a TV.

Some people complain that, because I don't have a cell phone, they can't instantly reach me. I suppose that that's true, but I don't feel that being instantaneously available 24/7 is one of the things that I have to do, and a cell phone is just one more thing to carry around and keep track of. People can always leave me messages on my answering machine or e-mail me, and I do eventually respond.

I don't have Internet service, because I now (2015) have, on my computer, over 1700 pages of material that's of no value to anyone else, but it means a lot to me. I don't want any damage to come to it.

So even though I dutifully back up my files every month, I'm just not interested in having my material destroyed by some virus or worm. Maintaining a security system is a pain, and they can protect you only from what they know, not what they don't know.

But the Internet is important. We've grown to depend on e-mail for one form of communication, and Googling for information is convenient.

Fortunately, the Internet is available at the library, so I can avoid the whole security mess by using the Internet at the library. And while I'm there, why not read the newspapers, which are also available?

I don't buy snacks and soft drinks, etc. for the same reason that I don't have a TV. If I did, I'd scarf down the stuff immoderately, so I follow the advice of the Roman church — I remove myself from the presence of temptation.

Magazines don't interest me. I love films, but between method acting and my failing hearing, I no longer catch enough of the dialogue to make going to movies an enjoyable experience for me.

And I don't care to travel. All that work to get organized and everything arranged, just so that you can live out of a suitcase and tromp around on other people's property. (If I want to find out something about a place, I read a book about it.)

A fourth opportunity to save is when you experience a windfall, such as receiving an unexpected bonus or coming into a small inheritance. When something like that happens, the tendency is to want to celebrate, and a good way to celebrate is to spend the money.

Resist the temptation. Put the money into your savings.

I'll now issue a probably unnecessary caveat. If you ever accumulate enough savings to cover all of your long-term needs, there's then no need to continue to save.

Instead, spend your income and enjoy it. That's what money is for. However, in building up my savings, I've never reached the point where I didn't need more, and to tell you the truth, I doubt that you will either.

There are people who don't earn enough to make ends meet, let alone save. And there are others who suffer some kind of catastrophe, such as a large medical bill or job loss, which wipes out their savings and then some.

It's argued that exhorting such people to save is, not only pointless, but also insulting. I agree.

Such people are candidates for welfare. But that doesn't relieve the rest of us of the responsibility to save for the purpose of meeting large expenses that we can anticipate in the future, such as educating our children and providing for our retirement.

Investing

OK. So now you're accumulating some savings.

You'd like that money that you're saving to earn a return so that your savings can be enhanced. That's what investing is all about. So, let's talk about investing.

Liquidity

If we're going to talk about investing, then the first thing that we have to do is to get some feeling for the concept of liquidity. Unfortunately, that isn't easy.

An asset is something that you own that has value. Liquidity is the availability of counterparties when you want to sell your asset.

As such, liquidity is essential. Without it, trading (the buying and selling of assets) would be impossible. Yet we have no workable definition of liquidity and we don't know enough about it to be able to quantify it. (D 47,48)

Liquidity has to do with the ease with which you can, on short notice, convert an asset of yours into money without significantly affecting the price at which the asset is currently selling. For example, in normal circumstances, if you own a stock, you can call up your broker and he'll tell you the price at which your stock is currently selling, and if you decide to sell, the sale will go through right away, and you'll get close to the quoted price for your stock.

What you get for your stock may be a little more or a little less than the quoted price, but it will be close to the quoted price. Your stock is a liquid asset. (The qualification, "under normal circumstances", is necessary, because if the stock market goes into panic, which it sometimes does, the price of your stock may drop significantly between the time that you get the quote and the time that you sell, no matter how short that time interval is.)

If you own a house, it has what's known as a market value. That is, you can have an appraiser come in, and he'll tell you what the going price for your house on the current market is.

The appraiser may be off a little. But he'll be pretty close to the mark, and if you wait long enough in a stable market, you'll probably be able to sell your house at or near its appraised value.

But that's the hooker. You can get the market price for your house, but you may not get it right away. Your house is a relatively illiquid asset.

The liquidity of an asset has nothing to do with whether you'll be able to realize a profit when you sell your asset. The instant that you buy a stock, its price may begin to fall and continue to fall for as long as you hold onto the stock. It's a loser.

But the stock is still a liquid asset. At any time that you decide to dump it, you can call up your broker, he'll tell you what your dog is currently selling for, and when you sell, you'll get close to the price quoted.

Profitability and liquidity are different things. Profitability has to do with whether you can sell your asset for more than you bought it for. Liquidity has to do with whether you can sell your asset quickly at the currently quoted price.

Our assumption here is that your circumstances are such that you're always going to be in the position where you may need to sell investments to raise cash on short notice. So you want to invest in liquid assets.

## Investment Types

There are three main types of investments: real estate (residential and commercial), collectibles (such as antiques, coins, jewelry, art work, baseball cards, and comic books), and securities. Real estate and collectibles are relatively illiquid.

The only liquid investment is securities. So, you want to invest in securities.

## Securities

There are three types of securities: stock, bonds and derivatives.

Derivatives

A derivative is a security that derives its value from the value of something else. The most common forms of derivatives are options and futures.

An option is the right to either buy or sell some specified asset, known as the underlying asset, on or before some specified future date, known as the expiration date, at some specified price, known as the contract price, but entails no obligation to do so. Suppose that you buy an option to buy a specified amount of cocoa. If before the expiration date the market price of cocoa becomes more than the contract price, then your option acquires value, since you can exercise the option, buy cocoa at the lower contract price, and sell the cocoa at the higher market price. The value of your option derives from the value of the underlying asset, which is why options are called derivatives.

But if the market price becomes more than the contract price, you don't have buy cocoa to make a profit. All that you have to do is sell your option, because since it has acquired value, investors will be willing to pay you more for it than you paid to buy the option. That's how option investors make their money.

However, if by the expiration date, the price of cocoa has remained below the contract price, then your option will expire without ever having obtained any value, and you'll lose all of your money that you used to buy the option. That can hurt, and options buyers have been known to be hurt badly.

A future is a contract that both gives you the right and obligates you to either buy or sell some specified asset at some specified price at some specified future date. Suppose that you buy a future to buy a specified amount of cocoa. If on the expiration date, the market price of cocoa is more than the contract price, then you'll buy the cocoa at the contract price, and you're then in a position to sell the cocoa at the market price and make a profit.

However, if during the life of the future, the market price becomes more than the contract price, your future has acquired value, and investors will be willing to buy it from you for more than you paid for it. The value of your future derives from the value of the underlying asset, which is why futures are called derivatives. Selling futures that you've previously purchased and that have acquired value is how futures investors make money.

However, if by the expiration date, the price of cocoa has remained below the contract price, then you're obligated to buy the cocoa at the specified price, even though the market price is less than the contract price. Actually, you don't have to really carry out the obligation. What you do is buy an opposite future option that cancels out your original future — you buy a second future to sell the same amount of cocoa that you contracted to buy in your first future. But because of market conditions, that sell future is going to cost you more than your buy future, and the differential can be severe.

All derivatives (futures, options, and all of their more complex relatives) come with the potential for devastating losses. This isn't where you want to invest your savings. As my ol' Daddy used to say, "Don't gamble unless you can afford to lose."

Stocks and Bonds

Both stock and bonds are viable investment vehicles. The debate is over which is the more desirable, a debate that revolves around what kind of term you should consider when investing.

Over the long term, stock returns about twice as much as bonds. On the other hand, stock is more volatile than bonds.

Beginning in 1929, the stock market went into a swoon, from which it didn't recover until 1952, 23 years later. If sometime during those 23 years, you needed to cash out your investments to meet your long-term needs, the stock market wasn't the place to be.

However, the Great Depression may have been an anomaly. Since 1970, the stock market has experienced a number of recessions, but none of them have come close to the length of the Great Depression. The market went seven years, from 1973 to 1980, before it recovered the losses incurred in the interim. It went into an eight-year slump from 1999 to 2007. From 2009 until 2013, it was in a six year down period.

Whether your can handle such volatility in the value of your investments, where you can see your savings shrink by one half, I won't venture to say. All I can do is tell you about my own experience.

I retired in 1993, and of course, at that point, I stopped contributing to my savings. At that time, my investments amounted to about $140,000.

In 1999, the market topped out, at which time, my investment had grown to about $453,000. The market then tanked, and when it had bottomed out in 2002, my investment had been reduced by about 50 percent.

In 2007, the market, once more, topped out, and by then, my investment had grown to about $485,000. By the time that the market next reached its bottom in 2009, my investment had, once again, shrunk to about half of that. Today (at the first quarter of 2015), my nest egg stands at about $797,000.

And each year, from 1993 until today, I withdrew between $10,000 and $25,000 from my savings to support my life style. So I've been able to live off of my savings without diminishing them, courtesy of the stock market.

The stock market is volatile, but if you can take the sickeningly dips in the value of your investments as the market gyrates through its roller coaster ride, the market can possibly be your friend.

Let's proceed on the idea that your investment strategy should be to concentrate on stocks. The question then is: What approach should you take to investing in stocks?

## Investing in Stocks

As we've observed, the stock market is volatile. One day, stocks are up. On another day, they're down.

But that isn't so bad. If we just hold onto our investment, day-to-day fluctuations shouldn't concern us.

What we want to avoid is an investment that goes down and then stays down, which unfortunately, can happen to any individual stock.

But that isn't true of the stock market as a whole. No matter how far it drops, it always recovers.

So your strategy should be to not invest in individual stocks but to, instead, invest in the market as a whole. And that's possible. You invest in an index fund.

(All right. I agree. I can't logically rule out the possibility that the market may go down and stay down for good. But I'll say that, if such a thing were to occur, there wouldn't be much left of the world, so it probably wouldn't matter where you stashed your money, which likely wouldn't be worth much anyhow.)

Most of the time, you're just going to keep your money in the market, grit your teeth and hold on when it goes into a slump, and rub your hands with glee when it goes up. But there are times when you're going to have to draw funds out of your savings, and you have to prepare for these events.

There are four such events — emergencies, buying a house, paying for your children's college education, and retiring. What you want to do is handle these events without having to draw money out of your index fund when the market is down, because that would mean selling your assets at the then current low price, which would be a real hit to your savings.

Emergencies

When you need money to cover emergency expenses and the market is down, what you need is a cushion of money on which you can fall back rather than tap your index fund. You need some amount of money in a money market account (MMA), where your money is always accessible.

The question is: How much should you stash away in your MMA? You don't want more in there than you need, because MMAs are notorious for not paying much of a return. On the other hand, you want enough to cover the cost of an emergency.

So, how much should you be setting aside for an emergency? I can't tell you. It has to be up to you.

I set aside $5000 for emergencies. That may be a little risky. But I think that I can handle it. In this matter, you have to make up your own mind about what kind of risk you can tolerate and then act accordingly.

The defining characteristic of an emergency is that you don't know when one will occur. That's why you need a cushion to fall back on.

Unlike emergencies, buying a house, paying for your children's college education, and retiring are things that can, to a considerable extent, be anticipated and, therefore, planned for.

## Buying a House

If you intend to buy a house, you're probably aware of intention long before you plan to make the purchase. When the house search gets serious, you're going to need to be able to put up the down payment on short notice.

If the stock market is up, there's no problem. You take the down payment out of your index fund.

But if the market is down, taking the down payment out of your index fund is what you don't want to do. So, some time before the house search gets serious, you want to have the down payment stashed away in your MMA, just in case that, when it comes time to make the down payment, the market is down. And of course, you want to stash the down payment away in your MMA when the market is up.

At some point before the house search becomes serious, the market is going to be up. This may be one year before you get serious about buying a house, or two years, or three, or what have you. At that point, do you want to stash away the down payment? Or do you want to wait a while?

After all, the market might continue to go up for some time yet, and if you wait, you can take full advantage of that bull market before you have to set aside the funds for the down payment. But suppose you wait and, instead of continuing to go up, the market turns around and goes down. Then what do you do?

So, what's the answer? Once more, I can't give you any advice. You're just going to have to make up your own mind in terms of your penchant for risk. If you're comfortable with risk, you might wait a while. If risk drives you crazy, you're better off setting aside the money now, getting it over with, and having some peace of mind.

## Paying for Your Children's Education

Here you want to have an investment that will pay off exactly when you need the money. For example, suppose that you have one child who's going to start college in 2018 and you anticipate that this college education is going to cost you $40,000 a year.

Assuming that you're not going to pay for this education out of pocket, then what you want is a $40,000 investment that's going to pay off in 2018, a second investment of $40,000 that's going to pay off in 2019, a third investment that's going to pay off in 2020, and a fourth that's going to pay off in 2021. The type of investment that fills this bill is bonds.

The type of bond that you want is one that isn't going to default — that is, not pay off when it comes due. The bond least likely to default is a Treasury bond. So that's the bond that you want to buy.

In the example above, what you want is $40,000 of Treasury bonds that are going to mature in 2018, a second set of $40,000 worth of bonds that's going to mature in 2019, a third set that's going to mature in 2020, and a fourth set with a maturity date of 2021. If you're going to meet some of the college expense for your child out of pocket, then you should adjust down the amount of bonds that you need accordingly.

You're going to pay for these bonds with money that you draw out of your index fund, and you want to make this withdrawal when the market is up. So, you now face the same question that you did when it was time to set aside a down payment for buying a house.

For example, suppose that it's 2015 and the market is up. Should you buy the bonds now, or should you wait another year, so that your money can earn more before you take it out to buy the bonds?

Waiting another year is a good idea … if the market stays up. But if the market goes down, then you've got a narrow window until 2018 before you're going to need $40,000 to pay for the first year of your child's college education. If the market is still down when that time comes, you're going to have to take this money out of your index fund, and your investments are going to take a hit.

So, what's the answer? Once more, I can't give you any advice. You're just going to have to make up your own mind in terms of your penchant for risk.

There's an alternative here that allows you to save part of your skin. If it comes time to start paying college education expenses, you haven't previously taken money out of your index fund to meet these expenses, and the market is down, you can avoid taking money out of your index fund by borrowing the money to pay the college expenses.

You can then carry this loan until the market turns up, at which time you can afford to take money out of your index fund to pay off your loan. But in exercising this alternative, at a minimum, you're going to experience interest costs on your loan, and if it's the only kind of loan that you can float (which is typically the case), you're going to have to periodically, usually monthly, pay down on the principal of your loan.

## Planning for Retirement

Finally, comes the day when you retire. At that point, you're going to stop contributing to your savings and start withdrawing funds from them to support yourself during retirement.

At that point, you want to have enough of a money cushion in your MMA so that you can withdraw your maintenance cash from your MMA during any period when the market is down. Once more, the amount that this should be is something that only you can decide.

First, you have to figure out how much you're going to need each year to support yourself. That shouldn't be too difficult to determine. For me, I figure that, taking my pensions into account, I need an extra $30,000 a year at a maximum.

Second, you have to decide how long you think that a market downturn can last. That's more difficult.

Your estimate is going to depend on your tolerance for risk. The less that you can live with risk, the longer the period on which you should count. I've chosen six years, which given the way in which the market has recently been behaving, is kind of risky.

Once you've made these two decisions, you just multiply the amount that you need each year by the number of years of down market that you think will be a maximum, and the product is how much you should have in your MMA. For me, that's $30,000 multiplied by six years, or $180,000. (Of course, that's in addition to the $5000 that I've set aside for emergencies.)

But you still have one more decision to make. When you retire, you want that cash cushion to be sitting in your MMA. So, you're going to have to build it up in the years before you retire, and the question is: When do you start building it up?

This is analogous to the question of when you should set aside funds for a down payment on a house and when you should start buying those bonds to provide for your child's college education. You want to do it when the market is up.

So, sometime before you retire, say ten years (the number that you actually use is one that you have to chose to suit yourself), you should start thinking about moving money from your index fund to your MMA. You want to do this in an up market.

You could be in an up market right at the start of the ten years. If not, your plan is that one will occur before you have to retire.

Once you're in an up market, you then have to decide how long you're willing to wait before transferring money from your index fund to your MMA. The later you wait, the more the amount in your index fund is going to grow ... provided that the market stays up.

But if you wait, and instead of staying up, the market goes down, then you've got a problem. Once more, you have to make this decision on the basis of what makes you feel comfortable.

## Managing Your Money in Retirement

When the market is down, you should rely on your MMA to provide you with your annual maintenance expenses. When the market is up, you can start shifting funds from your index fund to replenish the cushion in your MMA.

In addition, there are times when a real bull market takes hold. Here, even if you already have an adequate cushion in your MMA, my advice is to skim off some of the froth of the bull market and transfer the funds to your MMA.

Eventually, even the strongest of bull markets is going to lose steam, turn around, and begin a drop into bear territory. But the money in your MMA isn't going to lose value.

You've pocketed the proceeds of the bubble, and you can look forward to the recession with equanimity. And if you don't like all of that money sitting idle in your MMA, you can take some of it and buy Treasury bonds or bank CDs.

For example, according to the index that I follow (Total Stock Market), on October 9, 2007, the market made a high of 15806.69. It then dropped into the Great Recession.

On May 17, 2013, the market exceeded 17,387.59, more than ten percent above its previous all-time high of 15806.69. I promptly moved $30,000 from my index fund to my MMA.

On December 20, 2013, the market exceeded 18,968.03, more than 20 percent above its previous all-time high of 15806.69. I promptly moved another $30,000 from my index fund to my MMA. (I confess. One of my investment principles is to not let tax considerations influence my investment decisions. On December 20, I really wanted to move $60,000 from my index fund to MMA, but it was so close to the end of the year that I moved only $30,000. When 2014 rolled around, I promptly moved another $30,000 from my index fund to my MMA.)

On June 20, the market exceeded 20,548.70, 30 percent above its previous all-time high of 15806.69. I promptly moved $90,000 from my index fund to my MMA.

On April 24, 2015, the market exceeded 22,129.37, 40 percent above its previous all-time high of 15806.69. I promptly moved $120,000 from my index fund to my MMA.

The market is now slowing down, but it may continue to go up, and it may eventually exceed 23,709.14, 50 percent above its previous all-time high of 15806.69. When that happens, I'll move another chunk of money from my index fund to my MMA. And so on, until the market turns around.

## When Is the Market Up? When Is It Down?

Throughout this whole discussion, we've been talking blithely about when the market is up and when the market is down. But how do you tell when the market is up and when it's down?

Let's suppose that the market has just made a new high. Obviously, at this point, the market is up.

You then have to decide how far the market can drop before it's down. Again, this is something that you have to decide for yourself.

I consider the market down if it drops more than ten percent from its all-time high. (Besides being my own decision, this measure is a kind of industry standard. Thus, if the market drops more than ten percent from an all time high, the newspapers will start telling you that we're now in a bear market.)

For example, the index that I follow peaked at a new all-time high of 14,751.64 on March 23, 1999. A drop of ten percent from this all time high would be if the index dropped to 13,274.48. This index value of 13,274.48 became my boundary between an up and a down market.

As long as the index remained above 13,274.48, then as far as I was concerned, the market remained up. When the index dropped below 13,274.48, which it did on November 28, 2000, I decided that we were now in a down market.

From my point of view, the market would remain down until the index passed 13,274.48 on the way up, which it finally did on September 26, 2006. At that point, for me, the market was now up.

After September 26, 2006, the market remained up, and on October 9, 2007, the index made a new all time high of 15,806.69. At that point, I abandoned my previous boundary of 13,274.48 between up and down markets and computed a new boundary at 14,226.02, which was a ten percent drop from the all time high of 15806.69.

As of May 18, 2015, the market stood at 22,264.51, an all-time high. If that turns out to be the crest of the market boom, then when the market drops below 20,038.59 (10 percent below 22,264.51), I'll consider it to be down.

## Caveat

That's it. I have just one more thing to say.

What I've been describing here is my approach to investing. At least so far, it has worked for me. Whether it's something that you want to adopt only you can decide.

# Index